The Social and Political Thought of Noam Chomsky

The quality of Edgley's work is very high. The exposition of Chomsky's work is always clear and judicious. Edgley provides a sound treatment of the material and pays excellent attention to the broader context of the argument.... In the existing literature there is nothing quite like this in its treatment of Chomsky.

Professor David McLellan, University of Kent

This book explores the theoretical framework that enables Chomsky to be consistently radical in his analysis of contemporary political affairs. It argues that, far from Chomsky being a 'conspiracy theorist', his approach is embedded within a systematic philosophical understanding of human nature, combined with critical perspectives on the state, nationalism and the media. When compared to Marxist, liberal and cultural relativist thought, Chomsky's libertarian socialist thought provides coherent grounds for a militant optimism.

The Social and Political Thought of Noam Chomsky questions Chomsky's claim *not* to have a theory about the relationship between human beings and their society other than that which can be 'written on the back of a postage stamp'. Edgley compares Chomsky's vision of the good society with liberal and communitarian perspectives, and establishes that it is grounded in a hopeful belief about human nature. She argues that sympathy with this vision of the good society is essential for understanding the nature of Chomsky's critique of state capitalism, its inherent nationalism and the media. The author concludes that Chomsky's analysis is coherent and systematic when one acknowledges that he is not just a critic but a theorist.

One of the few serious academic studies of Chomsky's political writing, this volume addresses many key issues in political theory through an engagement with Chomsky's ideas. Subjects covered include equality and freedom, politics and the media, nationalism and state capitalism. *The Social and Political Thought of Noam Chomsky* is an essential resource for scholars of social and political thought.

Alison Edgley is Senior Lecturer in Social and Political Thought at Canterbury Christ Church University College. Her articles have been published in journals such as *Politics* and *Talking Politics*.

Routledge Studies in Social and Political Thought

The Social and Political Thought of Noam Chomsky

Alison Edgley

London and New York

First published 2000
by Routledge
11 New Fetter Lane, London EC4P 4EE

Simultaneously published in the USA and Canada
by Routledge
29 West 35th Street, New York, NY 10001

Routledge is an imprint of the Taylor & Francis Group

© 2000 Alison Edgley

Typeset in Sabon by
Florence Production Ltd, Stoodleigh, Devon
Printed and bound in Great Britain by
St Edmundsbury Press, Bury St Edmunds, Suffolk

British Library Cataloguing in Publication Data
A catalogue record for this book is available from the
British Library

Library of Congress Cataloging-in-Publication Data
Edgley, Alison, 1963–
   The social and political thought of Noam Chomsky /
   Alison Edgley.
      p.   cm.—(Routledge studies in social and political thought)
   Includes bibliographical references and index.
   ISBN 0–415–20586–7 (hb)
   1. Chomsky, Noam—Political and social views.   I. Title.
   II. Series.
P85.C47 E34 2000
410′.92–dc21   99–055601

ISBN 0-415-20586-7

For my father, Roy Edgley

Contents

Acknowledgements

I would like to thank Ian Forbes not only for his love, friendship and practical support but also for his relentless and rigorous intellectual criticism. Thanks too to Amy for sleeping so peacefully thereby allowing me to complete the final stages. I would also like to thank the following people: Noam Chomsky for corresponding and meeting with me; David McLellan for his encouragement of the project at its inception and for supervising these ideas in their doctoral form; Peter Wilkin and Fred Inglis for enthusiastic support and their comments on an earlier draft; Sean Sayers, Joe McCarney and the numerous others who attended David's Lentil Seminars for useful comments; my friend Sue Davies for her friendship and for the twilight editing we did. Lastly, I would like to thank my family but especially my father, Roy Edgley, who bought me my first Chomsky volume and who read everything and discussed the ideas at every painful stage of the book's development. Tragically for me he has not survived to see the book finally published.

Introduction
Chomsky – critic or theorist?

How are we to characterise Noam Chomsky's political writings? Certainly it is notable that Chomsky's political work is to a great extent marginalised within academic circles. His writings rarely appear on undergraduate reading lists nor do they, on the whole, enter the fray of mainstream debates about social and political organisation. There are perhaps only two areas where this is an exception: media studies and international relations. Given that Chomsky has been writing prolifically on just about every political issue one might care to think of for over thirty years, what reasons may be offered to explain this? It might be suggested that there is a degree of intellectual snobbery attached to the perhaps subconscious decision within the academic community not to give his ideas in this area serious consideration. In other words he is regarded first and foremost as a linguist, and it is therefore inappropriate that he should cross intellectual boundaries and enter debates about subjects that are deemed to lie beyond his academic expertise. Chomsky explains that this argument has indeed been used. Some academics from The University of Victoria in British Columbia for example tried to stop him speaking and 'they published letters in the press, etc., saying that since I'm a linguist, I shouldn't be allowed to talk about "their field"'.[1] This is perhaps paradoxical given that Chomsky is accorded wide acclaim as Professor of Linguistics at MIT and that he quite literally generated a revolution within his discipline. Indeed, he has been described by the *New York Times* as 'arguably the most important intellectual alive'.[2] How can it be that someone of such apparent eminence is not worthy of consideration when it comes to his views on social and political organisation? As Chomsky himself points out with some amusement, 'If you go back and look at the context of that remark, the sentence was: "arguably the most important intellectual alive, how can he write such nonsense about international affairs and foreign policy?"'[3] To have come to such a strong conclusion about Chomsky's work on issues unrelated to linguistics suggests one of two things. Either he does just dabble in political issues, and is therefore perhaps unaware of significant developments in the field. Or careful consideration has been given to his views, and they have been found wanting in some way. However, neither can be said to be the case. On the first point, one only needs to take a quick look at a list of the books and articles he has written on political issues over the years, to see that this is no passing interest. Within the books are copious references to numerous pieces of research and publications, both government sponsored and otherwise, demonstrating his prodigious appetite for knowledge in this area. As Alexander Cockburn notes 'The times I've stayed the night at Noam and Carol Chomsky's house in Lexington I've watched him at eventide working his way through a capacious box of the day's intake of tripe – newspapers, weeklies, monthlies, learned journals, flimsy mimeo-ed mailers – while Carol Chomsky does the same thing on the other side of the room'.[4] On the second point, we find that his books are rarely, if ever, published or reviewed in America. The following story about *The New York Review* is illustrative:

> A novelist who writes regularly for *The New York Times* and the *Washington Post* was greatly surprised by the reactions his idea of sending them a profile on Chomsky elicited from his usual contacts in those papers. This experience, unimaginable for him before he went through it, apparently stimulated his interest in finding out why *The New York Review* had stopped publishing Chomsky and tried to get the account of the editors. Robert Silvers refused even to answer the phone. Out of curiosity, he phoned Gore Vidal in Italy, asking him to intercede. He did, and Silvers was willing to take his call, but told him he'd have to check with his lawyers before answering. When Vidal called back, Silvers told him that their lawyers had advised them not to say anything. He later checked with Barbara Epstein, who told him that Silvers is constantly bombarded on this topic and is entirely paranoid about it.[5]

So here we have an eminent linguist, whose tracts on political issues are unpublishable and unreviewable in America, who also generates paranoia in editors. Could it be something other than intellectual snobbery that is at work here? As Shaun Harbord has argued, 'the United States does not lack for opportunities to debate positions such as Chomsky's, but it is tempting to conclude that such effort is not made because his [antagonists] fear that they could lose the argument ... An attempted rebuttal of Chomsky could be launched; that it is not is surely an indictment of American intellectual life'.[6] Chomsky's own view on this issue is not dissimilar to Harbord's. For Chomsky, in general, successful intellectuals on social and political issues within capitalist societies are merely 'experts in legitimation', to use Gramsci's term. As Chomsky's work sets out to uncover and attack the power structures within society, he is in effect seeking to question and even undermine this legitimation and thereby the individuals and interests associated with this particular position.

[T]he ones who labor to make what people in power do legitimate, are mainly the privileged educated elites. The journalists, the academics, the teachers, the public relations specialists, this whole category of people have a kind of an institutional task, and that is to create the system of beliefs which will ensure the effective engineering of consent. And again, the more sophisticated of them say that. In the academic social sciences, for example, there's quite a tradition, explaining the necessity for the engineering of democratic consent.[7]

Chomsky argues that, apart from a few notable and worthy exceptions, intellectuals have become a 'secular priesthood'.[8] '[T]his means worship of the state religion, which in the western democracies incorporates the doctrine of submission to the masters of the system of public subsidy, private profit, called free enterprise. The people must be kept in ignorance, reduced to jingoist incantations, for their own good'.[9] How does this work in a non-totalitarian society?

The way [this] works, with rare exceptions, [is that] you cannot make it through these institutions unless you've accepted the indoctrination. You're kind of weeded out along the way. Independent thinking is encouraged in the sciences but discouraged in these areas, and if people do it they're weeded out as radical or there's something wrong with them.[10]

In other words amongst intellectuals there is an elitist strain, which manifests itself through a form of state adulation, whereby the state is seen as *the* way by and through which to organise society. 'Limiting ourselves just to the United States, the intelligentsia – particularly, the dominant "liberal intelligentisa" – have, in my view, tended to be state propagandists'.[11]

To the ears or eyes of the European such a description of intellectuals as 'masters of the system of public subsidy, private profit, called free enterprise' may sound distinctly foreign. The objection may be raised that what Chomsky is describing may indeed be a characteristic of the American intellectual tradition, but can hardly be said to be true of European intellectual thought, which has a strong tradition in criticism of the capitalist system. Chomsky is aware of the differences between the United States and European intellectual traditions. As he argues:

The United States . . . is . . . one of the most deeply indoctrinated societies in the world and one of the most depoliticized societies in the world, and one of the societies with the most conformist intelligentsia in the world, in this respect more so than in western Europe.[12]

It is also notable, in the light of these claims, that Chomsky's political writings do get published and reviewed outside America. Nevertheless, the original point still stands: his ideas rarely enter mainstream debate, nor therefore are they given prominence to undergraduates (except in international relations and media studies). In Chomsky's view elitism is not just a feature of the American liberal tradition it is also a feature of much of the European left.

> The Leninist model has had great appeal to the intelligentsia in certain places and periods because, beneath a facade of concern for the welfare of the masses of the population, it offers a justification for the acquisition of state power by the revolutionary intelligentsia, who, as Bakunin perceptively observed a century ago, will exploit mass popular struggles to construct a regime of terror and oppresssion. As he wrote, they will beat the people with 'the people's stick'.[13]

So although the European, in contrast to the North American intellectual tradition, does focus on a critique of *capitalism*, this critique nevertheless masks and diverts attention from an institution which serves to prop up this system, namely the state. In Chomsky's view, for too many intellectuals the state is not seen as problematic in itself, but as problematic only as a reflection of the economic structure. That society is best organised through the state is deemed normal, part of the conventional wisdom. As such, Chomsky argues 'there is a very significant, if undeveloped, tradition that grew out of Marxism and anarchism. It presents a range of opinion which is important but hasn't been developed, since it's been carefully excluded. Anyone's chances of airing this viewpoint in the universities or elsewhere are pretty slight . . .'.[14]

Chomsky belongs firmly in this tradition. And certainly it seems that his own explanation is significant in accounting for the lack of serious consideration given to his political writings. However, it seems that there may be a further, but related, reason for his marginalisation. Chomsky's political writings take the form of political journalism. In other words he commentates on contemporary social and political events. From the Vietnam war onwards he looks at and analyses American foreign policy. He looks at proclaimed policy objectives and compares them with outcomes. And because, in his view, America's international relations are driven by the nature of America's internal social organisation, this also comes in for consideration. He compares America's policy with one country to its policy with another country and he looks at the way in which other nations support or challenge American actions and objectives. In other words he draws parallels between America's organisation and that of other countries in the west or east. He also looks at the way in which things are communicated to the public, the justifications used, the things that are suppressed and the things that are distorted or misrepresented. In so doing he looks at what is eventually to become the historical record. The pictures he paints are full of the intricacies and details of power struggles between oppressed and oppressor both small and large in scale. The pictures present the flux – the ebb and flow of a precarious existence. If we stand and reflect on his pictures, absorbing the complexity and detail, we also cannot fail to notice that the form and structure of these pictures remain the same. However, the form and structure are at once both clear and obscure. The clarity derives from the fact that these components are always there and yet, because of the sheer weight of detail, it is hard to concentrate upon them. The framework is never at the forefront of the picture, and neither is it intended to be.

The point is that Chomsky's work has an intended atheoretical quality to it. He wants us to concentrate on the detail, gruesome though it is. He wants us to remain in touch with the experiences of those in the picture and he wants us to feel the 'reality' of those experiences. He wants to expose us to the interconnectedness between those in the picture and us. He wants us to see ourselves in the picture so that we can recognise that we also shape the picture. We can be both its subject and its author. He wants to stop us from standing back from the picture so that we take in only its form and structure which allows us to remove our feelings about its content, precisely because we ignore the detail. In Chomsky's view, if we do stand back and consider only the structure, we end up with arcane discussion and debate. It is also likely to leave us with a muted and distorted picture which very few can properly see or understand.

It is this focus on the form and structure of a picture that concerns intellectuals of the social sciences. In Chomsky's view this process of obfuscation removes them from the real world, and allows them to feel comfortable with their positions of status and the label of expert. However, he wants to argue that the pictures they paint miss and corrupt the detail, because of this emphasis on form and structure, and so betray their elitist underpinnings. Chomsky himself then avoids the dominant intellectual tradition, just as much as it avoids him. When he offers us his interpretation on political events he does not begin by setting out his framework. (An exception to this is his work with Edward Herman – this exception is considered later.[15]) He does not set out the theory he employs and with which he selects the facts. Neither does he set out another's theory in order to knock it down, thereby contrasting it with his own. (Again there is another exception when he makes his attack on Skinner's *Behaviourism*. However, this attack comes from Chomsky the linguist – although as I shall try to draw out later, there are links between Chomksy the linguist and Chomsky the political commentator.[16]) He does make reference to other thinkers and their interpretation of the facts, demonstrating the possible elitist underpinnings for example, but he does not embark upon a full-scale attack of their theoretical framework. Readers of Chomsky's political work, then, are left with a general impression of a theoretical framework, noting perhaps vague parallels with the likes of Marx, but nothing more specific than that. Chomsky himself is of the opinion that nothing he, or anyone else in the social sciences, says even warrants the term theory. He regards most of what he has to say as being self-evident. In his view one could write his political theory 'on the back of a postage stamp'.[17]

This is perplexing because there seems plenty of evidence that a theory is being applied. The consistency with which he approaches different issues over the years is notable. The content and coherence of his framework was not always evident to me ... but then perhaps this might say more about me and my own intellectual 'indoctrination'. What is his political theory and why does he claim not to have one? If he does employ a political theory what are the implications? These are the questions I wish to raise. What this book does not cover is the history of ideas or intellectual context in which Chomsky's ideas should be placed. This would constitute a different project too vast for this book.[18]

In Chapter 1 I set out to discover what a political theory is and what it should look like. I consider various accounts of the necessary criteria and the implications of the various explanations. I then go on to question Chomsky's claim that he does not have a political theory, other than that which can be written on the back of a postage stamp. I look at why he makes this claim, and consider whether it is appropriate. The chapter explores the significance of his claim that any understanding of social and political organisation must be derived from an informed view of human nature. Furthermore, it examines his claim that as we know so little that can be scientifically verified about human nature, our ideas about social and political organisation can only be based upon hope and intuition. The chapter seeks to develop an alternative account.

The second chapter considers the way in which Chomsky is able to reconcile his libertarian socialist framework (or, as I establish, theory) with his vision of the good society and his view of human nature. In attempting to explicate his position, this chapter will also be looking at other interpretations of the 'good society' in an attempt to move beyond them. It will be argued that the frameworks employed by various political philosophers, when looking at the good society are flawed and they are flawed because they fall upon one side or other of a well-known, but virulent, dichotomy which plagues social and political thought. It will also be argued that Chomsky's theory can be interpreted as bridging this dichotomy. This dichotomy has many labels identifying it but they essentially amount to the same thing: it is the dichotomy between structure and agency.[19]

Whether thinkers acknowledge it or not, their work can usually be said to fall towards one or other side of the dichotomy. Both sides attack each other, and both have successfully wounded the other in the sense that both positions have difficulty in the face of the other's critique. And yet it is not just a case of taking a midway position for it then becomes difficult to remain logically coherent. On the one hand, there are those who look at the way in which the social structure and the respective social institutions within a society influence and determine human intentions, actions and outcomes. So from this perspective we might want to argue that we can account for Thatcher's formidable rise to power, and her subsequent ruthless policy agenda, as being the result of certain historically specific social and political conditions. And so here, thinkers in this perspective would begin with the social structure, namely capitalism, and look at the weakening of Britain's position within the international capitalist environment together with the perceived weakness of the British state, and conclude that it was these conditions that gave rise to her success. In other words, this perspective would not emphasise Thatcher the individual, focusing perhaps on the idea that it was her particular insight to have recognised the needs of British capitalism, and to have put together the necessary policies to facilitate a turnaround in Britain's fortunes. In general, it is feasible to argue that it is those within the Marxist tradition who have embraced this structuralist approach.

On the other hand, there are those who look at the way in which actors or groups of actors compete for power, perhaps turning to a consideration of the strategies and techniques utilised to succeed. Usually this perspective will see these battles in isolation and as discrete from the wider social and economic environment. Emphasis will lie on personalities and strategy – presupposing intentionality. By this view, structures and institutions are only in place because people *intend* them to be there. Again, very generally, one can say that those who employ this sort of perspective have tended to come from the liberal pluralist tradition.

Having said that Marxists are usually structuralists and that liberals are usually on the agency side of the debate, it is recognised that there are of course exceptions. Miliband, a Marxist, has been accused of offering an instrumentalist approach. This term 'instrumentalist' implies that capitalists use the state as an instrument with which to pursue their interests (in Miliband's analysis). That they use the state as an instrument implies intentionality, which in turn suggests an agency-orientated approach. Conversely, Skocpol offers a highly structuralist analysis of the state, but because she regards the state as autonomous from the social structure of capitalism her analysis cannot be Marxist. Of course many writers (perhaps unwittingly) hold within their ideas both aspects of the dichotomy. However, as critics are quick to point out, this represents a tension in their work. Marx is of course no exception here, and it is possible to suggest that the whole Marxist tradition has been concerned with this very conundrum. Despite what we may characterise as these political crossovers then, the fact remains that a possibly irreconcilable dichotomy is present. Layder reviews various attempts to overcome this dichotomy and shows how in various ways the attempts fail.[20]

From this dichotomy arise various methodological and philosophical ramifications. Methodologically, if one proceeds from a structuralist standpoint then one is not going to study the actions and intentions of actors, because by this view, these will only ever be regarded as being induced by certain structural conditions. Thus, methodologically the place to begin an analysis is with the social and economic environment. Alternatively, if our perspective is agency-orientated, then to study the machinations of the market, for example, is to reify the process and what we need to be doing is to look at the actions and intentions of the agents who generate market conditions. This, it is supposed, will give us a greater insight into its workings. However, it implies that agents operating within this structure have 'chosen' it intentionally.

Philosophically, if analysis begins with structural considerations then the implication is that human beings are malleable, for it is into structures that we are born, and it is the structures which therefore shape and socialise us. However, if our concern is with the action of social agents, then the implication is that agents have some kind of *a priori* intentionality.

The problems with each perspective, although perhaps readily apparent, are worth sketching. If structures socialise us, how are we to account for change? If, as Marx postulated, socialism is the epoch to follow capitalism, the question is do we just sit back and wait for it to come, or is consciousness to be raised – which then leads us to ask the question, who is to educate the educators? A structuralist perspective involves pulling out the typical characteristics of a structure, which then become its defining characteristics, which then in turn inform the selection and interpretation of the facts. Such a perspective risks the danger of becoming abstract, static and tautological. Another point to consider is just how comfortable we are with the idea that our natures are malleable and plastic. In Chomsky's view there is not much evidence to support such a conclusion, as his critique of Skinner demonstrates.[21] Conversely, if agents are the centre of things, the question is what gives rise to intentionality. By this view we can only be left with a metaphysical conclusion which is not open to explanation. Also we are in danger of accepting articulated intentions as being a true indication of intention, when in fact articulated intentions may serve to obscure some other perhaps less palatable intention. If we take the position that agents are rationally intentional how are we to explain power differentials in society? Is it just that some people are *a priori* more intelligent than others and/or more virtuous, ruthless or wicked?

In the light of this dichotomy in social and political thought it is possible to examine, in the remainder of this book, the way in which Chomsky's ideas have a direct relevance to this dichotomy. Chapters 3, 4, 5 and 6, therefore, examine the consequences of Chomsky having a political theory for an understanding of various forms of institutional and political behaviour. In other words, the implications of his 'theory' are considered for an analysis of society. In order to do this Chomsky's critique of society is contrasted with the critiques of others in the field. Once again the contrast demonstrates that the structure/agency dichotomy is prevalent within other theoretical positions. Because this book deals with a number of very different debates within different disciplines – ranging from political theory to political philosophy and media studies – this dichotomy will appear here under a variety of labels. As the debates are well-established this book will take the terms appropriate to their disciplines. While the structural side of the dichotomy remains constant in name, on the agency side this is also known (often pejoratively) as instrumentalism or voluntarism.

Chapter 3 compares Chomsky's ideas on the state and capitalism with those of Marx. Chomsky's methodology, which is to compare policy intentions with policy outcomes, demonstrates that the state is actively and instrumentally involved in so-called market economies, and that this is more than simply a reflection of an economic logic. Chomsky's evidence suggests that an analysis such as Marx's reifies the capitalist economy, thereby making it hard to comprehend the state's role internationally. Chomsky's analysis also raises questions about the way in which we define a state.

Having established the importance of the different emphases placed on the state by Chomsky, as compared to Marx, Chapter 4 considers the implications of Chomsky's theory for state theory generally, but particularly those theories influenced by Marxist ideas. This chapter looks at the problems of theorising about the state, in particular interpreting the relationship between the structure of the state and agency – business elites, state elites and the general public.

If, as Chomsky emphasises, the state and elites are conceived of as active agents in social, political and economic affairs then this raises questions about the nature of nationalism. States seek to secure the national interest, however narrowly conceived this might be. This suggests that the most powerful states of the so-called 'first world' must be most actively nationalistic. Chapter 5 looks at theories of nationalism, and finds that first world nations are curiously absent from the models, except, that is, to explain the birth of first world nations. Again Chomsky's analysis offers a way of questioning the theoretical assumptions underpinning this aspect of political theory.

Chapter 6 looks at Chomsky's analysis of the media, where he finds that much of the ideological obfuscation on these matters is achieved. Unlike most of his work, here he acknowledges a framework. However, most interpretations of this framework find it to be too agency-orientated and therefore 'instrumentalist'. This criticism suggests that Chomsky is a 'conspiracy theorist'. These claims are considered, as is his analysis of media content and the effect the media has on audiences. As with other chapters his general theory of human nature and his ideas on libertarian socialism are essential for an understanding of his critique of the media.

This book then is a comprehensive analysis of Chomsky as a social and political theorist. It covers his critique of contemporary state capitalism and his vision of the good society, together with his ideas on how to get there.

Notes

1 Chomsky, N. in Raskin, M. G. and Bernstein, H. J. (eds) (1987) *New Ways of Knowing: The Sciences, Society and Reconstructive Knowledge*, Totowa, New Jersey: Rowmen and Littlefield, p. 148. Chomsky does go on to note that 'I'm not a linguist either; I have no professional credentials in anything'.
2 See 'Noam Chomsky: An Interview' in *Radical Philosophy*, 53, Autumn 1989, p. 35.
3 Chomsky, N. in *Radical Philosophy*, p. 35.
4 Cockburn, A. in Barsamian, D. (ed.) (1992) *Chronicles of Dissent*, Stirling: A.K. Press.
5 See Otero, C. P. (ed.) (1988) *Noam Chomsky: Language and Politics*, Montreal and New York: Black Rose Books, pp. 72–3, n. 44.
6 Harbord, S. (1987) *A Historian's Appraisal of the Political Writings of Noam Chomsky*, MA Thesis, University of Kent at Canterbury, pp. 130–1.
7 Chomsky, N. in Otero, C. P. (ed.) (1988) *op. cit.*, pp. 674–5.
8 Chomsky, N. in Otero, C. P. (ed.) (1988) *op. cit.*, p. 372.
9 Chomsky, N. (1989a) *Necessary Illusions*, London: Pluto Press, p. 18.
10 Chomsky, N. in Otero, C. P. (ed.) (1988) *op. cit.*, p. 675.
11 Chomsky, N. in Otero, C. P. (ed.) (1988) *op. cit.*, p. 373.
12 Chomsky, N. in Otero, C. P. (ed.) (1988) *op. cit.*, p. 599.
13 Chomsky, N. in Otero, C. P. (ed.) (1988) *op. cit.*, p. 372.
14 Chomsky, N. in Otero, C. P. (ed.) (1988) *op. cit.*, p. 164.
15 Herman, E. S. and Chomsky, N. (1994) *Manfacturing Consent* (2nd edn), London: Vintage.
16 Chomsky, N. (1970) *For Reasons of State*, New York: Vintage Books, ch. 7.
17 Imagery drawn by Chomsky in personal conversation with him – 1994.
18 Aspects of this context are offered by Otero (1988) in the introduction to his book *Noam Chomsky: Language and Politics*.
19 Layder, D. (1981) *Structure, Interaction and Social Theory*, London: Routledge and Kegan Paul.
20 Layder, D., *op. cit.* He makes his own attempt to bridge the dichotomy, but not, in my view, successfully. At no point does he discuss human nature.
21 Chomsky, N. (1973) *For Reasons of State*, New York: Vintage Books, pp. 318–69.

1 Political theory

Introduction

This chapter critically examines Chomsky's claims that he does not have a political theory and that his analysis of contemporary political issues does not warrant the label of 'science'.[1] 'I never use the phrase "scientific knowledge" in dealing with any questions of history . . . [it is] neither science nor mere opinion'.[2] When we look closely at why he makes such claims we find him arguing that forms of human social organisation presuppose certain ideas about human nature but that as we know so little about human nature, we cannot describe our claims as having a theoretical and/or scientific content. In Chomsky's view we might never know much about human nature because of possible constraints on the capacities of the human mind that make such introspection impossible. However, such difficulty should not lead one to assume that we have no intrinsic nature, or that our natures are plastic and malleable. It is because of the difficulties in drawing connections between human nature and human organisation that Chomsky feels it is more intellectually honest not to claim that we are doing theory or science when we study human behaviour and organisation.

The notion that claims about human social organisation presuppose a framework of unverifiable views about human nature implies that any observation about human social organisation may be as good as any other, because they all rest upon theoretical frameworks that are incommensurable. In other words, there is some sense in which two theories can refer to the same reality and yet have no logical relations between them that allow inferences to be drawn. While Chomsky maintains that what we can know about political events is often unclear, secondhand and therefore difficult to verify, and also relies on an understanding of human need, he would nevertheless be unhappy with the conclusion that it is all a matter of interpretation. Human beings are not, in his view, hermeneutically sealed within their own interpretative frameworks. Human beings survive or not within social and political environments and these environments have effects for better or worse upon human behaviour. So while he would argue that observations and analyses of events presuppose interpretations about human need that cannot be verified, it is not the case that these often implicit claims about human need cannot themselves be tested. In other words it is possible for two commentators to have very different interpretations of the same event. The differences in their interpretations will ultimately stem from divergent understandings of human need and nature. While we may not be able to gain know-ledge about human nature, this does not mean that interpretation and its resultant action will not have real effects on human life. The precise nature of the relationship, however, has yet to be established, if it ever can be.

While Chomsky is clearly correct that we have yet to establish any deep understanding of human nature and its relationship to society, it will be argued that there are good grounds for rejecting his conclusions that his framework cannot be called a theory and cannot be tested.

The question then to ask of Chomsky is what are his grounds for claiming that his social and political thought is not scientific. Is it that his work is mere interpretation and that he holds a 'purer' definition of science than, say, phenomenologists? We might also ask why he takes the position that he does on theory, because something can be a theory without being scientific. Religious notions would be an example.

His view on this is important because in a postmodern world where anything goes and truth is elusive, Chomsky's social and political analysis appears to be challenging such a doctrine. When we consider his fastid-ious attention to detail and the scrupulous referencing of the 'facts', we trust that his work is just that, laying claims to the facts of the matter, to the truth. But then if this is the case why is this not science?

Science or interpretation?

Talk of science usually refers to the activity associated with the natural sciences. This activity involves the application of rational criteria to an understanding of events. Rational criteria include a combination of obser-vational evidence and logic. It is the use of these rational criteria that is seen to have provided the natural sciences with advancement, despite the fact that what is to count as an observation in evidence is often contested.

The question has been raised, however, whether the methods and tech-niques employed by the natural sciences are appropriate for the study of human behaviour. Those for 'naturalism' in the social sciences are asso-ciated with the positivist approach, believing the tools of the natural sciences are appropriate for the study of human behaviour. The classic opposition to this is put forward by phenomenologists in opposition to positivism. Phenomenologists argue that variables under consideration in the natural sciences are inanimate and non-sentient and so can be expected to behave in patterned law-like ways. By contrast, the key variable in the social sciences, the human being, is endowed with consciousness and hence subjectivity. As for the other variable within the study of social science – 'society' – this too is treated as having been shaped by human consciousness. This means that devising a theory in order to explain the relationship between variables, which is the job of a theory, is complicated in the social sciences because of the difficulty in reaching agreement on the status of subjectivity in an explanation of events. So, for example, positivists (naturalists) who see the 'aim of the social sciences [as] the same as that of the natural sciences'[3] thereby treat subjective states[4] as belonging outside the realm of social scientific activity, having more to do with value judgements. Value judgements are associated with morality and involve claims that '. . . something is good, or right, or such as . . . ought to be done'.[5] Some have come to regard these kind of statements as having a different meaning from statements of fact and description. But then as Hudson argues '[t]he question nevertheless remains: how are moral judgements and statements of fact *related* to one another?'[6] For positivists, however, facts and values are separate. For them a theory must consist of 'logically interrelated propositions which have empirical consequences'.[7] Behaviour is patterned and the social scientist can study these patterns and their relationship to society, seeking causal relation without reference to subjective intention.[8] Phenomenologists, by contrast, argue that as behaviour is informed by intentionality, it is the job of the social scientist to 'develop categories for understanding what the actor – from his [sic] own point of view – "means" in his actions'.[9] Phenomenology

> is not concerned with proving that others exist, but rather with how we come to interpret others and their actions; with the complex ways in which we understand those with whom we interact; and with the ways in which we interpret our own actions and those of others within a social context.[10]

Having said this, as Bernstein points out, phenomenologists are not claiming that what they do is not science, only that, counter to the view of positivists, subjectivity is a legitimate object for scientific study.

> Like all sciences, the social sciences make objective meaning claims. Yet what is distinctive about the social sciences is that these claims concern the subjective meanings that are constitutive of actions of individuals in the social world.[11]

Nevertheless phenomenologists, like positivists, separate facts and values and so as Bernstein points out, phenomenology fails to show how it is possible to adjudicate between competing interpretations of meaning, removing evaluative criteria thereby leaving unresolved the problem of the causal determinants of social action. If certain reasons cannot be established to be objectively more true than others, then this implies that explanations are always relative to the sociological or psychological conditions of the object under study. So depending on one's definition of science, we could object to the phenomenologists' claims that what they are doing is science, and argue instead that it is merely description. If phenomenologists are not doing science, because they do not adjudicate between competing interpretations of meaning, this suggests that contrary to the positivist claim, science does involve evaluative claims.

Is and ought

In social and political thought there are two categories or types of question one might ask. In the first instance one might ask questions about *what is*, and in the second instance one might ask questions about *what ought to be*. In other words one can provide explanatory accounts of social and political phenomena or one can make normative claims. Usually normative claims[12] are taken to be evaluative, whereas explanatory accounts are said to be factual. It is the relationship between *is* and *ought* questions which is controversial. But this is not just controversial for the social sciences, for as Zimmerman argues '[h]ow could they [naturalists, empiricists] talk about statements being "justified" only if supported by "is" statements, if by "justified" they mean "ought to be believed"?'[13] But both positivists and phenomenologists argue that normative or evaluative questions are unscientific and so cannot be answered by any sort of scientific theory. Particularly in the view of a strict empiricist, normative accounts should have no influence in a description of *what is*. In this sense the empiricist meets scientific strictures and can arrive at theories that are 'correct' precisely because they are objective, abstract and devoid of 'feeling'.

In political philosophy we find a concern with 'ought' questions. For example 'why we ought to obey the law and the government'.[14] For some this is a problem because 'the theoretical task of analysis and classification have rarely been separated or even satisfactorily distinguished from the evaluation questions'.[15] But as Keat and Urry show, Charles Taylor argues that

> [t]o show that some state of affairs leads to the satisfaction of human wants, needs or interests is to show that it is morally desirable. It is unintelligible, though not strictly self-contradictory, to deny that such a state of affairs is desirable, unless it can also be shown that it contains elements leading to non-satisfactions.[16]

Taylor it seems is keen to avoid neutrality in political science, and seeks to derive an 'ought' from an 'is'. However, despite his view that a judgement is *rationally* defensible he nevertheless also wants to claim, as Nielsen describes it, that '[t]here is no breaking out of the hermeneutical circle so that independently of some challengable, hermeneutic stance, we can verify any significant social science or political claim. Social science is a science of interpretation and not a science of verification'.[17] So, unlike phenomenologists, he is arguing that we can evaluate and that we can do this rationally, but ultimately, he wants to argue it is all interpretation.

It seems Taylor is caught in the same position as phenomenologists, because by describing human beings as being trapped hermeneutically, he is implying that we cannot establish a causal relation between human behaviour and society. Presumably Taylor cannot believe this, because otherwise he would not wish to produce value judgements in social science. He is presumably of the view that were we to make changes to our social organisation in the ways he considers appropriate, then there would be some beneficial effect on us as human beings. As such, we ought to be able to see and measure the effects, and not simply claim that what we are doing is interpretation.

Theory

Depending on the perspective one takes then, we find that this has implications for what is to count for a theory and this in turn affects the methodology employed. Theory in natural science refers to the set of principles or laws which seek to make connections between variables in order to explain the cause of various effects, across time and space. Reasons are found to explain and predict events, and from this it is considered possible to ascertain that certain reasons can be established to be objectively more true than others. The logic of this position is that certain ideas and explanations carry more authority than others. For phenomenologists such as Schutz, however, a theory in the social sciences can only meet three primary postulates: (1) the 'postulate of logical consistency' which means guaranteeing the 'objective validity of the thought objects constructed by the social scientist'; (2) 'the postulate of subjective interpretation' which means 'the possibility of referring all kinds of human action or their results to the subjective meaning such action or result of an action had for the actor'; and (3) the 'postulate of adequacy' which means that there must be 'consistency of the constructs of the social scientist with the constructs of common-sense experience of the social reality'.[18] As such then 'subjective states [are given] in the causal explanation of human action'.[19] But as has already been noted it is difficult from this to 'ascertain that certain reasons can be established to be objectively more true than others', other than by appeal to the 'postulate of adequacy'. As we have seen phenomenologists take the view that value judgements must be kept out of social scientific investigation. By contrast Keat and Urry argue '[f]or positivists, "understanding" is merely a psychological device by which we postulate the nature of other people's subjective states. The use of this device in no way establishes the validity of its results, and therefore it does not belong to the "logic of science"'.[20]

Theory for phenomenologists admits the variable of subjectivity but dismisses the possibility of prediction. Positivists by contrast see theory as necessarily predictive but do not regard subjective states as legitimate variables.

Structure and agency

What is problematic to this debate, is the question of what is to count as *evidence* in the social sciences. The answer to this question has implications for, or rather influences, the theoretical framework and methodology employed by this perspective. For example if we take a positivist such as Emile Durkheim, and look at his analysis of *Suicide*, we see he proceeds by observing existing patterns in externalised behaviour.[21] On this basis, he then makes inferences about the patterned behaviour and its relationship to society. In so doing he implies a causal relation from society to the human being. This type of analysis which begins with an analysis of society, in order to make causal connections between this and human behaviour, is also known as a structural approach.[22] A structural analysis has a 'commitment to the view that the relations between the constituent elements of a structure are more important than the individual elements; and indeed that all the elements themselves are comprised of sets of relations'.[23] This type of positivist structural approach is implying something about human nature. It implicitly employs the theory that human beings are without intrinsic behavioural characteristics because by this analysis they are shaped by the social structure around them. In other words human nature is conceived of as plastic and malleable.

By contrast, phenomenologists, such as Schutz, proceed also by observing existing patterns of externalised behaviour, but instead are concerned to interpret this behaviour, seeing it as the product of a subjective state. This type of analysis, which begins with an interpretative analysis of human behaviour, is also known as a social action approach, where the agent is the principle unit of analysis. Concern is with 'the ways in which human beings explain and justify their actions in the course of everyday life'.[24] For Weber 'in ascribing ... motives to the agents, we should be seen as attempting to give causal explanations of their actions'.[25] Although this is not stated explicitly this implies that the causal relation in the relationship between human beings and their society is from the actor to the society. Society is the product of actors' interpretations. Again this type of action approach is implying something about human nature. The theoretical suggestion is that human beings do have intrinsic behaviour characteristics, perhaps the product of psychological states, although these may be left unexplored.

It is recognised that these brief attempts to introduce the theoretical assumptions behind the structure/agency dichotomy do not do justice to the various complexities. So, for example, Keat and Urry argue that 'such outright rejections of the legitimacy of explaining social phenomena by reference to subjective states are rare amongst positivist sociologists'.[26] And, 'more often, both their [positivist's] methodological claims and their actual practice have displayed a considerable degree of ambiguity or inconsistency on this issue'.[27] This suggests that either a theoretical position is clear, consistent, unambiguous and therefore conforms to the canons of science (and we might want to say is not very realistic) or it is not, but then it cannot claim to be scientific.

The problem with both these positions is that each treats their principal object of analysis – structure or agent – as empirically separable from the other. Yet they claim effect occurs from one to the other, without being able to offer a satisfactory explanation of how or even why we should accept the claim of an effect.

It would seem that the study of social and political behaviour is fraught with difficulties. If we remove subjectivity from analysis, then although we may be able to meet a certain type of scientific rigour, we also remove from our analysis human subjectivity and intention. However, if we include in our analysis human subjectivity, then we give this some sort of metaphysical *a priori* status, which means we cannot explain and so evaluate it.

The way in which this debate has been couched implies that all is well in the natural sciences, but, as has been alluded to even in the natural sciences, there is a question about the use of evaluative criteria in the determination of facts. In other words the question is raised whether subjectivity can be removed from an analysis of the facts, even in the natural sciences. This raises the further question of whether it is the case that all things are relative (even this statement?).

Relativism

Feyerabend launches an attack upon what is in his view the arrogance of western science. He argues that science has become oppressive and rigid, and that scientific 'facts' are taught to the young in much the same way that religion used to be taught. Feyerabend attacks two assertions made by the philosophy of science: firstly, that it has found the correct method for achieving results; and secondly, that science has many achievements to prove this. Popper (1945) argued that theories that are empirically tested and falsified by the facts should be rejected while theories that have not been falsified can remain. However, absence of falsification does not establish the truth of the theory. As Feyerabend argues in his attack on Popper, an unfalsified theory 'may in fact be the best lousy theory there is'.[28] Feyerabend is expressly critical of such assertive pronouncements within the philosophy of science, because, as he demonstrates following Kuhn (1970), falsified theories may continue to thrive, and as history demonstrates falsified theories should not necessarily be rejected by science.

He goes on to argue that observation in science is itself theory dependent. As such, observation then cannot be a reliable tool for deciding between theories. Contrary to what philosophers of science argue, Feyerabend finds that struggles in science are determined not by adherence to the scientific method, but rather by propaganda, prestige, power, age, sex and polemic. Indeed, to assert that science has found *the* correct method is an argument that can only be sustained if it can also be argued that nothing else has produced results. Feyerabend argues that this is simply not the case. Alternative methods of, for example, medical diagnosis and therapy have been shown to be as effective as, if not more effective than, that offered by western medicine today. In his view 'the scientific method' is too restricting. For progress there should be methodological pluralism and scientists should adopt the motto 'anything goes'.

In Feyerabend's later work he considers social and political implications of western scientific hegemony. He expresses vehement objection to the way in which western ideals supported by science have been exported and imposed upon other cultures.

> I do not favour the export of 'freedom' into regions that are doing well without it and whose inhabitants show no desire to change their ways. For me a declaration such as 'humanity is one, and he who cares for freedom and human rights cares for freedom and human rights everywhere', where 'to care' may imply active intervention . . . is just another example of intellectual (liberal) presumption.[29]

For Feyerabend his 'concern is neither rationality, nor science, nor freedom – abstractions such as these have done more harm than good – but the quality of the lives of individuals'.[30] Feyerabend it seems is seeking to move away from abstract notions of truth and falsity towards concrete notions of good and bad: concrete in the sense that value is determined by those affected. Quoting Protagoras he argues ' ". . . [T]ruth lies with us, with our 'opinions' and 'experiences' and we, 'the many', not abstract theories, are the measure of things" '.[31] Feyerabend's relativism holds that knowledge is culturally specific and that truth therefore is relative.

For some opponents of Feyerabend's relativistic position the notion that 'anything goes' means in practice that 'everything stays'.[32] In other words it suggests that there can be no change or progress. But Feyerabend does believe that there can be change or progress, but only if decisions to move on from the bad are decisions taken by those affected.

> . . . perception and opinion, the customary measures of truth, are infallible measures and the worlds projected by different individuals, groups, nations are as they perceive and describe them – they are all equally real. However, *they are not equally good or beneficial* (to those who live in them). A sick person lives in a world where every-

thing tastes sour and therefore is sour – but he is not happy in it. The members of a racist society live in a world where people fall into sharply defined groups, some creative and benevolent, others parasitical and evil – but their lives are not very comfortable. A desire for change may arise in either case.[33]

The question now to be asked is whether Chomsky's claim not to be doing theory or science in his social and political analysis is associated with one or other of these perspectives.

The paradox of liberalism

Chomsky describes himself as a libertarian socialist.[34] A detailed discussion on what this constitutes can be found in the next chapter. For now, for the purposes of this discussion we can say that libertarian socialism for Chomsky means he believes that human beings can flourish best in, and should therefore have, conditions providing maximum freedom. In his view a key prerequisite to this involves the abolition of private property,[35] in other words a form of socialism. For many, such a prescription would mean placing the means of production in the hands of the state. However, his commitment to freedom precludes this as a possibility. A situation in which a central body decides upon the allocation of resources should be avoided at all costs, even if such decisions are supposed to be 'on behalf of the people'. Equally, there should be freedom from authority in the field of ideas. Freedom of expression must be defended while production is established through 'free association'.[36]

Chomsky's ideas then constitute a form of anarchism. Anarchism has various strands, but one element common to all strands is the belief that given adequate information people are able to make informed choices and so there should be no obligation upon them to obey authority. 'Authority' in this sense has traditionally referred to forms of political authority. Clearly Chomsky's views accept this as a basic feature of his anarchism, but in his view to be consistent in one's opposition to authority this must be extended to economic matters.[37] However, since Feyerabend, anarchism has been further extended and can also mean opposition to the authority accorded certain types of ideas, for example the authority given to western scientific rationalism.[38] In other words anarchism can also imply support for an anti-rationalist or a relativist position. Chomsky's anarchist or libertarian position could then involve what Gellner has called the paradox of liberalism.[39] Such a position, when taken to its logical conclusion, suggests a form of relativism.

Following the 'Faurisson affair', Chomsky has become renowned for his opposition to censorship and his defence of freedom of expression. In 1979 he signed a petition objecting to a decision which deprived Robert Faurisson of his job at the University of Lyon, and to a subsequent court conviction which found Faurisson to be an irresponsible historian. Faurisson's crime was that he had written a book denying the Nazi Holocaust against the Jews. Shortly after signing this petition, Chomsky wrote an essay defending freedom of expression. This essay was used as a preface to Faurisson's book but without Chomsky's knowledge or permission. Chomsky pointed out that some of his critics were guilty of confusing the defence of Faurisson's civil rights with the defence of his views.[40] More generous critics argued that Chomsky should only have defended Faurisson's right to freedom of expression if he had also denounced Faurisson's conclusions. But as Chomsky points out, this would 'require a careful analysis of his documentation ... [t]he demand that defence of civil rights requires an analysis and commentary on the views expressed would simply eliminate the defence of the rights of those who express unpopular or horrendous views ...'.[41]

Rationalism

In many ways Chomsky's position seems to have certain parallels with Feyerabend's position. However, as the Faurisson case shows Chomsky is not arguing that the truth is relative, rather that people should be free to express any idea however unpopular. Chomsky also explicitly describes himself as a rationalist. 'I think myself that it is rationalist approaches which provide the basis for a progressive world view ...'.[42] But what does it mean to describe oneself as a rationalist? For Chomksy '[t]he rationalist view assumes that there are certain intrinsic properties of human nature, and we have to find out what those are'.[43] Chomsky contrasts this with the empiricist view that finds that 'human beings are malleable, that they have no intrinsic characteristics ...'.[44] However, when Feyerabend describes himself as a relativist as opposed to a rationalist, his objection, as we've seen, is to the rationalist method rather than to whether human nature has any intrinsic characteristics. His objection is to rationalism in the sense of the claim that some ideas and actions are objectively more rational, and thus more acceptable, than others. For Feyerabend, to restrict knowledge to what survives submission to rationalist strictures like commensurability, universality, and non-contradiction is too restraining and unrealistic. 'A non-contradiction cannot be demanded in a world where an old woman is seen as having "the round, sweet throat of a goddess"'.[45] However, Chomsky is not just a rationalist in the sense that he is of the view that human nature has intrinsic properties. He is also a rationalist in the sense that he is of the view that reason can establish that some things are objectively more true than others; in other words that some ideas are more rational than others. 'I am a child of the Enlightenment. I think irrational belief is a dangerous phenomenon, and I try consciously to avoid irrational belief'.[46] Having said this Chomsky does demonstrate openness and a willingness to be persuaded

otherwise, which is something Feyerabend finds absent in science generally. Speaking about religion in the context of irrational belief Chomsky
continues:

> On the other hand, I certainly recognize that it's [religion] a major
> phenomenon for people in general, and you can understand why it
> would be. It does, apparently, provide personal sustenance, but also
> bonds of association and solidarity and a means for expressing
> elements of one's personality that are often very valuable. To many
> people it does that. In my view, there's nothing wrong with that. *My
> view could be wrong, of course,* but my position is that we should
> not succumb to irrational belief.[47] (my italics)

As we've seen in Feyerabend's later work, he objects to the way in
which other cultures, which are deemed to be pre-rational, are attacked
by western rationalism. His point is that there is no objective way of
deciding whether or not a belief is really rational or irrational. '...
[R]esearch is not a privilege of special groups and (scientific) knowledge
not a universal measure of human excellence. Knowlege is a local com-
modity designed to satisfy local needs and to solve local problems; it can
be changed from the outside, but only after extended consultations that
include the opinions of all concerned parties'.[48]

Chomsky, as his emphasis on American foreign policy indicates, like
Feyerabend, is also concerned about the west's relationship with other
cultures. However, even as a rationalist (in both senses of the term) and
despite objecting to what is in his view irrational belief, Chomsky is critical of any form of force being used in an attempt to get another person
or culture to drop certain views. In Chomsky's view persuasion and
demonstration are more effective tools. 'If the physics student believes
his [sic] professor doesn't understand which way is up, then he should
demonstrate this to the professor. It won't do any good to storm the
physics building. If the student knows which side is up I think he has a
fair chance of showing it'.[49] The difference, it seems, between Chomsky
and Feyerabend is that Feyerabend is content to accept the incommensu-
rability of systems of belief. This is because he feels that there is no way
of deciding which view is objectively more acceptable. Chomsky, by
contrast, holds that humans, given a better spread of resources and knowledge or information, will be able to agree and make a rational choice
within the circumstances.[50] In fact in Chomsky's view, despite the ideological manipulation justified by western rationalism, people are able to
see when what is justified as rational is in fact manipulation. Chomsky
documents the way in which people experience contradiction between
what they are told and their experiences. He argues 'I believe in Cartesian
common sense. I think people have the capacities to see through the
deceit in which they are ensnared, but they've got to make the effort'.[51]

For Chomsky what people lack are the political and economic structures necessary to expose the selective use of rationalist justification.

Despite the fact that in their declared positions Chomsky and Feyerabend appear oppositional, they nevertheless share many concerns. Having said this it seems to me that Chomsky offers a more sophisticated account of political realities. Feyerabend, in his analysis of western science and rationalism, tends to consider them in isolation. At no point does Feyerabend attempt to locate the scientific community within the wider social, political and economic climate. There is no question that the guise of objectivity and scientific method have been used to defend western attempts to meddle in the affairs of other countries, but there is nothing intrinsic to rationalism to mean that this should be so. Behind the interference Chomsky so graphically describes are always interests that are intimately linked with the political and economic structure of western state capitalism. As Chomsky argues, the double standards can easily be demonstrated by considering much intellectual response to the rationalists of 'enemy' states.

> [W]e despise the technocratic and policy-oriented intellectuals as 'commissars' and 'apparatchiks,' and honor the value-oriented intellectuals as the 'democratic dissidents.' At home, the values are reversed. Ways must be found to control the value-oriented intellectuals so that democracy can survive, with the citizenry reduced to the apathy and obedience that become them, and with the commissars free to conduct the serious work of social management.[52]

Chomsky regards Bakunin's warning, a century ago, of the emergence of a 'new class', in reference to those controlling technical knowledge, as particularly pertinent. Such a class, Bakunin predicted, would 'attempt to convert their access to knowledge into power over economic and social life'.[53] Chomsky argues that this has been possible with the type of convergence that has occurred between so-called socialist and capitalist societies in terms of centralised state power. In this context he notes the 'close links in the United States between corporate ownership and control on the one hand, and university-based programs in technology and industrial management on the other ...'.[54]

Feyerabend in his discussion of 'the reign of scientific intelligence'[55] does draw upon, as well as make explicit reference in a footnote to, Chomsky's piece 'Intellectuals and the State'.[56] However, Feyerabend's work fails to draw out the structural interconnections traced by Chomsky. Chomsky makes what is a key point in opposition to Feyerabend's relativism, namely, that it should not be concluded that because 'the technical intelligentsia make decisions on behalf of others in capitalist democracy, they therefore hold power'.[57] In other words, it is Chomsky's view that the power acquired by the technical intelligentsia is not something intrinsic to the form and character of production that they undertake. Rather it is conferred from without. The 'reign' referred to by Feyerabend simply refers to the period where intimate links were established (wittingly or unwittingly by the scientific community) between certain ideas and the political and economic dynamics of the era.

Indeed in Chomsky's view the intelligentsia can produce results that threaten the status quo: it is just that such intellectuals do not receive the same notice and acclaim as those whose findings do not challenge existing arrangements. In his view, this accounts for the popularity and acclaim accorded to, for example, the rationalist claims of empiricism.[58] Here Chomsky is referring to the behaviourist notion that humans are socialised and develop solely in response to external stimuli. As such, human beings are characterised as being malleable and as having no intrinsic characteristics. 'The empiricist concept of human nature has essentially nothing that supports it and much that goes against it. Why then is it accepted as virtually a kind of doctrine or dogma? Well, I think here we might ask the question how it serves the needs of those who accept it'.[59] It is important to point out that Chomsky objects to the empiricist concept of human nature, but not to the empirical method as such. Empiricism, then, claims rationalist credentials but relies upon unsubstantiated claims about human nature. Chomsky objects to its claims to be rational, rather than to the possibility of a rational explanation.

Feyerabend makes repeated reference to the lack of respect western science has had for tradition. '[S]tatements composed of concepts lacking in details could be used to build new kinds of stories, soon to be called proofs, whose truth "followed from" their inner structure and needed no support from traditional authorities. The discovery was interpreted as showing that knowledge could be detached from traditions and made "objective".'[60] But such 'detachment from tradition', as Feyerabend puts it, need not be something that occurs necessarily in using an empirical and therefore rational methodology. That 'detachment from tradition' does occur indicates that other interests are at play: interests that are not exclusively western either. We must question then Feyerabend's whole use of the term 'tradition', as though a tradition was homogenous and without internal conflict.

Chomsky it seems is a rationalist then in both senses of the term. He is of the view that human nature has intrinsic properties and he is of the view that some claims can be established to be objectively more true than others.

Re-describing reality

Up to this point Chomsky has been identified as a rationalist, but one who would defend another's right to make a 'wrong' or 'bad' statement. However, it seems, despite being a rationalist, Chomsky would be sympathetic to a more anarchistic approach in the sciences and social sciences. Perhaps, then, Chomsky seeks to break away from the over-theorising tendency of the social sciences in an effort to simply re-describe reality. Jaggar has argued that there are many similarities between radical feminist approaches and anarchism. In both traditions there is a mistrust of abstract principles and formalism.[61] '[P]olitical life should be judged by "personal" standards of caring, spontaneity and playfulness, "strength, vitality and joy".'[62] One such feminist argues that 'she no longer likes to use the word *theory* for our thought since that word implies a special kind of separation between thought, feeling and experience'.[63] '[R]adical feminists see their first task as being simply to redescribe reality'.[64] In other words not theorising about it. In many ways because Chomsky's work is a form of political journalism, and so he could be said to be doing just as the radical feminists did, re-describing reality. Like them he has been concerned to present an alternative picture of reality to that presented by the elite media.

Jaggar, however, makes the following objection to the radical feminist's suggestion that description or re-description can in a sense be purer or somehow more accurate:

> When social phenomena have to be explained, it is common to think of a theory as postulating certain underlying mechanisms that will provide a causal explanation of observed patterns of regularities in those phenomena. If one thinks of a theory in this way it is evident that an adequate theoretical account of any social phenomena presup-poses an adequate description of those phenomena: if the phenomena in question are misdescribed, if existing regularities are unrecognized or if regularities are asserted that are unimportant or even nonexistent, then the theoretical inquiry will be misdirected. For this reason, although it is possible to distinguish between theories and descriptions in terms of the levels of reality to which they refer, it is impossible to make a sharp separation between theory and description. Descriptions of reality are theory laden, at least in the sense that they are compatible or incompatible with certain theoretical accounts; similarly, although theories are supposed to explain rather than contradict observations or descriptions, they may imply that certain observations have been mis-interpreted or that the supposed data should be redescribed.[65]

Feyerabend would agree with her. In his view there is no pure unmedi-ated, theory-free, access to reality. Chomsky on the other hand would, it seems to me, hold a position that both accepts Jaggar's criticisms of radical feminism, yet demonstrates sympathies with the anarchist/radical feminist position, while at the same time remaining consistent and rationalist. This is significant because we begin to see why Chomsky wants to assert that his social and political analysis is not theory or science.

Human nature

As has been mentioned in social and political thought there are two categories or types of question one might ask. We can ask *what is* questions, when we wish to consider the present character of social and political affairs. From this we can then raise questions about *what ought to be*. In other words our findings about the current state of affairs may provide insight into the way things could be in the future. The first category of question seeks to provide an explanatory account, where the second offers normative claims. However, normative claims are evaluative and as we have seen there is a question about their status in relation to facts. This has been seen to present problems for the socialist. As the socialist is, in the first instance, defined by his or her view of *what ought to be*, this is deemed to colour their view of *what is*. As such, they can be accused of importing an evaluative premise into their explanatory accounts, leaving their accounts open to being discounted as unscientific, Utopian and idealist. In other words socialists are accused of having their explanatory accounts determined by their normative views.

Marx sought to overcome this problem by reversing the determinants. In his view, a careful study of the social and economic facts, i.e. *what is*, would reveal that there are internal contradictions within social relations. To put this at its briefest, these contradictions, he argued, would give rise to a set of conditions that would bring about conditions, if not an outcome, that are socialist: in other words an outcome which favoured his normative ideals. This enabled him to present his views as scientific socialism as distinct from Utopian socialism.

Chomsky, however, turns this argument on its head. In his view, whatever normative account one seeks to defend, even if it is to remain with the status quo, one presupposes a certain explanatory view about *what is*. One presupposes certain ideas about *what is* specifically of human nature.

> Suppose you have an opinion about what ought to be done. We think there has to be some revolutionary change. Anyone that advocates that kind of position at the root is basing the advocacy on some assumption about human nature. Maybe the assumption is not explicit, in fact, it almost never is explicit. But the fact is that if there is any moral character to what we advocate, it is because we believe or are hoping that this change we are proposing is better for humans because of the way humans are. There is something about the way humans fundamentally are, about their fundamental nature, which requires that this change we are advocating take place.[66]

The point is that in social and political analysis, even if an account of reality shies away from normative claims, preferring to stick to interpretive descriptive accounts, it is implicitly accepting the status quo. As

Gouldner points out, even those committed to the dogma 'Thou shalt not commit a value judgement' are simply supporting the status quo in terms of social organisation.[67] In other words, any description of *what is* is indicative of *what ought to be* but it is also theory-laden in terms of *what is* human nature.

Chomsky goes on to argue that as we know so little about human nature, any view that one holds of it, however implicit, can only be based on guess work, intuition or hope. As such then *what is* and *what ought to be* are both evaluative and are therefore unscientific. Thus he would agree with Jaggar that any explanatory view about *what is* is theory-bound. In his view any description of social and political reality ultimately has implicit within it certain assumptions about human nature. However, as far as he is concerned the notion that the often implicit views of human nature can realistically be called a theory or worse a science, is highly dubious. '... I am sceptical as to whether the fundamental problems of man and society can be studied in any very profound manner, at least in ways resembling scientific inquiry.'[68] Scepticism or an anarchistic approach then to abstract and theoretical accounts of human and social arrangements comes highly recommended.

Without the assurances of some more verifiable account of human nature, Chomsky resorts to a view that is hopeful. He argues that his 'beliefs are surely not scientifically well-grounded; they are a mixture of intuition, hope, and a certain reading of history'.[69] He refers to this view as Pascal's wager:

> Pascal raised the question: How do you know whether God exists? He said, if I assume that he exists and he does, I'll make out OK. If he doesn't, I won't lose anything. If he does exist and I assume he doesn't, I may be in trouble. That's basically the logic. On this issue of human freedom, if you assume that there's no hope, you guarantee that there will be no hope. If you assume that there is an instinct for freedom, there are opportunities to change things, etc., there's a chance you may contribute to making a better world. That's your choice.[70]

But to claim as Chomsky does that 'it's our choice' suggests perhaps that, as with phenomenologists, it is all a matter of interpretation, and that it is not possible to adjudicate between interpretations. Certainly his rejection of theory and a scientific approach in the social sciences is suggestive of this conclusion. However, it is hard to accept such a conclusion when we consider that Chomsky is of the view that intellectuals have a responsibility and should 'expose lies'.[71] Such a view suggests that some claims about the success or otherwise of certain forms of human social organisation can be established to be more true and therefore rational than others. Nielsen considers just this point when he assesses whether it is possible to adjudicate between Chomsky and his critics. Such disputes leave, for example, 'Schlesinger ... accus[ing] Chomsky of foreswearing "reasoned analysis" and of fabricating evidence, while Chomsky replies by denying this and accusing Schlesinger of deliberate and gross misrepresentation, invention and an "inability to get the simplest facts straight"'.[72] Nielsen makes a case for arguing that 'it is true enough that interpretations must be made, but it does not appear that we are inextricably caught in a hermeneutical circle from which we cannot break out'.[73] He goes on to argue:

> In trying to ascertain what the situation is, there are a myriad of phenomena which are not simply the creatures of practices, such as how many guns and tanks went from one border to another, how many Americans versus how many non-Americans hold jobs in a certain salary range in the so-called multi-national corporations, and how many missiles the Americans have and where they are placed, and how many missiles the Russians have and where are they placed.[74]

Clearly Nielsen is correct that we can establish the answers to these sorts of questions by reference to the facts. However, Nielsen fails to acknowledge that facts on their own 'mean' very little; they require interpretation, and tests of interpretation. Whether American missiles are interpreted as being defensive or aggressive will depend upon a whole framework of understandings about human and social affairs. Such interpretation will include, ultimately, a view about the way in which human beings *ought* to be living, which must, in Chomsky's view go back to a view of human nature. If Chomsky is accusing someone of misrepresentation, then either it is because they are misrepresenting the facts, or – and this is central to his analysis – it is because their professed claims about human social organisation (e.g. democracy) do not match their interpretation of the facts. It is for this reason that Chomsky argues that Hawks (Republicans) are often more honest than Doves (Liberals), even though he finds their claims about human social organisation to be inimical to his view of human need.

Chomsky's methodology

The crucial point about Chomsky's rationalism is his view that human nature is at the root of any critical analysis of social and political affairs, and claims in this direction cannot be verified. Despite this, Chomsky's view and practice is that in social and political analysis what we can do is look at policy intentions with their implied conception of human nature and compare them with policy outcomes in order to expose contradictions. So, for example, he observes the way in which elites usually couch their policy initiatives in terms of some sort of moral framework suggestive of a certain view of human nature. Chomsky's work then sets out to demonstrate the disparity between their purported morality and the outcome of policies. The disparity between the two, Chomsky suggests, is often suggestive not of their purported morality but rather indicates an alternative morality *rational* to an elitist view of human nature. As Chomsky shows here:

> The tactic of massive bombardment must be labeled 'counterproductive' in Pentagonese, and can be attributed only to advanced cretinism, *if* the United States goal had been to restrict American casualties or to win popular support for the Saigon government or to 'protect the population.' But it is quite rational as a device for demolishing the society in which a rebellion is rooted and takes refuge.[75]

Here we have then the methodology and theory behind Chomsky's social and political analysis. In all his work he employs what is essentially a fairly simple formula. This formula looks a bit like a phenomenological formula, in that he is concerned with motive and intention. However, unlike a phenomenologist he is not concerned to interpret intention from behaviour. He lets the actor speak for him or herself, and then compares this with the actor's action. So, as suggested, he compares claimed policy objectives with the outcome or consequences. This formula is not unlike that which he uses for his work in linguistics. Interestingly he does regard what he does in linguistics as having theoretical content.[76] It is a comparison between input and output that is indicative of the processes relating the two. He explains the methodology for studying the learning of language thus:

> The input–output situation is like this: a child who initially does not have knowledge of a language constructs for himself knowledge of a language on the basis of a certain amount of data; the input is the data, the output – which of course is internally represented – is the knowledge of the language. It's this relationship between the data available, and the knowledge of the language which results from the child's mental activities, which constitutes the data for the study of learning – of how the transition takes place from the input data to the resulting knowledge.[77]

So, in terms of political analysis, as the consequences of policy are often inimical to proclaimed intentions, this suggests a hidden agenda. In Chomsky's view the disparity between input and output suggests that elites have a rather different view of human need from the one they profess to hold.

One question this methodology raises is why should we accept Chomsky's interpretation of political outcomes. Here Chomsky is extremely careful about his choice of data. So for example he will often use 'official' data. This is not because he regards other sources as less accurate (although given the resources available to the state, it is likely that they will have a pretty full picture) but rather because official data is the elite's own record of their action. In other words their own interpretation of outcome can be found to contradict their own political rhetoric. In this sense official data become the most 'objective' source. An obvious example he uses relates to the American state's attempt to portray the USSR as having enormous and growing nuclear might, when at the same time US intelligence was producing evidence to suggest that this was far from the case.[78] In a sense, what the real figures are in terms of numbers of warheads etc. is beside the point. The really interesting issue is the observed disparity between official data and official rhetoric.

In his analysis of the media, Chomsky can also be seen employing a rigorous empirical method. He looks at the data available on a particular issue and compares it with that used and highlighted by the media. In what is clearly an empirical approach, he can be found measuring column inches and looking at where in a report an issue gets raised. Very often, he argues, all the available data on an issue are actually used by the media, but what is significant is the amount of attention given to some issues over others. Again it is the observed disparity which is important and indicative, rather than accuracy of some data over other data.

Chomsky then is extremely careful about claims to 'know' something. Even with the sort of 'facts' Nielsen wants to claim we must be able to verify, such as numbers of guns or tanks, Chomsky is careful to give us the source of this knowledge, because unless we are there counting them ourselves we cannot be said to 'know' the answer. And anyway the source of such information is often useful in his strategy of exposing the discontinuity of elite analysis in social and political affairs.

Chomsky's opposition to theory

It seems, however, that in Chomksy's view this methodology does not involve or is not constitutive of a theory and is therefore unscientific. In his view a theory is supposed to explain the occurrence of a range of phenomena in terms of something which is hidden, i.e. something not itself observable. 'Is there anything in the social sciences that even merits the term "theory"? That is, some explanatory system involving hidden structures with non-trivial principles that provide understanding of phenomena? If so I've missed it'.[79] And as early as 1969 he argues 'if there is a body of theory, well tested and verified, that applies to the conduct of foreign affairs or the resolution of domestic or international conflicts, its existence has been kept a well-guarded secret'.[80] In his view, what makes theories adequate is 'that they give some sort of insight into some domain of phenomena, provide some explanation for puzzling things, or come up with principles that are less than obvious that have empirical support'.[81]

The question is, why does he think that his political thought does not fulfil these criteria? Chomsky's own claim is that his arguments do not fulfil these criteria essentially because in his view the operations of our social system are obvious and apparent and, he argues, most people recognise them.[82] It is only the elite and the intellectuals who deceive themselves with ideologies. In particular, he argues, intellectuals have an interest in doing so.

> ... [I]n fact, social and political issues in general seem to me fairly simple; the effort to obfuscate them in esoteric and generally vacuous theory is one of the contributions of the intelligentsia to enhancing their power and the power of those they serve, as is the mindless 'empiricism' conducted in the name of 'science' but in fact in sharp contradiction to the methods of the sciences, which often succeeds in concealing major operative factors in policy and history in a maze of unanalyzed facts.[83]

Intellectuals become apologists when they generate theories and abstract tracts that ultimately obscure the fact that 'Americans steal food from starving children on a vast scale'.[84] Such obscurity is required because in his view 'most people are not gangsters. Few people, for example, would steal food from a starving child, even if they happened to be hungry and knew they could not get caught or punished'.[85]

His belief that non-elites do see through the 'propaganda' is derived not only from simply meeting ordinary people and being involved at the 'grass roots' but also because he studies opinion polls, which when interpreted 'correctly', demonstrate that people do very often have different views from the elites.

Developing this point a little, the obvious question to ask is: if people are aware that the system is exploitative and that economic and political arrangements perpetuate inequalities unjustly, then why do they not do something about it? The short answer as far as Chomsky is concerned is because they lack the political and economic power necessary and because of the difficulties of organising any such action.[86] He often refers to the more exploited groups as standing on the side-lines and watching.[87] In response to the observation that the student activism of the 1960s died because the issues which had fired students were no longer interesting to them, Chomsky argues '[t]hat students were no longer interested is not obvious; it is possible that they were simply no longer willing to endure beatings, imprisonment, vituperation, and idiotic denunciations for what was in fact courageous devotion to principle'.[88] In his view, because the more exploited groups in society are easier to repress, the middle class is 'a politically very important part of the population'. This is because they are 'difficult to repress, in the sense that there is a high political cost to the repression of these classes'.[89] For this reason he argues it is the middle classes that are the 'primary targets' for propaganda.[90]

In Chomsky's claim that his political work is atheoretical, the idea that 'hidden' things are exposed is obviously a key feature in any assessment of the explanatory power of a theory. However, despite the fact that he holds that ordinary people, with a little effort, can and do see the system for what it is, he does nevertheless seem to vacillate about the hidden nature or otherwise of social and political processes. At some levels he does seem to think that his work uncovers distorted and hidden features of the system. 'In talks and in print, I try to stress what I think is true: that with a little willingness to explore and use one's mind, it is possible to discover a good deal about the social and political world that is generally hidden'.[91] It seems quite accurate to argue that there is much about the workings of the social and political world that is hidden and so requires exposing, as Chomsky's work itself shows. Indeed his overall theory of the media is that its *raison d'être* is to hide the truth. For example it would appear that if I buy a newspaper, I am the consumer of that product. However, if one takes a closer look, as Chomsky does, at the political economy of newspaper production, it becomes apparent that in fact I am a product, in this instance part of an audience, which gets sold to advertisers, who are in fact the real consumers. These relations are obscured or hidden.

Clearly Chomsky is in a difficult position here. On the one hand he wants to credit ordinary people with recognising the exploitative nature of the system, and yet on the other, he seems to be suggesting that aspects of this system are, in fact, hidden. This can be taken to imply that some sort of theoretical framework is required to expose hidden characteristics. Chomsky is, it seems, inconsistent on this point, for as Rai quotes him, he can be found arguing that to change things some balance between theory and practice is required.

> Chomsky argues that the way to combat propaganda is not by isolated academic research, but by engaging in social struggle. Research and activism should operate in tandem: 'You don't sit in your room somewhere and dispel illusions.' You need to interact with others in order to develop ideas: 'Otherwise you don't know what you think. You just hear something, and you react to it or you don't pay any attention to it or something.' Learning comes from interest, and if the subject is the social world, 'your interest in it often involves, ought to involve at least, trying to change it'. Learning also comes from formulating programmes, and trying to pursue them, understanding their failures and limitations, gaining experience in various ways.[92]

In 1969 he can be found arguing that '[w]ithout a revolutionary theory or a revolutionary consciousness there is not going to be a revolutionary movement. There is not going to be a serious movement without a clear analysis and a theoretical point of view'.[93] And indeed Chomsky's very call for us to use our minds, implies a systematic, rule-bound activity, in other words an activity which is theory-based.

Naturalism

Chomsky's methodology restricts his analysis to looking at what people say they are going to do and then looking at what they actually do. In so doing he shows us things about the way in which our social and political institutions work. In other words he shows us the way policies shape and influence the social structure. But, as we have seen, in his view this is not science, nor does it involve theory. However, in employing this methodology he must also be employing certain theoretical assumptions. If we return to the theoretical assumptions concerning structure and agency within the debate between positivists and phenomenologists, Chomsky, it could be argued, takes the agency side of the dichotomy. As we have seen Chomsky is deeply critical of those on the structural positivist and empiricist side of the divide. In his view there is little evidence to support the view that human beings are totally malleable and have no intrinsic characteristics. In his view such political theories are highly dubious – as are the intelligentsia that hold them.

> For them it is very convenient to have an ideology which says that there are no moral barriers to domination, interference and control, because then they just add one or two assumptions such as: I am the obvious controller, I know what is good, and I will manipulate these people for their own benefit, because that is no interference with their essential rights since they have no essential rights, they are just some collection of properties, and I will therefore dominate them for their own good.[94]

We have also seen in his claim to be a rationalist, that Chomsky is of the view that human beings do have essential characteristics to their human nature. However, he makes it clear that any more specific claims than this about the more precise characteristics that this might entail are merely speculative. Chomsky is particularly reluctant to trace any connections between his work in linguistics and his political work. Nevertheless he concedes a 'loose connection', but

> certainly not a deductive one. Whatever connection there is lies more at the level of hope and aspiration than of firm result. We have good evidence that the human language capacity, which surely enters into thought, reasoning, human interaction, etc., in the most intimate fashion, is based on biologically-determined principles which underlie

(though they do not account for) the free creative use of language that is typical of normal speakers. I presume that the same is true in all cognitive domains, though knowledge elsewhere is sparse.[95]

In Chomsky's view we have many 'faculties of the mind'.[96] One such faculty is the language faculty. In his view we can be infinitely creative, but only within the limits of such a faculty which is itself finite.[97]

> It seems to me that what is now known indicates that language develops along an intrinsically determined path, involving specific mechanisms of the language system, which is, in this respect, rather analogous to a physical organ. As in the case of the visual system and others, the course of development is influenced by an interaction with the environment.[98]

By way of example he argues that '[o]ne can think of many formal operations which are simply not permitted in a natural language, even though they're very simple ...', such as that '... there's no natural language which forms questions by reading declarative sentences backwards'.[99] 'It's not so obvious why that should be so, because that's a very simple operation. It's a much simpler operation to state than the operation by which we formulate questions in English, let's say'.[100] Chomsky is asserting that there is some form of universal grammar, the structure of which, he argues, all human beings are born with in order that they may acquire language. Discovering the limits of language structure is the basis of his work in linguistics, and in his view could be suggestive for the study of other systems of knowledge.

In Chomsky's view the knowledge we can acquire about human knowledge will not necessarily be 'introspectible', a view with which Feyerabend sympathises.[101] Chomsky argues:

> I want to use 'knowledge' in the sense in which Leibnitz uses it: as referring to unconscious knowledge, principles which form the sinews and connections of thought but which may not be conscious principles, which we know must be functioning although we may not be able to introspect into them. ... You can think of these principles as propositional in form, but in any event they're not expressible. You can't get a person to tell you what these principles are. ... [I]n fact the one fundamental mistake that I think is made by the Leibnizian theory of mind is its assumption that one could dredge out these principles, that if you really worked hard at it and introspected, you could bring to consciousness the contents of the mind. I don't see any reason to believe that the sinews and connections of thought, in Leibnitz's sense, are even in principle available to introspection.[102]

Chomsky is of the view that the human mind can be studied in the same way as any other natural object. In this Chomsky is an advocate of naturalism.

> The thesis is that all should be studied in the same way, whether we are considering the motion of the planets, fields of force, structural formulas for complex molecules, or computational properties of the language faculty. Let's call this a 'naturalistic approach to mind', meaning that we seek to investigate the mental aspects of the world by the methods of rational inquiry characteristic of the natural sciences'.[103]

However, he goes on to say '[w]hether the results of a naturalistic approach merit the honorific term "science" depends on the results it achieves'.[104] Having made the point that our understanding of human nature is very limited, Chomsky's work in linguistics nevertheless leads him to draw some very tentative conclusions. The 'essential features of human nature involve a kind of creative urge, a need to control one's own productive, [for] creative labor, to be free from authoritarian intrusions, a kind of instinct for liberty and creativity, a real human need to be able to work productively under conditions of one's own choosing and determination in voluntary association with others'.[105]

If such a view of human nature and the requirement for freedom is deemed plausible then 'there should be an unending struggle to discover, understand, and overcome all structures of authority, domination, subordination, and restriction of the freedom to become and live as a full human being, who can fulfil the need for creative self-expression in solidarity with others'.[106] As such Chomsky moves from a description of the natural mind to a set of propositions about human behaviour and even predictions of a distinctly political kind. As an outcome, his analysis has all the hallmarks of a theory.

Essentialism and the responsibility of intellectuals

Chomsky's essentialism, the notion that human beings have certain essential characteristics that constrain or enable certain behaviour, is certainly crucial for understanding his social and political thought. In his view sociobiology is 'on the right track', although he warns that sociobiologists should be extremely cautious about the specific conclusions they draw from their research. Unfortunately, they 'often draw conclusions that are remote from evidence or theory'.[107] In resorting to biological categories Chomsky is not arguing that we are biologically identical as humans, behaviourally. Rather in his view humans 'differ markedly in their capacities, their interests, their aspirations' and that they do should be 'a source of joy, not concern'.[108] Some would argue (and Chomsky says particularly those on the left) that such views lend themselves to racism and or sexism and that these are unscientific factors. But as Chomsky argues there may well be a correlation between race and intelligence just as there may be a genetic tendency in Jews for usury, or for squirrels to collect too many nuts. However, such differences are only of significance if one believes that 'rights and rewards should accrue to ability and intelligence, [which is] a disturbing and elitist doctrine'.[109] Having said this, he argues that because we live in a racist and sexist society, attempts to find such correlations are extremely dubious. This goes back to his point that intellectuals should have an eye on the consequences of their research. As he argues:

> Hernstein mentions a possible correlation between height and IQ. Of what social importance is that? None, of course, since our society does not suffer under discrimination by height. We do not insist on assigning each adult to the category 'below six feet in height' or 'above six feet in height' when we ask what sort of education he [sic] should receive or where he should live or what work he should do. Rather he is what he is, quite independent of the mean IQ of people of his height category. In a nonracist society, the category of race would be of no greater significance. The mean IQ of individuals of a certain racial background is irrelevant to the situation of a particular individual, who is what he is. Recognizing this perfectly obvious fact, we are left with little, if any, plausible justification for an interest in the relation between mean IQ and race, apart from the 'justification' provided by the existence of racial discrimination.[110]

The onus then is on the scientist. As Chomsky argues: '[s]cience is held in such awe in our culture that every scientist has special responsibility to make clear to the lay audience where his expert knowledge actually yields scientifically verifiable results and where he is guessing, indulging in sheer speculation, or expressing his own personal hopes about the success of his research. This is an important task because the lay audience is in no position to make these distinctions.'[111] Chomsky, then, while making essentialist claims, warns of the dangers in such an approach.

Human nature, agency and social structure

Chomsky's essentialism has laid him open to the charge of having idealist views and for being reductionist. To these criticisms he responds:

> This characterization is so irrational that it is virtually impossible to discuss; plainly, there is no reason to doubt that the principles of UG [universal grammar] have a physical realization, as do the 'instructions' that lead to the growth of arms and legs, and that there is a

physical realization of the resulting grammar, somewhere in the neural system. The charge of 'idealism' is strange indeed ... As for the term 'reductionist,' if this means that we would like to explain mental functions in terms of physical mechanisms, I would certainly accept the characterization, though we should recognize, in all honesty, that there are many aspects of mental function (in particular, matters having to do with will and choice) for which we have not the slightest idea of what the relevant mechanisms or structures might be, even in principle.[112]

There is however a further crucial step to Chomsky's tentative essentialist claims about human nature that can be derived from his work in linguistics. Again we must return to the structure–agency dichotomy. Although he is clearly emphasising the importance of agency in social and political processes, he is nevertheless clear that the social structure *is* influential in the manifestation of human nature.[113] As social structure is influential, Chomsky concludes that when making decisions about human organisation our attention should be focused upon institutions rather than individuals. Chomsky distinguishes himself from the behaviourist approach because of his essentialism.

Human nature has lots of ways of realizing itself, humans have lots of capacities and options. Which ones reveal themselves depends to a large extent on the institutional structures. If we had institutions which permitted pathological killers free rein, they'd be running the place. The only way to survive would be to let those elements of your nature manifest themselves. If we have institutions which make greed the sole property of human beings and encourage pure greed at the expense of other human emotions and commitments, we're going to have a society based on greed, with all that follows. A different society might be organized in such a way that human feelings and emotions of other sorts, say solidarity, support, sympathy become dominant. Then you'll have different aspects of human nature and personality revealing themselves.[114]

Unlike the deep structures that constrain language acquisition, the social structures that constrain or enable political behaviour are not immutable.

Political and economic organisation could be different. It seems plausible to suggest that it is the mutability of social structures which again accounts for his reluctance to describe the process he uses for filling in and accounting for the observed disparity between input and output as 'theory' and as 'science'. For Chomsky it is important that we remember that although social structures are influential in the shaping and constraining of human social and political behaviour they are not static or law-like entities. We see then, a significant shift from much Marxist analysis where it can be argued that analysis of economic structures has become reified. Chomsky identifies within Marx a strand that has a view about human nature not unlike Chomsky's own, for example in the belief that work is a human need.[115] As Dupre argues of Marx '[l]abour is conceived of as the activity through which man realizes his own essence. "Labour is man's coming to be for himself." Man is not a static being – he *becomes* himself through his labor'.[116] And as McLellan argues, Marx writes of 'human need' and of 'man as species being, the individual as a social being, the idea of nature as, in a sense, man's body'.[117] However, Marx's claims to theoretical scientific status lie not in his observations about human nature, but rather in the observation that capitalism is inherently contradictory because of the conflict between owners and non-owners of capital. His theory of *what is* focuses upon the capitalist system or structure and seeks to show that it has a tendency for crisis. For Chomsky this reifies capitalism and produces a static account of *what is* which is mistaken. According to Chomsky, capitalism as it is theorised has never existed. Chomsky's analysis of *what is* rather than reifying the system or the structure, and in so doing misdescribing it, re-describes the conflict between non-owners and owners who are aided by the state. In his view what he is describing is relatively self-evident (except, that is, for many intellectuals), and so cannot be labelled a theory. His analysis describes human action within institutional constraints. However what he describes *does* involve a theory concerned with human need, but one that in unsubstantiated, and this theory informs his description.

Chomsky's own *belief* is that there are indeed influential connections between structure and agency, and that they do not go in one direction only. However, we are far from being able to explain them mainly because of the difficulty of introspecting on human nature. In his view human nature does have essential characteristics but that the development of such characteristics is facilitated or hindered by the nature of social organisation. Given this, we ought to have around us social conditions that reflect the best aspects of our natures. Social structures help to trigger certain human behaviour. But an exact understanding of human nature and its dialectical relationship with the social environment is yet to be, and may never be, within our grasp. In Chomsky's view not only are such tentative conclusions the most any social and political analysis can offer, it is also, in fact, all that social and political analysis offers. That analysts claim theoretical or scientific credentials is, in Chomsky's view, dishonest.

Critique

Despite the objections Chomsky has to calling his or anyone else's social and political thought theoretical, and therefore scientific, his social and political analysis conforms closely to a theoretical model that utilises scientific methodological tools of analysis. It is difficult not to come to this conclusion when one considers the main body of his political work which is principally concerned with *what is,* and takes the form of an analysis of contemporary political issues employing a clear methodology. When one comes to his other more tentative and therefore more peripheral ideas about *what ought to be* in the light of what are, in his view, only hopeful ideas about human nature, taken in isolation such views do appear more speculative and so less scientifically based. However, it cannot therefore be said that they do not employ a theoretical framework. And, if one places what Chomsky calls his 'hope' about human nature within the context of his theoretical and scientific findings in linguistics, then it could be argued that his observations about human social and political organisation are closer to 'science' than the observations of those who call themselves social or political scientists.

There is however a further point. Chomsky acknowledges that to establish causal relations between human beings and their society may be impossible in any precise sense. Nevertheless, he would not want to argue that were we to make changes to the structure, we would not be able to observe effects on human beings. Whether social and political arrangements are more or less suitable to the human condition is something we ought to be able to test empirically. This can be and is done when social scientists collect data on mortality rates or statistics on health. Chomsky's challenge to us must be to test his theory of human nature with these scientific tools.

It is the contention of this book that Chomsky's social and political analysis does employ a theoretical framework and that his collection of data does involve a rigorous methodological approach necessary to any scientific quest. The remainder of this book looks at this theory in the context of various debates about human social and political organisation. The next chapter seeks to establish the nature of his theoretical framework and in particular how his theory of human nature informs his 'hopes' for the future good society. In other words how his theory of human nature informs his libertarian socialism?

Notes

1 Chomsky, N. in Otero, C. P. (ed.) (1981) *Noam Chomsky: Radical Priorities,* Montreal: Black Rose Books, p. 236.
2 Chomsky, N. in Rai, M. (1995) *Chomsky's Politics,* London: Verso, pp. 200–2, n. 44.
3 Bernstein, R. (1976) *The Restructuring of Social and Political Theory,* Oxford: Methuen, p. 43.
4 These might be 'purposes, intentions, feelings, emotions, values, beliefs, and so on'. See Layder, D. (1981) *Structure, Interaction and Social Theory,* London: Routledge and Kegan Paul, pp. 2, 21.
5 Hudson, W. D. 'Editor's Introduction: The "Is-Ought" Problem' in Hudson, W. D. (ed.) (1969) *The Is/Ought Question,* London: Macmillan, p. 12.
6 Hudson, W. D., *op. cit.,* p. 12.

7 Bernstein, R., *op. cit.*, p. 9.
8 The famous example is Durkheim's study of suicide.
9 Bernstein, R., *op. cit.*, p. 138.
10 Bernstein, R., *op. cit.*, p. 141.
11 Bernstein, R., *op. cit.*, p. 154.
12 Plant, R. (1991) *Modern Political Thought*, London: Basil Blackwell.
13 Zimmerman, M. 'The "is-ought": An unnecessary dualism' in Hudson, W. D., *op. cit.*, p. 83.
14 See entry for 'political philosophy' in Urmson, J. O. (ed.) (1975) *The Concise Encyclopedia of Western Philosophy and Philosophers*, London: Hutchinson.
15 Urmson, J. O., *op. cit.*, p. 228.
16 Keat, R. and Urry, J. (1975) *Social Theory as Science*, London: Routledge and Kegan Paul, p. 199.
17 Nielsen, K. (1973) 'Social Science and Hard Data' in *Cultural Hermeneutics* 1, pp. 115–43, p. 118. See also Charles Taylor 'Neutrality in Political Science' in Peter Laslett and W. G. Runciman (eds) (1967) *Philosophy, Politics and Society*, Oxford: Basil Blackwell.
18 Schutz, A. in Bernstein, R., *op. cit.*, pp. 155–6.
19 Keat, R. and Urry, J., *op. cit.*, p. 161.
20 Keat, R. and Urry, J., *op. cit.*, p. 169.
21 Durkheim, E. (1952) *Suicide: A Study in Sociology*, John A. Spaulding and George Simpson (trans.), London: Routledge and Kegan Paul.
22 Not all structural approaches are positivist. Marx also offers a structural approach: Keat, R. and Urry, J., *op. cit.*, pp. 119–44.
23 Keat, R. and Urry, J., *op. cit.*, pp. 119–20.
24 Keat, R. and Urry, J., *op. cit.*, p. 151.
25 Keat, R. and Urry, J., *op. cit.*, p. 146.
26 Keat, R. and Urry, J., *op. cit.*, p. 162.
27 Keat, R. and Urry, J., *op. cit.*, p. 162.
28 Feyerabend, P. (1975b) 'How to Defend Society Against Science' in *Radical Philosophy*, Summer, p. 5.
29 Feyerabend, P. (1987) *Farewell to Reason*, London: Verso, p. 39.
30 Feyerabend, P. (1987) *op. cit.*, p. 17.
31 Feyerabend, P. (1987) *op. cit.*, p. 50.
32 Krige, J. in McCarney, J., Review of Killing Time: The Autobiography of Paul Feyerabend, unpublished.
33 Feyerabend, P. (1987) *op. cit.*, p. 51.
34 Chomsky, N. in Otero, C. P. (ed.) (1981) *Noam Chomsky: Radical Priorities*, Montreal: Black Rose Books, p. 245.
35 Chomsky, N. in Otero, C. P. (ed.) (1981) *op. cit.*, p. 249.
36 Chomsky, N. in Otero, C. P. (ed.) (1981) *op. cit.*, p. 246.
37 Chomsky, N. in Otero, C. P. (ed.) (1981) *op. cit.*, p. 246.
38 Feyerabend, P. (1975a) *Against Method*, London: New Left Books; Feyerabend, P. (1987) *op. cit.* Feyerabend was not the first to argue that ideas could be used to serve the interests of an elite. Bakunin had predicted 'the reign of scientific intelligence, the most autocratic, despotic, arrogant and elitist of all regimes' (Dolgoff, S. (1972) *Bakunin on Anarchy*, New York: George Allen and Unwin, pp. 319). However, Feyerabend was the first in the modern period to take such arguments into the realms of relativism.
39 Gellner, E. 'Concepts and Society' in Wilson, B. R. (ed.) (1970) *Rationality*, Oxford: Basil Blackwell, p. 30.
40 Chomsky, N. in Otero, C. P. (ed.) (1988) *Noam Chomsky: Language and Politics*, Montreal: Black Rose Books, p. 316.
41 Chomsky, N. in Otero, C. P. (ed.) (1988) *op. cit.*, p. 316.

42　Chomsky, N. in Otero, C. P. (ed.) (1988) *op. cit.*, p. 594.
43　Chomsky, N. in Otero, C. P. (ed.) (1988) *op. cit.*, p. 594.
44　Chomsky, N. in Otero, C. P. (ed.) (1988) *op. cit.*, p. 594.
45　Feyerabend, P. (1987) *op. cit.*, p. 9.
46　Chomsky, N. in Barsamian, D. (1992) *Noam Chomsky: Chronicles of Dissent* Stirling: A.K. Press, p. 159.
47　Chomsky, N. in Barsamian, D. (1992) *op. cit.*, p. 159.
48　Feyerabend, P. (1987) *op. cit.*, p. 28.
49　Chomsky, N. in Rai, M. (1995) *Chomsky's Politics*, London: Verso.
50　Rai, M., *op. cit.*, describes an occasion during the Vietnam war where such a contention can be seen to have worked in practice. 'At a RESIST meeting in New York, a hostile group of draft resisters came to demand control of RESIST's finances – apparently opposed to the "diversion" of money to draft counselling and advisory groups. After some acrimonious debate, Chomsky suggested that a representative of the group come to the RESIST office in Boston the next day and examine their files, and decide which groups should not have been given money. When the files were inspected, the resisters saw that money was being passed on to Black groups in Mississippi who wanted to develop anti-draft work and so on, and they withdrew their objections.' p. 195, n. 84.
51　Chomsky, N. in Achbar, M. (ed.) (1994) *Manufacturing Consent: Noam Chomsky & the Media*, London: Black Rose Books, p. 20.
52　Chomsky, N. (1982) *Towards a New Cold War*, New York: Pantheon Books p. 69.
53　Chomsky, N. (1982) *op. cit.*, p. 61.
54　Chomsky, N. (1982) *op. cit.*, p. 62.
55　Bakunin, M. in Feyerabend, P. (1987) *op. cit.*, p. 22, n. 3.
56　Feyerabend, P. (1987) *op. cit.*, p. 22.
57　Chomsky, N. (1982) *op. cit.*, p. 63.
58　Chomsky points out that he is referring to the 'empiricist concept of human nature and not to questions of how to do science', see Otero, C. P. (ed.) (1988) *op. cit.*, p. 595.
59　Chomsky, N. in Otero, C. P. (ed.) (1988) *op. cit.*, p. 595.
60　Feyerabend, P. (1987) *op. cit.*, p. 66.
61　The label 'radical feminist' does lump together many diverse feminist thinkers and is not meant to imply that there is homogeneity amongst thinkers in that tradition.
62　Jaggar, A. (1983) *Feminist Politics and Human Nature*, Brighton: Harvester, p. 268.
63　Barry, K. in Jaggar A., *op. cit.*, p. 267.
64　Jaggar, A., *op. cit.*, p. 268.
65　Jaggar, A., *op. cit.*, p. 268.
66　Chomsky, N. in Otero, C. P. (ed.) (1988) *op. cit.*, p. 597.
67　Keat, R. and Urry, J., *op. cit.*, p. 200.
68　Chomsky, N. in Otero, C. P. (ed.) (1981) *op. cit.*, p. 236.
69　Chomsky, N. in Otero, C. P. (ed.) (1988) *op. cit.*, p. 386.
70　Chomsky, N. in Barsamian, D. (1992) *op. cit.*, p. 355.
71　Chomsky, N. (1969) *American Power and the New Mandarins*, Harmonds-worth: Penguin, p. 257.
72　Nielsen, K., *op. cit.*, p. 135.
73　Nielsen, K., *op. cit.*, p. 141.
74　Nielsen, K., *op. cit.*, p. 14.
75　Chomsky, N. (1973) *For Reasons of State*, New York: Vintage, p. 78.
76　Chomsky, N. in Otero, C. P. (ed.) (1988) *op. cit.*, p. 118.

77 Chomsky, N. in Otero, C. P. (ed.) (1988) *op. cit.*, p. 102.
78 Chomsky, N. (1992a) *Deterring Democracy*, London: Verso, pp. 11, 26.
79 Personal communication and Chomsky, N. (1969) *American Power and the New Mandarins*, Pelican Books, p. 271.
80 Chomsky, N. (1969) *op. cit.*, p. 271.
81 Chomsky, N. in Otero, C. P. (ed.) (1988) *Noam Chomsky: Language & Politics*, Montreal: Black Rose Books, p. 464.
82 Chomsky's evidence for this claim is derived from among other things a close analysis of opinion polls. See ch. 6 on Chomsky's analysis of the media.
83 Chomsky, N. in Otero, C. P. (ed.) (1988) *op. cit.*, p. 373.
84 Chomsky, N. in Otero, C. P. (ed.) (1988) *op. cit.*, p. 373.
85 Chomsky, N. in Otero, C. P. (ed.) (1988) *op. cit.*, p. 373.
86 Chomsky, N. (1992a) *op. cit.*
87 Chomsky, N. in Otero, C. P. (ed.) (1988) *op. cit.*, p. 685.
88 Chomsky, N. (1973) *For Reasons of State*, New York: Vintage, p. vii.
89 Chomsky, N. in Otero, C. P. (ed.) (1988) *op. cit.*, p. 135.
90 Chomsky, N. (1989) *Necessary Illusions*, London: Pluto Press, p. 47.
91 Chomsky, N. in Otero, C. P. (ed.) (1988) *op. cit.*, p. 389.
92 Rai, M. (1995) *Chomsky's Politics* London: Verso, p. 59.
93 Chomsky, N. in Otero, C. P. (ed.) (1988) *op. cit.*, p. 140.
94 Chomsky, N. in Otero, C. P. (ed.) (1988) *op. cit.*, p. 595.
95 Chomsky, N. in Otero, C. P. (ed.) (1988) *op. cit.*, p. 385–6.
96 Chomsky, N. in Otero, C. P. (ed.) (1988) *op. cit.*, p. 112.
97 Chomsky, N. (1966) *Cartesian Linguistics*, New York: Harper and Row, pp. 29, 41.
98 Chomsky, N. in Otero, C. P. (ed.) (1988) *op. cit.*, p. 385.
99 Chomsky, N. in Otero, C. P. (ed.) (1988) *op. cit.*, p. 104.
100 Chomsky, N. in Otero, C. P. (ed.) (1988) *op. cit.*, p. 106.
101 Feyerabend, P. (1987) *op. cit.*, p. 27.
102 Chomsky, N. in Otero, C. P. (ed.) (1988) *op. cit.*, p. 111.
103 Chomsky, N. (1996a) *Powers and Prospects: Reflections on Human Nature and the Social Order*, London: Pluto Press, pp. 31–2.
104 Chomsky, N. (1996) *op. cit.*, p. 32.
105 Chomsky, N. in Otero, C. P. (ed.) (1988) *op. cit.*, p. 594.
106 Chomsky, N. in Otero, C. P. (ed.) (1988) *op. cit.*, p. 386.
107 Chomsky, N. in Otero, C. P. (ed.) (1988) *op. cit.*, pp. 412–13.
108 Chomsky, N. in Otero, C. P. (ed.) (1988) *op. cit.*, pp. 386–7.
109 Chomsky, N. in Rai, M., *op. cit.*, p. 190, n. 61. See also Chomsky, N. in Otero, C. P. (ed.) (1988) *op. cit.*, p. 386.
110 Chomsky, N. (1973) *op. cit.*, p. 362.
111 Chomsky, N. in Otero, C. P. (ed.) (1988) *op. cit.*, p. 413.
112 Chomsky, N. in Otero, C. P. (ed.) (1988) *op. cit.*, p. 383.
113 Edgley, R. (1970) 'Innate Ideas' in Royal Institute of Philosophy Lectures, Volume III *Knowledge and Necessity*, London: Macmillan. Edgley sets out the logical problem with making a claim such as Chomsky's about innate ideas, pp. 1–33.
114 Chomsky, N. in Otero, C. P. (ed.) (1988) *op. cit.*, p. 773.
115 Chomsky, N. in Otero, C. P. (ed.) (1988) *op. cit.*, p. 177.
116 Dupre, L. (1966) *The Philosophical Foundations of Marxism*, New York: Harcourt Brace, p. 122. Inner parenthesis Karl Marx, *Economic and Philosophic Manuscripts of 1844* (Merlin Milliagan (trans.), Moscow, 1959), p. 155.
117 McLellan, D. (1971) *Marx's Grundrisse*, St Albans: Paladin, p. 23. See also Arthur, C. J. (1986) *Dialectics of Labour*, Oxford: Basil Blackwell, p. 1.

2 The 'good society'

This chapter looks at what is a constitutive aspect of Chomsky's contribution to social and political thought, namely his vision of the good society. Chomsky constructs a libertarian socialist account. Just as human nature is integral to the political theory he employs in his critique of society, so too is it crucial for an understanding of his libertarian socialism. The nature and content of his account is revealed in this chapter by a series of explorations of competing accounts of the good society in contemporary political thought provided by the liberal–communitarian debate, particularly Nozick, Rawls and Sandel, and Foucault in relation to human nature.

Chomsky declares himself to be a libertarian socialist.[1] For some, such a claim constitutes a contradiction in terms. This chapter begins by looking at the problems traditionally associated with being committed to both libertarian and socialist values – most specifically the values of liberty or freedom and equality. The chapter then turns to look at the way in which the libertarian socialist or anarchist tradition has itself attempted to defend logical consistency when these two values are conjoined.

Having attempted to show that the values of liberty and equality are not only logically consistent with each other but that they are logically interdependent concepts (if, that is, their meanings are taken in their fullest sense), the question still remains whether such values are realisable in any concrete sense. In other words it is all very well to argue at an abstract philosophical level that such concepts are mutually interdependent, but it is quite another to then assume that human beings are capable of behaving or willing to behave in accordance with such values. To make claims about the possibility or otherwise of organising society in a way which is radically different from what we have now depends upon one's view about the possibilities and constraints on human behaviour. So, the argument might be that if people have maximal freedom, they would act in ways that serve their self-interest, and thereby compromise egalitarian ideals. Conversely, it might be argued that so long as society is organised in the appropriate way, egalitarian ideals are actually fostered in human behaviour. Of course, if human behaviour is malleable in this way, then the value of freedom becomes redundant. Both positions then carry with them, if only implicitly, a view about human behaviour, entailing a view about human nature. In the first, human beings are deemed capable of self-interest, which implies that they are separable from the society in which they live. In the second, human beings are seen as formed by the society from which they come, and as such their natures are plastic, or at least contingent.

It is argued in this chapter that the point about Chomsky's vision of the good society is that he does not begin by asking what is just and fair, in order to then preach and justify his case, rather he takes what we might call a more scientific stance. He asks what are the conditions most suitable for human beings to realise their full potential. In other words, he begins with a premise about human nature. As has been established in the preceding chapter he is sceptical about ever being able to verify such an account, despite the fact that his work in linguistics is suggestive of his account. Then given this premise he takes the view that libertarian socialist ideals of freedom and equality are not only consistent with human behaviour, but are indeed necessary for human beings to have the opportunity to live to their full potential. Therefore, libertarian socialism is not simply a morally worthy ideal, it is a necessary state for the human condition.

In order to draw out the significance of Chomsky's ideas on human nature and their relationship to social organisation, it is worth looking at his views within the context of other thinkers who have pondered on the good society. As we shall see, all views on the good society begin with a concern about justice and fairness. By looking at the debate between liberals and communitarians we can see that questions of justice and fairness are either a matter of concern in terms of the rules of life, or they are applied to questions concerning the outcome in life. In both cases however we can see that within this debate the protagonists concern themselves at the outset with justice and fairness which they then seek to defend – often by employing or manipulating questionable, contradictory and/or assumptive notions about human nature.

The chapter begins by considering Rawls' liberal attempt in his book *A Theory of Justice* (1972) to put forward a view of social organisation that sees justice and fairness in terms of an attempt to reconcile the values of freedom and equality. In Rawls' view, justice and fairness must show a concern for both rules and outcome. His claims however employ certain assumptions about human nature. This prompts a libertarian critique from Nozick and a communitarian critique from, among others, Sandel. Both critiques attack Rawls' attempt to reconcile the two values, arguing ultimately that he fails. Importantly, both critiques accept their irreconcilability, and because they see an attempt to find fairness in rules and/or outcomes as being irreconcilable with human nature. The libertarian attack argues that the redistribution required by the value of equality would ultimately undermine freedom. For the libertarian, justice and fairness can only be achieved by ensuring that the rules are fair, even if the outcomes are not. The communitarian attack offered by Sandel explicitly finds Rawls' conception of human nature suspect. In Sandel's view Rawls tries to extrapolate from a suspect view of human nature a fair form of social organisation, given this human nature, but ultimately fails. Sandel, by contrast, argues that the process should be the other way round. We should begin by establishing a form of social organisation that nourishes communitarian values because this will, in his view, appropriately socialise human behaviour so that there is greater justice and fairness. Sandel is broadening his notions of justice and fairness beyond rules to outcomes, but in so doing he has to employ a very different view of human nature, notably one where human nature is malleable, and constructively so. (If human nature was malleable, we may wonder why the outcome was important to anyone.) Very roughly it can be argued that Rawls' and Nozick's positions ultimately associate themselves more closely with the value of freedom, whereas Sandel's position can be said to be more closely associated with the value of, if not equality, at least fraternity.

By following this debate between liberals and communitarians we are left with a rather stark choice for our vision of the good society. Rawls does not, it is argued, offer a vision that coherently reconciles the values of equality and freedom. As his critics show, one value is always in danger of undermining the other. The alternative seems to be an abandonment of any reconciliation to the libertarian position where justice is a concern for freedom, or to the communitarian position where justice is a concern for the outcome of egalitarianism or fraternity. Given that all views rest upon stated or unstated assumptions about human nature, I turn to Chomsky's vision of the good society, which begins with an alternative premise about human nature and shows this nature as requiring both equality and freedom. To this end, the chapter considers a debate Chomsky has with Foucault on the question of human nature. Foucault's views on the subject are not dissimilar to those of the communitarians, whereas Chomsky's are, on first sight, perhaps closer to the liberal position. However, I shall argue that although Chomsky is concerned with liberty, it is not because, as with many liberals, he sees human beings as autonomous self-seeking individuals. Rather, in Chomsky's view, liberty is necessary for us as human beings because our natures make us creative, social beings. Liberty and mutual interdependence are not therefore conceived of as being mutually exclusive as suggested by the libertarian/communitarian positions.

The chapter concludes by illustrating that Chomsky's views on human nature allow for the values of both freedom and equality to be preserved in practice. Of course, this leaves open the question of whether we are to accept Chomsky's assumptions about human nature. Although, as

Chomsky argues, our understanding of human nature is far from known,
I have argued, in Chapter 1 that it should not be concluded from this
that all forms of social and political organisation are as suitable as one
another to our nature. Debates about more or less freedom, or more or
less equality, are not just questions about the relative value of certain
concepts. Their relative employment in practice has an effect upon the
quality and longevity of human life, and can be measured with more or
less success. Such effects must be seen to be indicating something to us
about our nature as human beings, something Chomsky seems reluctant
to acknowledge.

The libertarian socialist

What is it to be a libertarian socialist? As much of the history of ideas
within the two traditions of liberalism and socialism attests, if freedom
is the chief value of liberalism and equality is the chief value of socialism
then are the two not mutually exclusive? To put the debate crudely, if
society is organised to ensure equality then this will necessarily infringe
upon people's freedoms. Conversely, if society is organised to ensure that
people have maximum freedom, then an egalitarian outcome is impossible. And at the centre of both questions, there lies a series of concerns
about the state. The liberal tradition has sought to establish the legit-
imising principles as well as the necessary scope of the state in order to
maintain conditions of maximum freedom. The socialist tradition, on the
other hand, has debated the state's role in redistributing resources to
ensure equality during and after the transition from capitalism to socialism.
The question is then, to what extent it is practical and coherent to claim
to be a libertarian socialist?

To couch the debate in this way is already to assume something, namely
that the argument is about the way in which society *ought to be* organised. However, for many the nature of this dispute raises, and not always
explicitly, a further question, namely, *what is* human nature and what is
its relationship to society. Within the liberal tradition, the emphasis on
freedom generates an explicit conception of human beings as autonomous,
rational and self-determining. This tradition is sometimes labelled idealist
because these traits are taken to be *a priori* characteristics of human beings
because they are not seen as having been derived from material existence.
Chomsky as we have seen questions this supposition (see note 112 in
Chapter 1). By contrast, within the socialist tradition human beings are
seen as essentially social and cooperative in nature, and, although there
are different degrees of emphasis on this point, the social or historical
material determines the human condition. This tradition, especially its
Marxist variant, is labelled materialist.

This (often-implicit) view of what constitutes human nature is important, because it informs the respective traditions in their view of the vehicle

for getting from *what is* to *what ought to be*. To cast the debate crudely again, if, as in the liberal conception, human beings are autonomous, rational and self-determining, then to achieve the good society requires changing or raising people's consciousness. In other words, it means changing their ideas. Conversely, for socialists, the social, economic and political, in other words the material, requires revolutionising for fundamental change to occur.

To set up the debate in these terms is without doubt to prioritise a certain reading in the history of ideas. In particular, the term 'socialist' here is recognisably drawing upon its form within the Marxist tradition. Libertarian socialists and some anarchists would automatically object to the umbrella use of the term 'socialist' to defend the above positions.[2] They regard themselves as socialists without subscribing to such a view of the state, of human nature, and of how to move to the good society. Indeed to even ask the question to what extent is the libertarian socialist tradition coherent, is to suggest that this tradition does not itself attempt to establish its coherence.

Equally, Marxists might object to the failure to identify the possibility of freedom with their position. Indeed, they would want to argue that freedom is important but that it can only be established once people have equality. It is without doubt a defining characteristic of what it is to be Marxist, to identify a role for the state in establishing and defending the appropriate material conditions during a transitional period between capitalism and socialism. However, in time the state would 'wither away'. Bakunin and subsequent anarchists by contrast have balked at both the theory and the practice of the state's role, on the grounds that the preservation of the state would only give rise to a new political or bureaucratic elite, compromising both goals of freedom and equality.[3] As Bakunin argues 'the State and all its institutions . . . corrupt the minds and will of its subjects and demand their passive obedience'.[4] By taking this position, anarchists are thereby seen to give greater weight to freedom than the so-called authoritarian socialists.

Having briefly considered the various complexities associated with the use of labels such as 'liberal' and 'socialist' in terms of their respective values, it also becomes apparent that the values themselves are contested concepts. Socialists principally concerned with equality may be mainly thinking in terms of material resources. However, equality may be present or absent in political participation or other decision-making processes, in which case it is closely associated with the other concept under consideration – *freedom* – in terms of *freedom* of expression. Further, material equality does not necessarily mean everyone should have the exactly the same number or type of resources. It may not involve, as Nozick takes it to involve, 'patterned outcomes'.[5] People have different needs and so equality may refer to equal *freedom* or opportunity to determine and produce things to satisfy their respective needs.[6] There is also the question of whether inequality is merely a material injustice or whether the cultural injustices of ethnicity and gender are separate and stem from different political activity. As Fraser asks '[u]nder what circumstances can a politics of recognition help support a politics of redistribution? And when is it more likely to undermine it?'[7]

Similarly, debate surrounds the concept of freedom. Is freedom a positive or negative concept?[8] As a negative concept, it implies freedom from external constraint. However, if it is a positive concept, it means giving people the conditions to realise their freedom. So it gets closer to the concept of equality, because it involves giving people equal conditions in order to be free. Thus, what constitutes liberal and socialist values is by no means clear. Given their contested nature I propose now to look at what libertarian socialists themselves have to say about the two concepts and their relative values, and to see just how they reconcile them, and why.

Equality and freedom: the libertarian socialist tradition

Libertarian socialism and anarchism are labels that are commonly used interchangeably. Anarchism argues for a society that can spontaneously organise itself without the coercive authority of the state. As libertarian socialists distinguish themselves from so-called authoritarian socialists by their attack on the maintenance of the state, it is possible to see why this interchangeability occurs. However, as Chomsky points out, 'the term anarchism is used to cover quite a range of political ideas', which is why he prefers to describe himself as a libertarian socialist.[9] Chomsky here is presumably acknowledging that in identifying oneself by a label that simply means no state, one is open to being interpreted as merely opposing coercion in terms of the state. If one merely opposes the state, it is not logically inconsistent to maintain this position with a support for private property and capitalist relations of production and exchange. The coercive authority of private property is not of concern to some anarchists. Indeed Nozick utilises the term anarchy in just such a way.[10]

However, it would seem from those who have attempted to trace the history of ideas in anarchist thought that anarchism is principally to be associated with the socialist tradition.[11] This means that anarchism, as it is generally conceived, is an attack on authority and not just the authority endowed in the government and the state but also the authority endowed by private property. James Joll has gone as far as to argue that 'decentralization . . . [and] the abolition of property [are] both prerequisites of all anarchist conceptions of society.[12] And Guerin argues '[t]he anarchist is primarily a socialist whose aim is to abolish the exploitation of man by man'.[13]

An attempt to trace the roots of anarchist thought has proved contentious. Woodcock is sceptical of attempts by anarchists to trace the roots of their thought to (among others) the stone age, or Jesus Christ.[14] In his view 'anarchism as a developed, articulate, and clearly identifiable trend appears only in the modern era of conscious social and political revolution'.[15] In Woodcock's view attempts to trace anarchist thought to prehistory 'springs from the belief that anarchism is a manifestation of natural human urges, and that it is the tendency to create authoritarian institutions which is the transient aberration'.[16] Nevertheless he concedes that the 'core attitudes can certainly be found echoing back through history', these core attitudes being 'faith in the essential decency of man, a desire for individual freedom, an intolerance of domination'.[17]

Woodcock wants to distinguish between a view of anarchism as identified by ongoing 'core attitudes' to be found throughout history and a view of anarchism as a movement with a 'clearly identifiable trend' apparent in social and political revolutions of the modern period. While Chomsky would presumably not disagree with the observation that anarchism's 'core attitudes' are to be found throughout history, he also clearly identifies his own ideals as closely connected with those stemming from the 'modern era' and more particularly the Enlightenment. '[I]t is libertarian socialism that has preserved and extended the radical humanist message of the Enlightenment and the classical liberal ideals that were perverted into an ideology to sustain the emerging social order'.[18] For Chomsky these classical liberal ideals have their roots in 'Rousseau's *Discourse on Inequality*, Humboldt's *Limits of State Action,* Kant's insistence, in his defence of the French Revolution, that freedom is the precondition for acquiring the maturity for freedom, not a gift to be granted when such maturity is achieved'.[19]

The classic liberal tradition, with its emphasis on freedom, is central for Chomsky in any definition of libertarian socialism. Indeed he argues '[i]f one were to see a single dominant idea, within the anarchist tradition, that might be defined as "libertarian socialist," it should ... be ... liberty'.[20] That liberty and freedom are the essence of classic liberal thought is, in Chomsky's view, a result of the particular historical moment in time in which they were born. In other words, they were a product of an age when feudal hierarchy and monarchical despotism were being questioned and attacked. These ideals were not extended to an attack on the inegalitarian development of property relations under capitalism, which are also constraints on liberty and freedom, because this had not yet become a feature of the society which produced such ideas. As Chomsky says of Humboldt's ideas '[t]his classic of liberal thought, completed in 1792, is in its essence profoundly, though prematurely, anti-capitalist'.[21] And elsewhere, again referring to Humboldt's work, he argues:

> he doesn't speak at all of the need to resist private concentration of power: rather he speaks of the need to resist the encroachment of coercive State power. And that is what one finds also in the early

American tradition. But the reason is that that was the only kind of power there was. I mean, Humboldt takes for granted that individuals are roughly equivalent in their private power, and that the only real imbalance of power lies in the centralized authoritarian state, and individual freedom must be sustained against its intrusion . . .[22]

As such, in Chomsky's view, these liberal enlightenment 'ideas must be attenuated beyond recognition to be transmuted into an ideology of industrial capitalism'.[23] Even Locke, who is associated with those hallowed liberal ideals that can be read as a defence of modern state capitalist arrangements – 'life, liberty and property' – argued:

> [t]he measure of property nature has well set by the extent of men's labour and the conveniency of life. No man's labour could subdue or appropriate all, nor could his enjoyment consume more than a small part; so that it was impossible for any man, this way, to encroach upon the right of another or acquire to himself a property to the prejudice of his neighbour, who would still have room for as good and as large a possession (after the other had taken out his) as before it was appropriated. Which measure did confine every man's possession to a very moderate proportion . . .[24]

With these Enlightenment thinkers, then, the central threat to freedom was seen to come from the state, but the private property enshrined in capitalist relations of production are only nascent. Chomsky also draws upon thinkers such as Bakunin, Rocker, Pannekoek and others who, in his view, correctly draw upon the earlier Enlightenment ideals so fundamental to the classic liberal thinkers. Just as it is possible to recognise that the emphasis in Humboldt's ideas on coercive state power was a product of the particular social and historical conditions in which he was working, so were these later thinkers that Chomsky draws upon working and responding to specific social and historical circumstances. In particular they were responding to a different form of coercive state power from that apparent in Humboldt's day, namely authoritarian socialism, or in the case of Bakunin, centralisation within the First International. However, although for these later thinkers the state is seen as a threat to freedom, it is just an emphasis – for, as Bakunin succinctly puts it, '[l]iberty without socialism is privilege, injustice; socialism without liberty is slavery and brutality'.[25]

Fleming argues that '[a] reconsideration of the principles of late nineteenth-century European anarchism, will I feel certain establish that the emphasis upon government and the state *is secondary to* the interest in the social-economic structure of society' (my emphasis).[26] But this is to impose on anarchist thought a typically Marxist prioritisation. If, as Rocker and Chomsky seem to think, historical materialism cannot account for the development of capitalist relations of production, but rather can be accounted for by the effect of centralised state power on the forces of production, then presumably any prioritising ought to be the other way around.[27] To stand a Marxist adage on its head: destroy the state and capitalism should 'wither away'.

Anarchists are committed to liberty, and claim history shows one key threat to this has been the state. However, Chomsky recognises that for today '[a] consistent anarchist must oppose private ownership of the means of production and the wage slavery which is a component of this system, as incompatible with the principle that labor must be freely undertaken and under the control of the producer'.[28] The growth of private power and the attendant economic concentration is clearly also a threat to liberty and freedom. Liberty and equality then become synonymous or interdependent concepts. As Bakunin argues:

> I am a convinced advocate of economic and social equality because I know that, without it, liberty, justice, human dignity, morality, and the well-being of individuals, as well as the prosperity of nations, will never amount to more than a pack of lies. But since I stand for liberty as the primary condition of mankind, I believe that equality must be established in the world by the spontaneous organization of labor and the collective ownership of property by freely organized producers' associations, and by the equally spontaneous federation of communes, to replace the domineering paternalistic State.[29]

And as Jacques-Rouz, an *Enrage* in the late eighteenth century argued, 'freedom is but an empty phantom if one class of men can starve another with impunity. Freedom is but an empty phantom when the rich man can through his monopoly exercise the right of life and death over his fellow men'.[30] However, if we see liberty and equality as synonymous, what are we to make of Nozick's argument that liberty is an empty concept if the 'socialist society . . . forbids] capitalist acts between consenting adults'.[31] As far as Nozick is concerned, the consistent anarchist cannot, as Chomsky does, 'oppose private ownership of the means of production'. It suggests to Nozick a contradiction.[32] Here we have the often referred to problem that for there to be equality under socialism there would have to be coercion or compulsion. Such equality would involve curtailing people's freedom.

It can be argued that Chomsky is using the word 'oppose' here in a particular way. 'Oppose' does not mean deny, but in order to be consistent *the anarchist* must 'oppose private ownership of the means of production'. In Chomsky's view it is farcical to describe capitalist relations of production as 'free enterprise'. What one is describing, he argues, is 'a system of autocratic governance of the economy in which neither the community nor the workforce has any role – a system that we would call "fascist" if translated to the political sphere'.[33] What the people do with their liberty then is presumably a matter for them. However, if we bring in Chomsky's views on human nature we see that these inform his claims about the cogency of a libertarian socialist position. He argues,

> I would like to believe that people have an instinct for freedom, that they really want to control their own affairs. They don't want to be pushed around, ordered, oppressed, etc., and they want a chance to do things that make sense, like constructive work in a way that they control, or maybe control together with others'.[34]

In other words, in his view, under conditions of freedom people would not 'choose' to engage in acts that are constitutive of capitalist economic relations. He recognises he has no way 'to prove this. It is really a hope about what human beings are like'.[35]

Chomsky's view that 'people have an instinct for freedom' is, however, one that recognises that '[h]ow the freedom works depends on what the social structures are'.[36] If the structures facilitate vast concentrations of property ownership, then those without property will probably 'choose' to sell their labour power, and so capitalist acts will occur between 'consenting adults'. If, however, workers take control of the production process, then such a structure would facilitate other possibilities. For example, Chomsky argues, it might be possible to make meaningful tasks that are currently onerous and unpleasant so that the question of compelling people to do the rotten jobs in a socialist society does not arise. 'Let's recall that science and technology and intellect have not been devoted to examining that question or to overcoming the onerous and self-destructive character of the necessary work of society. The reason is that it has always been assumed that there is a substantial body of wage-slaves who will do it simply because otherwise they'll starve'.[37] Further, he argues that if work is organised according to the principle that it gives workers satisfaction, it will not necessarily mean that the things that are useful to people will not get produced. '[I]t's by no means clear – in fact I think it's false – that contributing to the enhancement of pleasure and satisfaction in work is inversely proportional to contributing to the value of the output'.[38] 'My feeling is that part of what makes work meaningful is that it does have use, that its products do have use'.[39] So the notion that people will have to be compelled to produce certain useful products under socialism does not arise. Even were it to arise he goes on to argue that, at that point, society, the community, has to decide how to make compromises. 'Each individual is both a producer and a consumer, after all, and that means that each individual has to join in those socially determined compromises – if in fact there are compromises. And again I feel the nature of the compromise is much exaggerated because of the distorting prism of the really coercive and personally destructive system in which we live'.[40]

The notion that compulsion would have to occur in a socialist society to ensure that capitalist acts do not occur or to ensure that certain necessary products get produced is principally a result of extrapolating from observations about human behaviour within a society that is manifestly unfree. '[O]ur characteristic assumption that pleasure in work, pride in work, is either unrelated to or negatively related to the value of the output is related to a particular stage in social history, namely capitalism, in which human beings are tools of production. It is by no means necessarily true'.[41]

Libertarian socialists, then, defend their commitment to both equality and liberty. They argue that on the one hand liberty is meaningless without material equality because compulsion occurs when people do not freely have access to resources, and on the other hand to secure material equality without liberty is to involve compulsion in determining the terms and conditions of that material equality. Such compulsion involves a form of inequality. Equality in other words must include equality in decision-making processes, as part of the realisation of liberty. For libertarian socialists then the two terms are logically interdependent. This aspect of Chomsky's thought distinguishes him from strands of Marxism associated with Leninism.

One may want to conclude from the above discussion that libertarian socialists do offer logically coherent reasons for arguing that liberty and equality are not necessarily mutually exclusive. Indeed one may even want to conclude, as libertarian socialists do, that it is logically inconsistent to separate them. However, it is one thing to argue at an abstract level that one concept is logically incoherent without the other, but it is quite another thing to argue that these ideals separately or together are realisable in any concrete sense. The problem of extrapolating possibilities from human behaviour under certain historical circumstances has already been raised. However, success or failure in realising certain ideals is going to be determined by the perceived bounds of human behaviour. When Nozick, a self-declared libertarian, concerns himself with protecting society from the 'free rider' by introducing institutional frameworks that involve compulsion, he is obviously working with a certain conception as to the bounds of human behaviour.[42] Similarly, when Chomsky, also a self-declared libertarian, discusses the need for 'free association' to replace waged labour contracts and institutional obligations, he is working within a certain conception of the bounds of human behaviour. Thus, the very different conclusions reached by Nozick and Chomsky are determined ultimately by their different conceptions of what we might call human nature. Whether the question be about liberty, equality or both, any discussion about the way in which society ought to be organised, or even criticisms of the existing one, contain, more often than not only implicitly, certain fundamental assumptions about the human condition and its relationship to society.

It is a central proposition of this chapter that disagreements about the nature of society and its proper organisation (particularly concerning notions of freedom and equality) fail to resolve themselves because they are founded upon different conceptions of human nature. This is often the case even when such foundations are not explicitly recognised. The concept of human nature is here taken to refer to a set of factors that is shared by all fully human beings, and thus marks out the range and limits of human possibilities. It is also contended that the often-implicit conceptions of human nature usually involve one or other side of a dichotomy that is presented in such a way as to make the dichotomy mutually exclusive. Very crudely, the dichotomy is either humans are rational, self-determining and autonomous agents (which leads to the view that they thereby require freedom to be fully human), or they are 'blank sheets' onto which things can be written (so the value of equality can be inculcated into the human condition).[43] Human nature is viewed then, again often only implicitly, as having either one or the other of these forms. It will be suggested in what follows that Chomsky's libertarian socialist views on human nature transcend this dichotomy. Although he is explicitly concerned with the condition of freedom, it is not because he takes human beings to be autonomous, individual agents, as in the liberal picture, but rather that they are rational, mutually interdependent, creative and social beings. In holding such a conception, Chomsky is more adequately able to reconcile what have traditionally been seen as mutually exclusive political ideals: freedom and equality.

The proposition that debates about freedom and equality, the nature of society and the way it ought to be organised, contain within them certain assumptions about human nature that can be amply demonstrated by looking at the debate between so-called liberals and communitarians. This is a useful debate to consider, not only because aspects of the discussion do explicitly raise the issue of human nature, but also because they do this within the context of a debate about freedom and equality. However, for many commentators the debate only serves to highlight the irreconcilability of the two concepts. It is to this debate that this chapter now turns.

The liberal versus communitarian debate

Despite its richness and tradition, libertarian socialist thought has to some extent remained on the fringe. Indeed it has not systematically engaged with the more hegemonic debates of the day, even those explicitly concerned with the values of freedom and equality, such as the aforementioned debate between liberals and communitarians. Of course, as is the case with Chomsky, this will in part be for political reasons (see Chapter 1). It seems possible to suggest that Chomsky would say that a discussion about the relative merits of more or less freedom and/or equality in terms of what is just and fair is to be asking the wrong sort of question. It is to be asking the wrong sort of question because, as Feyerabend points out, notions like freedom are an abstraction; what we should be concerned with is 'the quality of the lives of individuals'[44] in order that we should not try to bend human beings to our abstractions. By this view it is crucial to begin by explicitly stating the view of human nature we wish to work with, accepting of course that we might be wrong, in order that we then find the conditions most beneficial to that nature. Having said this, I would argue that this silence on the part of libertarian socialists contributes to debates about fairness and justice remaining wedded to the supposed conundrum of freedom versus equality, thereby failing to transcend the polarity. It is possible, as Peter Wilkin[45] suggests, that Chomsky's views from the libertarian socialist tradition, which harness a particular conception of human nature, may contribute to this debate.

The liberal position on justice

The contemporary version of the debate between so-called liberals and communitarians was sparked by the publication of Rawls' book *A Theory of Justice*.[46] As the title of his book indicates Rawls is concerned with justice. According to Rawls, justice is: 'All social values – liberty and opportunity, income and wealth, and the bases of self-respect – are to be distributed equally unless an unequal distribution of any, or all, of those values is to everyone's advantage.'[47] Here Rawls makes clear that he is attempting to put forward a view of justice that reconciles the concepts of equality and freedom. Part of the communitarian critique involves the view that although the values of freedom and equality are important, the Rawlsian attempt to reconcile them fails. As Mulhall and Swift argue the 'worry is . . . the degree to which Rawls' theory focuses so exclusively upon them, and the degree to which they are compatible'.[48]

How does Rawls then propose a system of justice that is both free and equal? The first thing to note here concerns Rawls' use of the terms 'equal'. For Rawls 'equal' does not carry its socialist meaning, i.e. equal access to resources in a concrete sense. 'Equal' is used in a hypothetical sense to designate people in the 'original position', referred to by Hobbes as the 'state of nature'.[49] People in the original position would be equal in the sense that no one would have any idea of the social location that they might occupy in society and so with this 'veil of ignorance' they would have no reason to favour or discriminate against anyone. Working from the original position people would be able to rationally establish the just and fair principles for organising society. In Rawls' view, under these conditions people would come to agree to the following principle of justice: 'Social and economic inequalities are to be arranged so that they are both (a) to the greatest benefit of the least advantaged, and (b) attached to offices and positions open to all under conditions of fair equality of opportunity.'[50] When Rawls is not referring to the 'original position', equality is to mean equality of opportunity. As such, those in the worst-off position will have it as good as it can be and equality will be sought, unless inequality will actually help those that are worst-off. Clearly then, although in one sense Rawls can be said to be engaging with the concepts of equality and freedom, his conception of the former is limited as he accepts the maintenance of material inequalities. Rawls' second contention is that, under the veil, people will also be ignorant as to what their conception of the good life will be. As such people will be free to live their conception of the good life, and none will be given special favour. Again, then, under the veil of ignorance people would also agree to this further principle of justice: 'Each person is to have an equal right to the most extensive total system of equal basic liberties compatible with a similar system of liberty for all.'[51]

Rawls' two principles are however to be ranked so that the above latter principle takes what he calls 'lexical priority' over the former. Rawls is concerned here to make clear his objection to utilitarianism and so he argues that 'liberty can be restricted only for the sake of liberty' and that '[t]he second principle of justice is lexically prior to the principle of efficiency and to that of maximizing the sum of advantages'.[52] While justice for Rawls involves some concern for certain ends and outcomes, justice needs to be protected by ensuring that the proper procedures are maintained. 'We cannot, in general, assess a conception of justice by its distributive role alone'.[53] Rawls' conception of equality is weak therefore, and is in danger of having little meaning in the face of the primary principle, liberty. Despite Rawls' own intentions 'his theory of justice was widely perceived to be biased towards liberalism'.[54]

The libertarian critique

Rawls' thesis prompted most notably two divergent responses. On the one hand, there was the response from the libertarian camp represented by Nozick[55] and on the other, there was the critique from the communitarian position. Nozick's objection is to the redistributive character necessary to Rawls' theory. In Nozick's view this would involve the presence of more than a 'minimal state'. For Nozick the minimal state is the most likely outcome of individuals acting freely within the state of nature to ensure that no harm comes to one's 'life, health, liberty, or possessions'.[56] Beyond defence, exacting compensation and punishment the state must not go. 'Any state more extensive violates people's rights'.[57] It must certainly not involve itself in the economy or violate the principle of private property. Private property

> increases the social product by putting means of production in the hands of those who can use them most efficiently (profitably); exper-

imentation is encouraged, because with separate persons controlling resources, there is no one person or small group whom someone with a new idea must convince to try it out; private property enables people to decide on the pattern and types of risks they wish to bear, leading to specialized types of risk bearing; private property protects future persons by leading some to hold back resources from current consumption for future markets; it provides alternate sources of employment for unpopular persons who don't have to convince any one person or small group to hire them, and so on.[58]

In other words, as with Hayek before him, Nozick's principle objection to a Rawlsian position of redistribution, which in Nozick's view brings about a patterned outcome, is that it compromises freedom. Not only this, it also compromises a society's efficiency.[59] Thus Nozick is suspicious of Rawls' claim to fairness. In Nozick's view Rawls 'devotes much attention to explaining why those less well favored should not complain at receiving less', but devotes only one passage to explaining why the better endowed should find the 'terms satisfactory', which fails to 'show that these men have no grounds for complaint'.[60] Nozick regards patterned outcomes to be the height of unfairness, amounting to a restriction of freedom unless they are coincidental, which would be, in his view, highly improbable:

> ... patterned principles of distributive justice involve appropriating the actions of other persons. Seizing the results of someone's labor is equivalent to seizing hours from him and directing him to carry on various activities. If people force you to do certain work, or unrewarded work, for a certain period of time, they decide what you are to do and what purposes your work is to serve apart from your decisions. This process whereby they take this decision from you makes them a *part owner* of you; it gives them a property right in you.[61]

For Hayek, even for those less well endowed, patterned outcomes present a problem in terms of fairness:

> There will always exist inequalities which will appear unjust to those who suffer from them ... But when these things occur in a society which is consciously directed, the way in which people will react will be very different from what it is when they are nobody's conscious choice. Inequality is undoubtedly more readily borne, and affects the dignity of the person much less, if determined by impersonal force, than when it is due to design. In a competitive society it is no slight to a person, no offence to his dignity, to be told by any particular firm that it has no need for his services, or that it cannot offer him a better job.[62]

Both Hayek and Nozick celebrate the unfettered but invisible hand of the market, in which people can freely exchange their possessions as long as the rules of acquisition are just.[63] The outcome may not be, indeed will not be, egalitarian, but the rules are just. Neither Hayek nor Nozick is committed to equality because in their view human beings would not freely behave to achieve this. Both then are implicitly employing a view of human nature that is classically liberal. So, although Rawls and Nozick both claim to be committed to liberty and freedom, they cannot agree on what constitutes fairness. For Nozick fairness is simply about the rules by which people play, whereas for Rawls the outcome is also important.

The communitarian critique

Rawls' thesis prompted another well-known controversy, with those described as communitarians. The communitarian position is not a united one. However, it does seem that most from this tradition have two key objections to the liberal position. Firstly there is an objection to the liberal conception of the person, or in other words to the often-implicit assumptions made by a liberal position about the constituent factors of human nature. Communitarians reject the notion of the autonomous, separate, self-determining individual who is capable of detachment from their community and its traditional practices. This conception is apparent in Nozick and Hayek. Rawls recognises that 'society is a cooperative venture for mutual advantage'. Nevertheless, he is of the view that 'men are not indifferent as to how the greater benefits produced by their collaboration are distributed, for in order to pursue their ends they each prefer a larger to a lesser share'.[64] This emphasis on *their ends* suggests that these ends can be said to be autonomous from their community or society. Communitarians want to ask about the extent to which an individual's interests and values are conditional upon the type of culture from which they come. Communitarians take, in other words, an anti-rationalist stance and they insist that we 'can know a good in common that we cannot know alone'.[65]

The second objection they make is to the purported universalism and objectivism behind liberal propositions. In question is the appropriateness of positing a framework for organising society that does not take into consideration the particularities of different sorts of cultures. Of course this question is interrelated with the first because a communitarian might ask whether people from all cultural backgrounds have an interest in their capacity to *choose* how to live their life. Communitarians in other words highlight the paradox that a liberal position traditionally supports tolerance towards another's views, while at the same time seeking to find universal and objective reasons for defending their particular claims and views.

It is in the light of this debate between the liberals and communitarians that I intend to consider Chomsky's ideas. In particular I am interested in Chomsky's views about the first of the two areas of contention; namely that concerning the conception of the person, or rather, human nature. I shall begin by considering a communitarian critique of Rawls' conception of the person. At root two things are claimed. First, Rawls' implicit conception of human nature is inconsistent with his concern for fairness and equality, and secondly that anyway this conception of human nature is faulty. My view is that it is on this question of human nature that the protagonists on both sides of this debate have difficulties with reconciling justice, fairness, equality and liberty. By clarifying the libertarian socialist position, or at least the Chomskyan version of it, it is possible to see that notions of equality and freedom need not remain mere abstractions, but rather can be seen to be necessary to the human condition.

In Rawls' conception of justice, primacy is given to the rights of the individual: these rights cannot be undermined by other rights, such as those of a group or of a community. Justice therefore derives its foundational principles independently of the community. This, according to Sandel, makes Rawls' view of justice deontological rather than teleological.[66] In other words it does not presuppose any end conception of the good life. That the right of the individual has independent foundational principles is what justifies its primacy. Because individuals are capable of exercising free will, this capacity takes primacy over any possible aim or group of aims that the exercise of the will or wills may desire. The ability to choose has priority over the choice. According to Sandel, Rawls' conception of justice defends the foundational character of the right over the good, thereby giving it primacy, on the grounds that this is what it is to be fundamentally human.[67] It is fundamentally human to exercise free will or choice. Therefore any society organised to sanction or discriminate in favour of or against any particular choice in terms of the good life would ultimately constrain some individuals from exercising their capacity for *choosing* their own particular conception of the good life.

The liberal conception of human nature and its critics

Sandel's claim is that because Rawls attributes absolute moral worth to an individual's capacity for choice he is implicitly supporting a conception of what it is to be a human being. In other words he is making certain claims about human nature. To go against the Rawlsian priority of right is to contradict our essential nature as human beings. As such, because the subject has priority over its ends and its ends are autonomously chosen, the self is already constituted and its bounds are fixed. The self cannot therefore be constituted by the ends chosen. No matter the nature of socialisation, the self is irreducibly prior. According to Mulhall and Swift, this is making a metaphysical noumenal claim, because it implies that 'human beings ... [are] dual-aspect beings, a part of nature and yet simultaneously possessed of faculties that transcend nature'.[68] Mulhall and

Swift, by making this point, seem to be implying that free will is a metaphysical concept and as such cannot be accounted for in the same way as other things in nature. Or to put this another way, because we cannot explain or verify the existence of free will, it cannot therefore be part of nature and so it must be a metaphysical concept. This is a point, as will be discussed later, which Chomsky questions.

This metaphysical character in Rawlsian liberalism is apparent, according to Sandel, not only because of the implications of certain statements he makes, but also, Sandel argues, because it is an assumption necessary to the original position. When, behind the veil of ignorance, people are deciding upon the nature of the institutions that society ought to have, there must be some notion of how they stand in relation to one another and society. Rawls attaches certain motivations to the subject behind the veil of ignorance, such as 'mutual disinterestedness', and then claims that although, when the veil of ignorance is lifted, such motivations may not emerge, they provide his model with possible human weakness to guard against. Certainly it does seem that Rawls, having envisaged the way people might make decisions behind the veil of ignorance, seems to assume people would engage in capitalist acts once the veil is lifted. Sandel, however, wants to argue that motivational assumptions such as 'mutual disinterestedness' necessarily derive from Rawls' conception of the subject as an autonomous chooser of ends, and as such Rawls is embedding certain questionable empirical generalisations. Sandel argues that the original position is 'implicated too deeply in the contingent preferences of, say, Western liberal bourgeois life plans' but that it also 'achieves too much detachment from human circumstances, that the initial situation it describes is too abstract to yield ... any determinate principles at all'.[69]

Sandel is also concerned that although subjects may be autonomous choosers of ends, it is of course possible that in the plurality ends may overlap, in which case there can be cooperation. In Sandel's view, because such overlapping is merely a coincidence of circumstance, such cooperative relationships cannot be regarded as constitutional of the self in the Rawlsian picture. For Rawls 'the plurality of distinct persons with separate systems of ends is an essential feature of human socieities, [and so] we should not expect the principles of social choice to be utilitarian'.[70] Interests are interests of an autonomous individual who is an already constituted self. Identities are fixed prior to any relationship they have to another or to circumstance.

Sandel's key objection then to Rawlsian liberalism is that it involves a conception of the person as antecedently individuated, in other words as having an *a priori* fixed identity that is autonomous and self-determining which, according to Sandel, cannot escape arbitrary transcendentalism.[71] Sandel objects to this firstly because it suggests a voluntaristic way of conceiving of an individual's relationship to their ends. In other words an individual autonomously exercises his or her will and chooses an end. Individuals do not then choose ends from the experience gained during intersubjective cognitive processes. His second he calls the 'sociological objection' is that no matter how committed an individual is to an end, the end can never be constitutive of the self.[72] The individuated self will always stand apart from its values and ends. Thus it is not possible to feel divided between values or ends, or to feel torn between identities. The problem is not that an individual will not make 'the good of another' their end, but rather that such an end can only be said to be in that individual's interest. In other words the good of the community can never be said to be a motivation integral to or shaping of an individual's identity.

According to Sandel, not only does Rawls rely upon a particular conception of human essence which is controversial, but he also, despite his ambition to conceive of a society which is maximally neutral between competing notions of the good, draws up a far from neutral conception of political society. In other words, his non-neutral, idealist and metaphysical assumptions about human essence infect and necessarily colour his picture of political society. If the self is assumed to be antecedently individuated, and the good reflects that, then this excludes versions of the good that presuppose selves with constitutive attachments to community, for example. This means a communitarian conception of politics is ruled out. A person's commitment to a community or goal cannot be conceived of as part of their identity. People would be forced to see mutual cooperation, for example, as being in their own interest, because it offers greater reward than solitary effort. It is not possible to see mutual cooperation in liberal society as constitutive of the self. The liberal claim to preserve as wide an area as possible for conceptions of the good, conceals the actual imposition of constraints on those who believe that their constitutive self can only be realised by organising society for the good of the community. By this view it is not possible to see our goals or ends, indeed the community, as contributing to our identity. As Sandel observes '[m]aybe for some it is asking much more to ask that they act selfishly rather than benevolently'.[73]

On the one hand conceptions of the good that regard the community as the main organising principle are precluded, and on the other the extent to which identity is formed by the community is also denied. Hence the liberal is not as neutral as he or she might think.

Sandel is of the view that Rawls' conception of the antecedently individuated self also has implications for his understanding of the process by which individuals choose ends. Individuals choose ends by rationally weighing up the pros and cons and possible outcomes. Rawls discusses the process in terms of people making rational plans in order to realise their main desires.[74] According to Sandel, this means desires are reflected upon, but the self as a product of those desires is not.

While the plan of life or conception of the good most appropriate to a particular person is said to be 'the outcome of careful reflection', it is clear that the objects of this reflection are restricted to (1) the various alternative plans and their likely consequences for the realization of the agents desires, and (2) the agent's wants and desires are themselves, and their relative intensities In neither case does reflection take as its object the self *qua* subject of desires.[75]

Sandel objects to the idea that who we are cannot be reflected upon in terms of the choices we make. Such bounds are not within the scope of the agent; we cannot transform the self, we can only reflect upon our choices and these are contingent not integral to the self. Choices can be nothing more than an expression of personal preference. 'As long as it is assumed that man is by nature a being who chooses his ends rather than a being, as the ancients conceived him, who discovers his ends, then his fundamental preference must necessarily be for conditions of choice rather than, say for conditions of self-knowledge'.[76]

For Sandel, Rawls' conception of the person as antecedently individuated comes up against a serious problem when Rawls employs the difference principle. In Rawls' view, social organisation should not permit those endowed with advantage to gain more than those without. 'We see then that the difference principle represents, in effect, an agreement to regard the distribution of natural talents as a common asset and to share in the benefits of this distribution whatever it turns out to be'.[77] An individual with talent or intelligence needs to be conceived of as having those assets only as a matter of contingency. Since talent is conceived of as merely contingent it follows that an individual should not be the rightful possessor of rewards that flow from such talent. However, Rawls' society recognises the need to cultivate talent, so institutions need to be designed accordingly, but with the difference principle in mind. This means that institutional arrangements evaluate talent with socially cooperative principles in mind, and as such talent cannot have value independently of those institutional arrangements. However, Sandel argues that if an individual cannot be regarded as the rightful pre-institutional possessor of reward due to talent, it is actually not just because these attributes are contingent or arbitrary, it must be because such attributes cannot be regarded as being essential characteristics of the self.

Sandel's objections are two-fold. First, he is unhappy with the distinction between people and their talents. '[G]iven his sharp distinction between the self, taken as the pure subject of possession, and the aims and attributes it possesses, the self is left bare of any substantive feature or characteristic ... the self *itself* is dispossessed ... the self, strictly speaking, *has nothing*.'[78] Second, Sandel is unhappy with the view that just because the individual does not possess his or her natural attributes, there is no reason why society should.[78] As such Rawls' difference principle cannot be justified. If he wants to justify the position that society is more deserving of an individual's assets than the individual, then he must offer a very different conception of the self. '[T]he difference principle commits Rawls to an intersubjective conception he otherwise rejects ...[80] The point that Sandel is making is that Rawls' conception of the individual is not consonant with his concern for fairness and redistribution. The notions he is trying to reconcile of equality and freedom fail to be reconciled as one value will always undermine the other. Using Sandel's critique of Rawls it is possible to argue that this failure is due to his conception of the self.

In defence of a communitarian position, Sandel argues that the difference principle works more effectively with an intersubjective conception of the self.[81] This intersubjective conception of the self is also more effective for an understanding of the process that might go on behind the veil of ignorance in order to reach agreement.

> What matters is not what they choose but what they see, not what they decide but what they discover. What goes on in the original position is not a contract after all, but the coming to self-awareness of an intersubjective being.[82]

Rawls' objective for using the hypothetical veil of ignorance to describe the process that individuals might go through in order to determine the shape of social institutions is to ensure that the outcome is fair. Because none of the parties behind the veil holds any power or knowledge of outcome, the process they go through in order to reach agreement is merely procedural.[83] If the original position guarantees that the agreement is fair, to what extent can it be argued that individuals exercise choice? If no one has any power or knowledge with which to bargain, everyone's interests must be identical. In other words if the veil of ignorance were more than hypothetical, it would be experienced as extreme constraint. As Sandel argues

> ... what it means to say that the principles chosen will be just 'whatever they turn out to be' is simply that, given their situation, the parties are guaranteed to choose the *right* principles. While it may be true that, strictly speaking, they can choose any principles they wish, their situation is designed in such a way that they are guaranteed to 'wish' to choose only certain principles.[84]

However, in Sandel's view, if we had an intersubjective understanding of the self as bound to the community, then it might make sense for us to accept the constraints of the veil of ignorance.

In Sandel's view Rawls needs to accept the community as constitutive of the self in order to defend his principles of justice. However, this is impossible, given that Rawls regards the individual's right to autonomy as having priority. In other words Sandel argues that Rawls only in fact produces a contradiction in attempting to reconcile a society that is both free and just, where the right is prior to the good, but where outcomes are the product of procedural justice and equality of opportunity. Sandel instead offers a view whereby our sense of self cannot be separated from the community to which we belong, and it is rather that interaction with the community develops and refines our sense of self.

> On this strong view, to say that the members of a society are bound by a sense of community is not simply to say that a great many of them profess communitarian sentiments and pursue comminitarian aims, but rather that they conceive their identity – the subject and not just the object of their feelings and aspirations – as defined to some extent by the community of which they are part.[85]

If equality was conceived of as in the interests of the community and so was put before the autonomy of the individual, this would not be experienced as constraint, because the intersubjective character of the individual would ensure that this could come to be accepted as integral to the person. And so to use his phrase again, Sandel asks us not to forget 'the possibility that when politics goes well, we can know a good in common that we cannot know alone'.[86]

This discussion has sought to show that debates around the organising principles for the good society are derived upon or infer, even if this is not explicitly acknowledged, a view of human nature. This debate between the so-called liberal and communitarian suggests a polarity between the two positions on the question of human nature. To sum up, if autonomy and self-determination of the individual is deemed worthy of protecting, then such a claim carries with it the assumption that human beings are capable of self-determination. Rawls, taking this as his starting point, then assumes that people will act self-interestedly, which brings with it inequality, against which the worst-off will have to be protected. In attempting to defend the logic of redistribution Rawls must undermine his conception of the autonomous individual. As such it seems that Rawls fails to reconcile the primacy of self-determination with his desire for redistribution.

Sandel, by contrast, is of the view that community interests can become constitutive of the self. While Sandel's work is less concerned than Rawls with establishing *the* princples around which society can be organised, his critique nevertheless proposes that empirically speaking persons do have 'qualities of character, reflectiveness, and friendship that depend on the possibility of constitutive projects and attachments'.[87] Were society organised to encourage such qualities a more egalitarian outcome may be possible. Sandel's conception of the good society suggests a more malleable conception of human nature. Self-determination and therefore freedom in Sandel's framework, then, is only ever a phantom generated by a certain form of social organisation.

Returning to the original conundrum. If absolute autonomy of the individual is defended then it becomes difficult to justify equality in any redistributive sense without somehow infringing the priority of autonomy. Conversely, if autonomy is not taken as constitutive of the self, but as something merely fostered, then an alternative fostering could take place. Egalitarian ends could be sought, to which the individual could become amenable. However, under such fostering the liberty of the autonomous individual would have to be reduced to facilitate resocialisation.

Chomsky's views on human nature

At an earlier stage in the chapter it was shown how the libertarian socialists or anarchists defended the view that the concepts of equality and freedom were logically consistent and even interdependent. From the above discussion the question still remains whether human beings are capable of, indeed have natures that allow, the realisation of such a possibility. The liberal/communitarian debate suggests the two concepts can never become conjoined in practice for reasons of human nature. Can the libertarian socialist, or more precisely the Chomskyan, view of human nature add anything to this debate, and in so doing transcend the dichotomy between the two principles: freedom and equality?

In clarifying Chomsky's views on human nature, we can look at a debate he has with Foucault on the subject.[88] Foucault's work is concerned with power, and in particular, the notion that power lies in discourse.[89] He looks at the change and development of, for example, the medical discourse during the seventeenth and eighteenth centuries and exposes its covertly oppressive character which, in his view, serves to construct the subject. Foucault explores the rise and fall of discourses, to demonstrate his contention that 'the mad' and 'the homosexual' are examples of the historical construction of the medical discourse. It seems likely that it is precisely because the conclusions drawn from Foucault's historical study of discourses result in a conception of the subject as constructed that he is chosen to debate the subject of human nature with Chomsky, for whom humans have certain *a priori* or antecedent, innate characteristics. As Wilkin argues '[Foucault's] dismissal of human nature as yet another construction of bourgeois civilisation, when coupled with his understanding of the socially constructed subject, raises grave difficulties for any substantive account of human agency'.[90] Chomsky, on the other hand, is openly committed to the notion of a human nature, despite his own acknowledgment that our understanding of precisely what constitutes human nature is only at an extremely formative stage, and may never be something we can know.[91] In the light of my account of the debate between the liberals and the communitarians, Foucault can be seen to be taking a position on human nature not dissimilar to that of the communitarians. Chomsky, by contrast, is clearly more in line with the Rawlsian view that there are substantive antecedent elements to human nature.

However, what is striking when one actually looks at the debate between Chomsky and Foucault, is the degree of agreement between them. This may seem paradoxical given the outline of their presumed positions on human nature. In recognising why there is agreement, it is possible to appreciate Chomsky's view of human nature and its complexities. The position Chomsky takes on human nature can be said to derive from his work in linguistics, although, as has been discussed, he is reticent to make any formal claims of this nature. Very briefly, his argument is that the 'normal' adult has acquired a sophisticated array of abilities that allow communication with others to take place. This leads us to consider the data available to that adult to try to establish how they go about acquiring such sophistication.

> [H]aving done so, in principle we're faced with a reasonably clear and well-delineated scientific problem, namely that of accounting for the gap between the really quite small quantity of data, small and rather degenerate in quality, that's presented to the child, and the very highly articulated, highly systematic, profoundly organised resulting knowledge that he [sic] somehow derives from these data.[92]

Chomsky goes on to argue that '[t]here is only one possible explanation, which I have to give ... for this remarkable phenomenon, namely the assumption that the individual himself contributes a good deal, an overwhelming part in fact.'[93] And so Chomsky concludes, 'I would claim then that this instinctive knowledge ... is one fundamental constituent of human nature'.[94] He tentatively takes the argument further when he argues: 'I assume that in other domains of human intelligence, in other domains of human cognition and behaviour, something of the same sort must be true'.[95]

Foucault, on the other hand, acknowledges '[i]t is true that I mistrust the notion of human nature, *a little*' (my emphasis).[96] It is important to note that he is reticent because he goes on to argue that his reason for this mistrust is that he finds 'it difficult to see in this a scientific concept'.[97] Because he argues *historically* human nature has not played a scientific role. 'In the history of knowledge, the notion of human nature seems to me mainly to have played the role of an epistemological indicator to designate certain types of discourse in relation to or in opposition to theology or biology or history'.[98] Chomsky makes two points in response. First, even though human nature has not been scientifically employed *in the past,* there is no reason to suppose that it cannot be regarded as a useful organising concept for *future* attempts to explain knowledge acquisition and human behaviour. However, in his second point he accepts Foucault's skepticism and concedes that it may not be possible to give the notion of human nature any scientific content:

> Can we explain in biological terms, ultimately in physical terms, these properties of both acquiring knowledge in the first place and making use of it in the second? I really see no reason to believe that we can; that is, it's an article of faith on the part of scientists that since science has explained many other things it will also explain this.[99]

Foucault goes on to accept human nature may be a useful organising concept for new advances to be made in the area of understanding human behaviour.

Chomsky and Foucault then, appear to agree. But how can there be agreement when the implication of Foucault's work is that subjects have historically been structured by oppressive exclusionary discourses, whereas Chomsky's work claims to uncover the extraordinary creativity of human capacity, which he concludes must be innate? Foucault then identifies why it is they agree whereas their writing suggests they should not. It seems that Foucault and Chomsky are fighting different ghosts, and it is this that leads them to a difference of *emphasis*. Foucault is fighting two ghosts in the history of knowledge. The first he calls 'attribution'. He objects to the way in which discoveries in knowledge are standardly attributed to an individual, which has the effect of devaluing what he calls 'collective phenomena'. When these 'collective phenomena' enter history they are usually characterised as responsible for holding back the inventor. His second *bête noire* is the way in which the history of knowledge conceives of truth as waiting to be revealed rather than as possibly being consti-tuted by history itself. '[S]o that it won't be compromised by history, it is necessary not that the truth constitutes itself in history, but only that it reveals itself in it; hidden to men's eyes, provisionally inaccessible, sitting in the shadows, it will wait to be unveiled'.[100] It seems that Foucault is not necessarily trying to take any firm position on this question of truth and its relation to social context, but more that he is only trying to redress the balance in the history of ideas, for he goes on to say:

> And what if understanding the relation of the subject to the truth were just an effect of knowledge? What if understanding were a complex, multiple, non-individual formation, not 'subjected to the subject', which produced effects of truth? One should then put forward positively this entire dimension which the history of science has nega-tivised; analyse the productive capacity of knowledge as a collective practice; and consequently replace individuals and their 'knowledge' in the development of a knowledge which at a given moment func-tions according to certain rules which one can register and describe.[101]

Foucault argues that Chomsky, on the other hand, 'has been fighting against linguistic behaviourism, which attributed almost nothing to the creativity of the speaking subject: the speaking subject was a kind of surface on which information came together little by little, which he afterwards combined'.[102] And so Foucault concludes 'I have, *in appearance at least*, a completely different attitude to Mr. Chomsky apropos creativity, because for me it is a matter of effacing the dilemma of the knowing subject' (my emphasis).[103] It seems then that in Foucault's view their differences lie in the fact that they are asking different types of questions, but this does not necessarily make their claims incompatible. Certainly Chomsky seems to accept the motivation Foucault has to question the history of knowledge in the way he does. He argues:

> Now, as far as what you say about the history of science is concerned, I think that's correct and illuminating and particularly relevant in fact to the kinds of enterprise that I see lying before us in psychology and linguistics and the philosophy of the mind.
>
> That is, I think there are certain topics that have been repressed or put aside during the scientific advances of the past few centuries.[104]

However, Chomsky would take the view that just because some 'knowledge' is dubiously constucted, it does not follow that the knowledge itself is necessarily false. One of Foucault's specific concerns is the way in which the discourse of medicine has pathologised homosexuality. Chomsky is also concerned about the way in which society has pathologised certain groups within society. But as he says of the attempts to link race and intelligence: '[i]t is . . . possible that there is some correlation between race and intelligence. But *in a non-racist society*, these differences – if shown to exist – would be of no significance.'[105] The point is that it is not the fault of the knowledge that it is used perniciously. Rather it is due to the character of the society in which the knowledge is acquired and then used.

Chomsky is certainly not as sceptical as Foucault about the possibility of seeking truth, although he is also aware that a truth need not be absolute. New knowledge can and does alter our understanding of something. As Wilkin argues: 'Chomsky's *Post-cartesianism* leads him to recognise that there are no absolute certainties or truths in science or knowledge generally, such a position is not open to us. However, this does not mean that we are forced to adopt the position of . . . scepticism.'[106] Wilkin then quotes Chomsky as saying: '[t]he lack of indubitable foundations need not lead us to reject the working assumption that there is an objective reality to be discovered, of which we have at best a partial grasp.'[107]

Returning to the debate between Chomsky and Foucault and the question of human nature, we see that what causes the appearance of irreconcilable differences between them is the result of the temporal difference in the questions they are asking. Foucault is concerned with the oppressive way in which knowledge is and has been used in the *past and present*: in other words during a time in which society is and has been hierarchically organised. Chomsky's political writings are also concerned with the oppressive way in which knowledge has been used in the past and present. However, his work in linguistics leads him to the view that in language human beings are creative within certain innate structural rules.[108] While he makes no pretence that he has any scientific evidence to support it, it is reasonable to *believe* that this creativity is a more general feature of human nature. Given this belief, he takes a further step by arguing for 'a conception of human nature which emphasises as essential to it the need for creative work under one's own control, solidarity and cooperation with others'.[109] If it could be established, or at least accepted, that creativity was indeed a feature of human nature, then such a feature ought to inform any view of the way in which society might be organised in the *future*. While Chomsky would not disagree with Foucault that societies have been and are organised in such a way that does not allow the full character of our human natures to flourish, producing some quite distorted results in human behaviour, this does not mean that this need always be the case. Chomsky's concern lies not only with the *past and present* but also with the *future*. He not only studies *what is* but from this suggests *what ought to be* or rather *what might be*. In this way, Chomsky lays the ground for an important element of any political theory – a vision of the future informed by an account of human nature.

> [H]aving this view of human nature and human needs, one tries to think about the modes of social organization that would permit the freest and fullest development of the individual, of each individual's potentialities in whatever direction they might take, that would permit him to be fully human in the sense of having the greatest possible scope for his freedom and initiative.[110]

Foucault, by contrast, because of his scepticism towards establishing any sort of truth, let alone truth about human nature, stops short of any sort of prescriptive agenda. The temporality of their questions, then, affects their emphasis, and distinguishes them – Foucault as critic, Chomsky as theorist.[111]

But is it really possible to reconcile Foucault's constructed subject with Chomsky's creative subject? Chomsky is not making any categorical claims about the specific content of human nature, apart from claiming that it is creative. Of course creativity can manifest itself in many different ways, both good and bad, constructive and destructive. In his view humans do demonstrate creativity, despite the odds, and his research in linguistics provides evidence to support such a contention. And as Wilkin argues, this creativity is evidenced in Chomsky's political writings, which 'are filled with snapshots of peoples who have struggled against [hideous abuses] and who have established international solidarity in defense of peoples they have never met and whose cultures they have never directly experienced'.[112] However, that human nature has a creative capacity does not mean that this capacity will necessarily manifest itself, and here is where the oppressive character of class societies works with more or less success, to construct a subject, suppressing what may otherwise be natural tendencies. In the context of language development Chomsky argues:

> Language development, like all human development, will be heavily determined by the nature of the environment, and may be severely limited unless the environment is appropriate. A stimulating environment is required to enable natural curiosity, intelligence and creativity to develop, and then enable our biological capacities to unfold. The fact that the course of development is largely internally determined does not mean that it will proceed without care, stimulation, and opportunity.[113]

For Chomsky then, it is not inconsistent to agree with the Foucauldian and communitarian position that takes the view that the environment constructs the subject, and to agree with those arguments attributed to the liberal Rawlsian position that individuals nevertheless have a specifiable human nature of politically relevant dimensions. However, there is a crucial difference between the Rawlsian antecedently individuated self and Chomsky's antecedent self. For Rawls the self is autonomous, self-determining and individual. Whereas for Chomsky what is antecedent is creativity, and from this he derives the view that human beings require conditions that are free *and* cooperative. So for Chomsky, as for Rawls, freedom is crucial but for very different reasons.

Naturalism and human nature

Chomsky is deeply sceptical of those who hold the view, as Sandel's view suggests, that humans do not have an intrinsic nature, thereby suggesting they are empty vessels into which knowledge and values can be poured.

> I would like to assume on the basis of fact and hope on the basis of confidence in the human species that there are innate structures of mind. If there are not, if humans are just plastic and random organisms, then they are fit subjects for shaping behavior. If humans only become as they are by random changes, then why not control that randomness by the state authority or the behaviourist technologist or anything else? Naturally I hope that it will turn out that there are intrinsic structures determining human need and fulfillment of human need.[114]

In his view the idea that the human brain or mind and thereby our human nature does not have an intrinsic structure to it, is the stuff of myth.

> The background myth is that the human brain is radically different from any other object in the physical world: namely, it's diffuse and unstructured. There's nothing else in the physical world like that ... Nothing is just some big amoeba. Well, a standard picture is – and it's the same as the picture of human malleability – that the brain is different. Even though it is (or maybe because it is) the most compli- cated object that we know of in the universe, somehow it's unstructured. That means every aspect of it is the same as every other aspect, and it's malleable and pliable and so on. Well, that just cannot be true. Everything we know is completely counter to it. Everything we know points to the fact that it's like other physical objects that develop in the natural world. And if it is, we're not going to find that one system has the same structural properties as other systems. You don't expect to find it in the other parts of the body. Why should it be true above the neck?.[115]

Mulhall and Swift find the Rawlsian picture of the self-determining indi- vidual problematic because it implies that free will is a metaphysical concept and as such cannot be accounted for in the same way as other things in nature. Thus 'human beings ... [are] dual-aspect beings, a part of nature and yet simultaneously possessed of faculties that transcend nature'.[116] Chomsky would suggest this is a questionable assumption. Just because we cannot explain free will naturalistically does not mean we have to resort to the conclusion that it is therefore metaphysical.

Similarly he is of the view that just because we are a part of nature, this does not mean that our social and political environment is not also extremely important for human development (see note 114 in Chapter 1).

These views on human nature can then in Chomsky's view be logically associated with certain social and political assumptions and claims. Because of their natures, human beings need liberty to develop their creative capac- ities as well as equality in terms of access to resources in order to sustain themselves and so to develop their innate capacity for creativity in a constructive and cooperative rather than an individually acquisitive and destructive way.

What sort of light do such claims throw upon the liberal communi- tarian debate which at root contain a fundamental disagreement about human nature? Rawls is criticised for giving foundational priority in any organising principles for society to an individual's capacity for choice, such that an individual's capacity to exercise free will must be protected over and above any other conception of the good, such as the good of the community. In Sandel's view, Rawls is not only making claims about what ought to be the case, but he is assuming certain fundamental characteristics actually are the case for human beings. Chomsky would, it seems, accept the Rawlsian position that the individual's liberty must be protected, precisely because individuals are capable of exercising free will. However, Chomsky does not seek to protect individual liberty simply because free will exists. Free will is valued because it is *expressive* of human nature, and liberty is therefore *functional*. Free will provides the necessary conditions for the exercise of the creative capacities. As ever, he is cautious about claiming to have anything but the most rudimentary evidence to support such a claim:

> Now, I don't think that there's any scientific grasp, any hint of an idea, as to how to explain free will. Suppose somebody argues that free will is an illusion. Okay. This could be the case, but I don't believe that it's the case. It *could* be. You have to be open-minded about the possibility. But you're going to need a very powerful argument to convince me that something as evident as free will is an illusion. (Original emphasis.)[117]

Reconciling the naturalistic individual and community

How would Chomsky defend himself against Sandel's objection that simply holding such a conception of human nature necessarily entails a conception of *the* good, which ought to be precluded if individuals are supposed to have the liberty to choose their own ends? In other words is it necessary to conclude that the liberal and Chomskyan view of human nature, by definition, precludes the choice of organising society based upon the view that a person's identity is constituted by their commitment to a community?

It has already been argued that even though on Chomsky's view humans have certain innate capacities, these capacities are triggered (or not) depending upon the environment. As such, even though Chomsky wants to argue that human creativity requires freedom for its expression, the environment or community in which a person operates is going to be crucial. The character of the community then is a matter of self-interest. Given that it is also Chomsky's view that different people will show flair for different skills and have different aptitudes, it is likely that an individual with a particular skill will recognise the need for cooperation with others who have skills that are different and perhaps complementary. The freedom of others to develop their own talents is of interest to every individual *qua* individual.

> My own hopes and intuitions are that self-fulfilling and creative work is a fundamental human need, and that the pleasures of a challenge met, a work well done, the exercise of skill and craftsmanship, are real and significant, and are an essential part of a full and meaningful

life. The same is true of the opportunity to understand and enjoy the achievements of others, which often go beyond what we ourselves can do, and to work constructively in cooperation with others.[118]

Chomsky makes a similar point with reference to language. Just as language has, in his view, an innate biological basis it also, crucially, has social uses. 'I think that the use of language is a very important means by which this species [human beings], because of its biological nature, creates a kind of a social space, to place itself in interaction with other people.'[119]

An immediate objection can be anticipated. Suppose I do not perceive someone else's skills and talents as useful or necessary to me or my community? Suppose in my view I feel an individual or group of individuals could be something more useful or necessary. Here it seems to me that Chomsky is right not to make any claims about some ideal society where such conflicts would not arise. Clearly it is possible to envisage times where certain resources become scarce and then decisions concerning relative production versus relative consumption would have to be made. Compromises would have to be made. But, as has already been mentioned, Chomsky argues '[e]ach individual is both a producer and a consumer, after all, and that means that each individual has to join in those socially determined compromises'.[120] In his view we do not 'need a separate bureaucracy to carry out governmental decisions'.[121] Decisions can be 'made by the informed working class through their assemblies and their direct representatives, who live among them and work among them'.[122] Of course, 'in any complex industrial society there should be a group of technicians whose task is to produce plans, and to lay out the consequences of decisions ... [b]ut the point is that those planning systems are themselves industries, and they will have their worker's councils and they will be part of the whole council system, and the distinction [with state socialism] is that these planning systems do not make decisions'.[123] Chomsky does not then regard such libertarian ideas as being applicable only to pre-industrial or rural society. In his view 'industrialization and the advance of technology raise possibilities for self-management over a broad scale that simply didn't exist in an earlier period'.[124] Community choices and compromises, then, involve individuals as both producers and consumers.

Chomsky's reference to social space raises the question of how humans can be within a social context. It is suggested here that libertarian and communitarian ideals need not be mutually exclusive, not only in terms of their view of human nature, but also in terms of political practice. A person can be both antecedently individuated in the sense that identity is or could be both given and at the same time intersubjectively constituted through cooperative relationships. The individuated self need not stand apart from its values and ends. Communal ends facilitate and enhance individual ends, just as following individual ends benefit the community.

Sandel objects to Rawls' conception of justice giving priority to the right over the good, but the right in Chomskyan terms would involve cooperatively determining the good. It is important to note that the good would never be absolute or fixed. Chomsky's conception of the good is not a restrictively prescriptive sense of the good, but neither is it elusive or amorphous. His conception of the good insists that individuals should be free to determine their own creative ends within the limits of the resources available to their society at any particular time. Freedom then is relative to the objective conditions at any historical point in time. Thus conceptions of the good will vary according to objective conditions and cultural backgrounds. Even this weak conception of the good is never going to be absolute. In Chomsky's view it is always going to be something that individuals and communities will have to strive towards. This view serves to delineate his political position, and thus sympathy with anarchist approaches.

> What I think is most important about anarchism . . . is its recognition that there is and will always be a need to discover and overcome structures of hierarchy, authority and domination and constraints on freedom: slavery, wage-slavery, racism, sexism, authoritarian schools, etc., forever. If human society progresses, overcoming some of these forms of oppression, it will uncover others . . .[125]

So in Chomskyan terms it makes no sense to prioritise an absolute ideal or blueprint of the good. 'Anarchism does not legislate ultimate solutions to these problems.'[126] Indeed to consider doing so is, for Chomsky, highly suspect. It is suspect firstly because any deviation from Chomsky's weak conception of the good would imply by definition relative degrees of lack of freedom. But then if freedom is not conceived of as being necessary to human nature in order for its creativity to flourish, indeed if as communitarians seem to think ends, goals or the good can be and should be constitutive of the self, then this presumably is not of concern. However, the thesis that human beings are infinitely malleable opens up the whole possibility of reaching totalitarian conclusions, benevolent and egalitarian or otherwise. The second reason why prioritising the good is suspect is that it carries the presumption that we are aware of all the possible constraints on and abundance of resources. 'We will each commit ourselves to the problems we feel most pressing, . . . many of which we are in no position even to identify under the intellectual and material constraints of our present existence.'[127] Chomsky here again is emphasising that our knowledge and hold on truth must always be flexible, that we must be open to the possibility that new problems will present themselves which will give rise in turn to new and possibly superior knowledge. We must never therefore conceive of a static solution to human problems of social organisation. The most we can do is give people the freedom with which to facilitate the triggering of creative solutions to the problems faced at any particular historical time. This means that Chomsky's view of freedom is not simply a permissive one, but a politically demanding one, requiring judgement and caution in our political arrangements.

Conclusion

This chapter has argued that Chomsky is not inconsistent, as some have tried to show, when he claims to be both a libertarian and a socialist. His socialism poses no particular problems: it is about the need for and the way in which humans organise and live together collectively as individuals. The values of freedom and equality are not mutually exclusive. Indeed, as the libertarian socialist or anarchist tradition has itself always maintained, equality should not only mean equality in terms of access to resources, but to remain meaningful should also include political equality so that individuals are given the liberty to take part in decision-making processes. In other words, for libertarian socialists, equality is shorn of its progressive value if it is to simply involve a body such as the state determining productive output and distribution. Similarly, freedom or liberty is meaningless if the distribution of resources in a society is inegalitarian, because a lack of resources by definition will constrain an individual's freedom.

Chomsky's views on human nature lend his particular position on libertarian socialism greater authority. Liberty and equality are not only interdependent and progressive values, since, in Chomsky's view, they are also necessary to or preferable for the healthy development of the human condition. Chomsky's evidence for such a necessity is far from concrete, as he admits. However, his work in linguistics is certainly suggestive of such a claim. The liberal and communitarian debate has also grappled with the concepts of liberty and equality, raising serious problems about the possibility of reconciling the two values. This suggested the interesting possibility of looking at Chomsky's views in the light of this debate and specifically the aspect of the debate between Rawls and Sandel. A key feature of this debate directly concerns itself with this question of human nature. According to Sandel the liberal position on social organisation implicitly posits a conception of the person. The liberal individual is autonomous, rational, self-interested and self-determining. These characteristics are *a priori* given, and as such are not influenced by the nature and character of the society in which individuals co-exist. Sandel, in criticising Rawls' conception of the individual, raises the possibility of a very different conception of the individual. In so doing Sandel questions the whole notion of a human nature in any *a priori* sense. For the communitarian, human beings are to a large extent formed by the society from which they come. Subjects are, in this view, constructed, and the goals or ends chosen are constitutive of the self. In Sandel's view it is Rawls' conception of human nature which makes it impossible for him to reconcile the values of equality and freedom. Of course Sandel's conception of human beings does not bring him any closer to reconciliation either, but then that objective is not on his agenda.

This chapter has also argued that Chomsky's conception of human nature shows that the values of equality and freedom are not mutually exclusive. Chomsky offers a hybrid version of the liberal and communitarian conception of human beings. Freedom is a requirement for human creativity, not a requirement for autonomous individuals. Subjects are or can be both self-determining and determined. Whilst the environment in which individuals grow is crucial to their development and of course objective conditions will affect and or constrain choices, it is Chomsky's view or hope that human nature is by no means totally plastic. Human beings are capable of self-determination and so the freedom to develop their creative capacities ought to be protected. However, at the same time it must be recognised that there always are objective constraints, such as periodic scarcity of a material resource. In Chomsky's view, human beings are capable of collectively determining how best to manage resources, given the objective constraints. Freedom and equality, then, are not absolute concepts but are always relative to objective reality. As such Chomsky cannot be accused of teleology. By this view, there is no 'end' to history – but there can nevertheless be progress.

We first set out to consider Chomsky's claim not to have a political theory. His claim is significant because it acknowledges very real gaps in our knowledge, and yet, it seems, despite this, his ideas do, nevertheless, constitute a theory. His theory establishes that any aspirations for social and political organisation must rest upon a view of human nature. It has been established that his libertarian socialist ideals are informed by his observations of human behaviour which in turn inform his suggestions about our human nature. Having ascertained that he has a solid coherent theoretical framework, we now turn to consider how he employs this theoretical framework in his critical analysis of society.

Notes

1 Chomsky, N. in Otero, C. P. (ed.) (1981) *Noam Chomsky: Radical Priorities*, Montreal: Black Rose Books, p. 245.
2 I say some anarchists, to distinguish between left and right wing anarchists. Left wing anarchists are those associated with the socialist tradition. Right wing anarchists are critical of the presence of the state, but accept private property and capitalist relations of exchange.
3 Bakunin, M. (1973) in Dolgoff S. (trans. and ed) *Bakunin on Anarchy*, New York: George Allen and Unwin, p. 268.
4 Bakunin, M. in Dolgoff S., *op. cit.*, p. 256.
5 Nozick, R. (1986) reprint *Anarchy, State and Utopia*, Oxford: Basil Blackwell.
6 Baker, J. (1987) *Arguing for Equality*, London: Verso.
7 Fraser, N. (1997) in Phillips, A., 'From Inequality to Difference: A Severe

Case of Displacement?' in *New Left Review*, no. 224, July/August 1997, p. 151.

8 Berlin, I. (1969) 'Two Concepts of Liberty' in *Four Essays on Liberty*, Oxford: Oxford University Press.

9 Chomsky, N. in Otero C. P. (ed.) (1981) *op cit.*, p. 245.

10 Nozick, R., *op. cit.*

11 Guerin, D. (1970) *Anarchism*, New York: London: Monthly Review Press; Joll, J. (1969) *The Anarchists*, London: Methuen; Woodcock, G. (1986) *Anarchism* (2nd edn), Harmondsworth: Penguin; Carter, A. (1971) *The Political Theory of Anarchism*, London: Routledge and Kegan Paul; Fleming, M. (1979) *The Anarchist Way to Socialism*, Totowa, New Jersey: Rowmen and Littlefield.

12 Joll, J., *op. cit.*, p. 26.

13 Guerin, D., *op. cit.*, p. 12.

14 Woodcock, G., *op. cit.*

15 Woodcock, G., *op. cit.*, p. 37.

16 Woodcock, G., *op. cit.*, p. 35.

17 Woodcock, G., *op. cit.*, p. 37.

18 Chomsky, N. (1973) *For Reasons of State*, New York: Vintage Books, p. 375.

19 Chomsky, N. (1973) *op. cit.*, p. 375.

20 Chomsky, N. (1973) *op. cit.*, p. 374.

21 Chomsky, N. (1973) *op. cit.*, p. 375.

22 Chomsky, N. (1981) *op. cit.*, p. 248.

23 Chomsky, N. (1973) *op. cit.*, p. 375.

24 Locke, J. (1986) in Stewart, M. (ed.) *Readings in Social and Political Philosophy*, New York: Oxford University Press, p. 12.

25 Bakunin, M., *op. cit.*

26 Fleming, M., *op. cit.*, p. 21.

27 See my chapter on Chomsky and the state. See also Rocker, R. (1938) (1972) *Anarcho-Syndicalism*, New York: Gordon Press p. 21.

28 Chomsky, N. (1973) *op. cit.*, p. 376.

29 Bakunin, M., *op. cit.*, p. 262.

30 Joll, J., *op. cit.*, p. 28.

31 Nozick, R., *op. cit.*, p. 163.

32 Nozick. R., *op. cit.*, p. 345, n. 6.

33 Chomsky, N. in Otero, C. P. (ed.) (1988) *Noam Chomsky: Language and Politics*, Montreal: Black Rose Books, p. 204.

34 Chomsky, N. in Otero, C. P. (ed.) (1988) *op. cit.*, p. 756.

35 Chomsky, N. in Otero, C. P. (ed.) (1988) *op. cit.*, p. 756.

36 Chomsky, N. in Otero, C. P. (ed.) (1988) *op. cit.*, p. 758.

37 Chomsky, N. in Otero, C. P. (ed.) (1981) *op. cit.*, p. 254.

38 Chomsky, N. in Otero, C. P. (ed.) (1981) *op. cit.*, p. 257.

39 Chomsky, N. in Otero, C. P. (ed.) (1981) *op. cit.*, p. 256.

40 Chomsky, N. in Otero, C. P. (ed.) (1981) *op. cit.*, p. 258.

41 Chomsky, N. in Otero, C. P. (ed.) (1981) *op. cit.*, p. 257.

42 Nozick, R., *op. cit.*

43 Hollis, M. (1977) *Models of Man*, Cambridge: Cambridge University Press; Forbes, I. and Smith, S. (1983) *Politics and Human Nature*, London: Frances Pinter Publishers.

44 Feyerabend, P. (1975) 'How to Defend Society Against Science' in *Radical Philosophy*, Summer, p. 17.

45 Wilkin, P. (1995) *Noam Chomsky: On Knowledge, Human Nature and Freedom*, PhD thesis, University of Southampton, p. 206.

46 Rawls, J. (1972) *A Theory of Justice*, Cambridge, Massachusetts: Harvard University Press.
47 Rawls, J., *op. cit.*, p. 65.
48 Mulhall, S., and Swift, A. (1996) (1996 reprint) *Liberals and Communitarians*, 2nd edn, Oxford: Blackwell Publishers, p. 67.
49 Hobbes, T. (1973) *Leviathan*, London: Everyman's Library.
50 Rawls, J., *op. cit.*, p. 302.
51 Rawls, J., *op. cit.*, p. 302.
52 Rawls, J., *op. cit.*, p. 302.
53 Rawls, J., *op. cit.*, p. 6.
54 Parekh, B. (1996) 'Political Theory: Traditions in Political Philosophy' in Goodin, R. E. and Klingemann H-D (eds) *A New Handbook of Political Science*, Oxford: Oxford University Press, p. 510.
55 Nozick, R., *op. cit.*
56 Nozick, R., *op. cit.*, p. 19. Nozick employs what he calls an 'invisible hand' explanation to account for the minimal state's presence. This 'explains what looks to be the product of someone's intentional design, as not being brought about by anyone's intentions' (p 10).
57 Nozick, R., *op. cit.*, p. 149.
58 Nozick, R., *op. cit.*, p. 177.
59 Hayek, F. A. (1944) (1986) *The Road to Serfdom*, London: Routledge and Kegan Paul.
60 Nozick, R., *op. cit.*, pp. 195–6.
61 Nozick, R., *op. cit.*, p. 172.
62 Hayek, F. A., *op. cit.*, p. 79.
63 Nozick, R., *op. cit.*, p. 151.
64 Rawls, J., *op. cit.*, p. 126.
65 Sandel, M. J. (1982) *Liberalism and The Limits of Justice*, Cambridge: Cambridge University Press, p. 183.
66 Sandel, M. J., *op. cit.*, p. 18.
67 Sandel, M. J., *op. cit.*, p. 19.
68 Mulhall, S. and Swift, A., *op. cit.*, p. 45.
69 Sandel, M. J., *op. cit.*, p. 27.
70 Rawls, J., *op. cit.*, p. 29.
71 Sandel, M. J., *op. cit.*, p. 13.
72 Sandel, M. J., *op. cit.*, p. 11.
73 Sandel, M. J., *op. cit.*, p. 46.
74 Rawls, J., *op. cit.*, p. 417.
75 Sandel, M. J., *op. cit.*, p. 159.
76 Sandel, M. J., *op. cit.*, p. 22.
77 Rawls, J., *op. cit.*, p. 101.
78 Sandel, M. J., *op. cit.*, p. 85.
79 Sandel, M. J., *op. cit.*, p. 96.
80 Sandel, M. J., *op. cit.*, p. 80.
81 Sandel, M. J., *op. cit.*, p. 97.
82 Sandel, M. J., *op. cit.*, p. 132.
83 Rawls, J., *op. cit.*, p. 136.
84 Sandel, M. J., *op. cit.*, p. 127.
85 Sandel, M. J., *op. cit.*, p. 151.
86 Sandel, M. J., *op. cit.*, p. 183.
87 Sandel, M. J., *op. cit.*, p. 181.
88 Elders, F. (1974) *Reflexive Water*, London: Souvenir Press.
89 Foucault, M. (1981) *The History of Sexuality: An Introduction*, Volume 1 Harmondsworth: Penguin.

90 Wilkin, P. (1995) *op. cit.*
91 Chomsky, N. in Otero, C. P. (ed.) (1988) *op cit.*, pp. 415–16.
92 Chomsky, N. in Elders, F., *op. cit.*, p. 136.
93 Chomsky, N. in Elders, F., *op. cit.*, p. 137.
94 Chomsky, N. in Elders, F., *op. cit.*, p. 137.
95 Chomsky, N. in Elders, F., *op. cit.*, p. 138.
96 Chomsky, N. in Elders, F., *op. cit.*, p. 139.
97 Foucault, M. in Elders, F., *op. cit.*, p. 140.
98 Foucault, M. in Elders, F., *op. cit.*, p. 140.
99 Chomsky, N. in Elders, F., *op. cit.*, p. 141.
100 Foucault, M. in Elders, F., *op. cit.*, p. 148.
101 Foucault, M. in Elders, F., *op. cit.*, p. 149.
102 Foucault, M. in Elders, F., *op. cit.*, p. 148.
103 Foucault, M. in Elders, F., *op. cit.*, p. 149.
104 Chomsky, N. in Elders, F., *op. cit.*, p. 152.
105 Chomsky, N. in Rai, M. (1995) *Chomsky's Politics,* London: Verso, p. 190, n. 61.
106 Wilkin, P. (1995) *op. cit.*, p. 54.
107 Chomsky, N. in Wilkin, P. (1995) *op. cit.*, p. 57.
108 Chomsky argues 'I think creativity means free action within the framework of rules' in Otero, C. P. (ed.) (1988) *op. cit.*, p. 144.
109 Chomsky, N., 'An Interview', *Radical Philosophy*, Autumn 1989, p. 31.
110 Chomsky, N. in Otero, C. P. (ed.) (1988) *op. cit.*, p. 144.
111 Chomsky, N. in Otero, C. P. (ed.) (1988) *op. cit.*, p. 145.
112 Wilkin, P. (1997) *Noam Chomsky: On Knowledge, Human Nature and Freedom,* London: Macmillan, p. 244.
113 Chomsky, N. in Otero, C. P. (ed.) (1988) *op. cit.*, p. 502.
114 Chomsky, N. in Otero, C. P. (ed.) (1988) *op. cit.*, p. 144.
115 Chomsky, N. (1989a) *Radical Philosophy*, pp. 32–3.
116 Mulhall, S. and Swift, A., *op. cit.*, p. 45.
117 Chomsky, N. in Otero, C. P. (ed.) (1988) *op. cit.*, p. 415.
118 Chomsky, N. in Otero, C. P. (ed.) (1988) *op. cit.*, p. 394.
119 Chomsky, N. in Otero, C. P. (ed.) (1988) *op. cit.*, p. 401.
120 Chomsky, N. in Otero, C. P. (ed.) (1981) *op. cit.*, p. 258.
121 Chomsky, N. in Otero, C. P. (ed.) (1981) *op. cit.*, p. 259.
122 Chomsky, N. in Otero, C. P. (ed.) (1981) *op. cit.*, p. 259.
123 Chomsky, N. in Otero, C. P. (ed.) (1981) *op. cit.*, p. 259.
124 Chomsky, N. in Otero, C. P. (ed.) (1981) *op. cit.*, p. 248.
125 Chomsky, N. in Otero, C. P. (ed.) (1988) *op. cit.*, p. 395.
126 Chomsky, N. in Otero, C. P. (ed.) (1988) *op. cit.*, p. 395.
127 Chomsky, N. in Otero, C. P. (ed.) (1988) *op. cit.*, p. 395.

3   State capitalism

Introduction

Chomsky is said to write and speak about American foreign policy and specifically about America's relations with Latin America and the Middle East. Although this is true, it is to conceive of his work too narrowly. Certainly his relentless, tirelessly documented, combing and interpreting of historical and contemporary events does focus upon the American state and its international relations. However, his work is full of ideas about the man-made structures and relations in society that establish and perpetuate inequality, injustice, inefficiency and the potential for global destruction. In this chapter, I look at what is, as has already been mentioned, Chomsky's principal focus – the American state. However, from this I want to see if his ideas add anything to our understanding of the state, from those who have attempted to theorise about this human construction.

The initial thing to strike one about Chomsky's analysis of the American state is he is deeply critical of actions carried out in the name of the state. In particular we quickly see that his general view is that the state appears to act in the interests of the more powerful in society. The general view then that serves to frame his understanding of the state, is that state actions are on the whole inimical to the needs and aspirations of large numbers of people. When we think about this in the context of his ideas on human nature, we see that he is concerned to strip away social structural constraints to human creativity and emancipation. The state then becomes an obvious target for critical analysis.

The method I employ to explicate and assess Chomsky's views on the state is to look at his views by comparing and contrasting them to Marx's on the subject. I have relied upon the work of McLellan, Maguire and Evans to help interpret Marx's position. My purpose in taking this approach is to consider whether Chomsky's observations and analysis belong and/or contribute in any way to this critical theoretical tradition. In so doing I hope to establish therefore whether he can be said to employ a theoretical framework, Marxist or otherwise.

I begin by looking at some of the general claims he makes about the way in which the state functions and consider his emphasis on its role internationally. I look at what the international role can tell us about the state, both as an institution and more specifically within its national context. Chomsky's analysis shows us that, in contrast to Marx's view, the state's role is not just judicial, ideological and at times coercive (although these are important enough). Rather, the state is also an important economic agent in a capitalist economy. Indeed Chomsky wants to argue that the state plays an absolutely crucial role in the maintenance of a capitalist economy, both nationally and internationally. By comparing Chomsky ideas in the light of Marx's on the subject, we see that the framework Marx employs – which sees the state as mostly subsumed to the workings of the economy – does not enable us to recognise its persistently proactive character or indeed the violent manifestations of this activity. If we consider the state in the light of Chomsky's emphasis we can question not only the way in which states are conventionally defined, we can also question the consequences for political thought of a theory which reifies state activity by reference to a reified economy.

State defined by function

What is the state? The state is that body of institutions – specifically the civil service or bureaucracy, the legislature, the judiciary and the military – that provide governance of a given territory. Not a very extraordinary statement and certainly not one many would want to argue with. However, Chomsky himself never actually explicitly defines the concept. Indeed he rarely defines any of his concepts, something his critics are eager to challenge him on.[1] It is unlikely that such omissions are mere oversight, especially given that his other specialism is linguistics. Rather for him debates about the meaning of a concept such as 'the state' are less important than asking questions about how this entity under its 'common sense' conception actually conducts itself and what its functions, interests and actions are. Answers to such questions provide illuminating ways to conceive of the state that can go beyond definitions offering tighter and perhaps more neutral (and therefore less disputable) conceptions. Skillen makes this point when he argues that political philosophy has a tendency to deal with timeless, abstract philosophical categories without consideration of empirical practices. When this happens a concept such as the state is under consideration, its 'ideal type' is put under scrutiny. Assumptions are made about it being the locus of power, able to bring about order, liberty and peace, and so are untroubled by the reality of oppression and war.[2]

Certainly, even a relatively cursory review of Chomsky's work would suggest that while he would not dispute the fact that the state is in the business of governance, a more illuminating characterisation of the state is that its function is actually control. This avoids the blander connotations associated with governance, such as 'direction', 'guidance' and 'influence'. How is it, then, that Chomsky could not disagree that the state is about governance and yet also explicitly demonstrate that actually the state is concerned with control? Are the two claims compatible? The answer is yes, because Chomsky employs a class analysis, although he rarely uses the term class. Chomsky's work is wholly concerned with state policy and its effects on populations both domestic and foreign. The population for Chomsky is distinct from the elites, which are groups of anyone with power, economic and/or political. Evidently then, the population, or 'rascal multitude' – as Chomsky prefers to characterise them in *Year 501*, to signify the view elites commonly have of the population – are controlled. On the other hand, elites who are not themselves directly involved in policy-making are subject to direction, guidance and influence. '[C]ontrolling the domestic population . . . that problem [is] a central one facing any state or other system of power.'[3] For Chomsky, then, the state is in no sense an embodiment of some general interest as Hegel had supposed, or for that matter an arbiter between multiple competing interests, as pluralists would have it. Its function is unreservedly to protect the interests of the rich and powerful and, in so doing, to control the 'rabble'. 'To those in power, it seems obvious that the population must be cajoled and manipulated, frightened and kept in ignorance, so that ruling elites can operate without hindrance to the "national interest" as they choose to define it'.[4] Chomsky's early work focuses on the more obvious ways in which the state can exercise control through the military and through the judiciary.[5] He has also always had an eye upon the way in which intellectuals are quick to accept such control as natural, thereby justifying the process. His later work advances on the analysis of control by exposing the more subtle aspects of state control, through, for example, the media.

State autonomy

If the state's function is protecting the interests of the rich and powerful does this mean its role is merely superstructural? In other words is it simply servile to the rich and dominant interests in society or does it have some autonomy? For Chomsky the rich and powerful of a society are those with business interests. They are those who acquire the private profit made in the process of financial and industrial production. They are also those who are in positions of political power. In *Year 501* he regularly refers to the 'state corporate nexus',[6] which suggests a direct connection or link between the state and those with private business interests. This link is made more explicit when he argues, with reference to the foreign policy of the American state, that: 'those segments of the corporate system that are particularly concerned with international affairs typically exert an overwhelming influence on the design and execution of foreign policy. You can see that simply enough by just who staffs the executive and the top decision-making positions. They're overwhelmingly drawn from major corporations with international interests.'[7] He makes the same point in his 1973 work *For Reasons of State*.[8]

However, does this nexus mean that the state is subordinate to business interests and that the corporate elite is monolithic? In terms of state subordination and in connection with domestic policy, Chomsky argues that the Reagan/Bush years represent a period of serious 'pathology' because of the entrenchment of 'a two-tiered society in which large sectors are superfluous',[9] to such a degree that '[s]ome corporate circles are awakening to the fact that "a third world within our own country" will harm business interests'.[10] Of course this could mean either that the state is autonomous and therefore does things contrary to business interests or that in pursuing business interests it might be making a mistake about the means by which to do this. That Chomsky regards the two as a nexus suggests the latter, and implies a degree of subordination. However, it is not as simple as that because the corporate elite is not monolithic. Chomsky notes that in connection with foreign policy, for example, there will be 'second order considerations' which expose conflicting elite interests. Nevertheless, in terms of a 'first approximation', a consensus of interests will be found concerning, for example, opposition to any form of nationalism that excludes foreign investment. In other words there will be universal opposition among the American elite to any country attempting to exclude foreign investment, and specifically American investment.[11] The means by which to achieve conditions suitable for American business interests can be among those 'second order considerations', and this is the point at which some might argue the state exercises a degree of autonomy. However, it is unlikely even then that it could be shown that the state acted in a way contrary to business interests.

Chomsky, then, regards the American state as operating to serve American business interests, but recognises that interpretation of these interests is by no means straightforward. However, he is also aware that the state is susceptible to other pressures, for example pressure from the public at large, such as rebellion against a particular policy, as in the case of opposition to the Vietnam war. In such an instance it may have to reject its initial business-orientated policies. Of course responding to instability and attempting to reassert the status quo is still in the interests of business, but instability also has the potential of threatening the state's own survival. The state can be said, then, to have a relative autonomy and Chomsky would argue that at times it even has interests of its own. Indeed, state management can have an interest in 'enhancing its own power'.[12] Perhaps the best way to characterise the relationship then is one of mutual support. It is a partnership, the two spheres being symbiotic, even if this relationship is very unequal.

The necessity of the state under capitalism

The most telling point Chomsky makes to illustrate the symbiotic nature of the relationship between business and the state lies in his assertion that free market capitalism is dead. The free market model as a system, he argues, has been abandoned: 'take note of the broad – if tacit – understanding that the capitalist model has limited application; business leaders have long recognised that it is not for them'.[13] Of course the notion of free market capitalism is threatened with contradiction. 'Free market' means both 'competitive' and 'independent of the state'. Given that there is a tendency towards monopoly, because monopoly profits are higher than profits under competition, the state's anti-monopoly legislation is necessary to maintain free (competitive) markets. But Chomsky's point goes beyond this. He wants to argue, first, that industrial societies in no way conform to the free market model and that this is why they are successful. Lenin makes a similar observation in his study of capitalism's tendency towards monopoly.[14] But, second, Chomsky wants to say that the business community is also dependent to a large extent upon the economic support rather than the purely legislative support of the state. 'Business circles have long taken for granted that the state must play a major role in *maintaining* the system of private profit' (my emphasis).[15] The central point then is that the state has a necessary economic role for the functioning of a system based upon the pursuit of private profit.

Chomsky's point is that business has to be induced to invest, especially in conditions of slump, or the threat of slump. The best inducement is a guaranteed market and/or public subsidy of aspects of business such as research and development. As far as Chomsky is concerned the only aspects of the American economy that remain competitive are those which depend upon state intervention in the form of public subsidy or a guaranteed market: for example advanced technology, capital intensive agriculture and pharmaceuticals. The state then is crucial, in its role as tax collector, to enable it to offer businesses the possibility of securing private profit. Keynes was not wrong to come to British capitalism's rescue with his solution of 'demand management'. However, what was wrong was his focus on welfare and job creation, in order to prop up demand to ensure healthy profits. These aspects of state expenditure, Chomsky argues, start to give workers security, powers and expectations that interfere with the pursuit of profit. He also makes the point that '[i]f the government gets involved in carrying out activities that affect the public existence directly, people will want to get involved in it'.[16] Erik Olin Wright and Claus Offe observe the same contradiction: that the functions of the welfare state undermine the process of private accumulation.[17] Offe, in an attempt to suggest a resolution to this contradiction, suggests the possibility of reducing the state's productive activity, but concludes that this would be inconsistent with his basic assumption that the accumulation process *requires* the state's involvement in the production process. Both Offe and Olin Wright spot the contradiction but neither can come up with a resolution.

America however, according to Chomsky, resolves the contradiction. It does this by engaging in what Chomsky calls 'military Keynesianism' or the 'Pentagon system', which is still public subsidy, private profit, but has the added advantage of strengthening the powers of the government and state rather than the welfare of the general population. Under this system the state creates demand for military hardware. This makes it necessary for America to constantly identify 'enemies', and the Cold War was the perfect pretext for this. The state engages in research and development for high technology in order to sustain the edge militarily, and this filters into other industries. But the state also buys military products. '[The] private sector tak[es] over when there are profits to be made. This crucial gift to the corporate manager has been the domestic function of the Pentagon system; benefits extend to the computer industry, electronics generally, and other sectors of the advanced industrial economy.'[18] '[T]he Pentagon system . . . has long been the engine for economic growth and preserving the technological edge.'[19]

For Chomsky, then, the state is essential to the survival of a system driven by capital in its pursuit of private profit. The state not only provides the legislative conditions for a capitalist economy, but it is also itself a major economic agent. The 'hidden hand' after all belongs to the state. The idea that the state is an economic agent in bourgeois society is missing from Marx's analysis of the state. In view of the similarities between Marx and Chomsky, this difference is worth exploring.

Marx and Chomsky on the state

Maguire argues that in Marx's early writings there is a tendency for him to 'downgrade' or 'dismiss' politics.[20] In *The Communist Manifesto*, Marx makes his famous statement that 'the executive of the modern state is but a committee for managing the common affairs of the whole bourgeoisie'.[21] Some commentators have argued that this claim supports the view that the 'normal' posture of the state is one of servility to the bourgeoisie, or that the state is merely a reflection of the economic base. But as Miliband points out, to say the state acts 'on behalf of' the dominant class is not to say that it acts 'at the behest of' that class, and 'the notion of common affairs assumes the existence of particular ones'.[22] Of course Marx's statement does not in itself preclude Chomsky's position; 'managing the common affairs' could mean ensuring a market and subsidising production. But Marx, being more concerned with the legal and constitutional roles of the state, it seems does not have this in mind.

Both Maguire and Skillen argue that Marx regarded the dynamics of a capitalist economy as 'autonomous', and as having its own 'rationality' and 'self-regulatory' powers. '... [A]ccepting the "economists'" myths about a self-regulating society, Marx and Engels presented society as abandoned to naked economic struggle'.[23] In different ways Maguire and Skillen both ask the same question. If the economy is self-regulating, why did politics not 'wither away' after the bourgeois revolution?[24] Skillen quotes Marx's observation that 'the dull compulsion of economic relations completes the subjection of the labourer to the capitalist',[25] and argues that the conception of politics as being actively engaged in only by the state is too narrow as political activity is present in all aspects of society. This does not mean, as Poulantzas (and Althusser before him) would have it, that the state is everywhere in society, but that many other institutions in society, the family being one, also have political relations and a political role in contributing to the maintenance of the economic system. Skillen's point is that Marx does tend to identify bourgeois politics and political struggle with the state – as if politics is only concerned with the state and the state is only concerned with politics. But turning Skillen's own argument onto itself, Skillen too can be accused of having too narrow a conception of the state as concerned only with politics, i.e. not recognising it as an economic agent.

Maguire, on the other hand, argues that politics did not 'wither away' precisely *because* of activity such as Marx's, in other words, precisely because capitalist society is itself open to radical questioning. Maguire argues that the state has an important function simply in maintaining its role as a bourgeois state, i.e. one that is taken to represent a 'communal interest'. Marx recognises that this 'communal interest' is illusory. However, capitalist social order and hierarchy is a reality, and so, in the maintenance of that reality, the state can be taken to represent the 'general interest' as defined by that reality, which happens to be one that serves the interests of the ruling class. Workers, then, do have a sphere in which they can see themselves as equal and free alongside the bosses, and for bourgeois civil society to be self-maintaining this conception is crucial. Maguire calls this the state's 'repressed ideological' function. But there is also its repressive function or 'suspended coercive' role, if this ideological tool fails.[26]

Maguire identifies another important reason for the continued presence of politics (Maguire also seems to take politics to be synonymous with the state and so falls foul of Skillen's criticism that politics is conceived of too narrowly), and this goes beyond the need to legislate against monopoly. It is that '[e]ven if they were the only human inhabitants of a world of profit-producing machines, the bourgeoisie would need a state in order to regulate their own affairs',[27] because as they are in competition with one another, the temptation would be to break their own rules. In other words capitalism is by nature predatory, so that without the state businesses would need to resort to warlords and mafiosi to protect their patch. Lenin makes the same point – that war is a feature of capitalism.

Lenin's concern is with the imperialistic nature of capitalism and a nation's international face, but his analysis also applies within a society.[28] The state then is not only necessary to regulate individuals.

Although Marx in his early work and in *The Communist Manifesto* seemed to regard the sphere of politics and the state as peripheral and therefore servile to the unproblematic momentum of the market, he characteristically revised his view in the light of the events in France and post-1848 Germany. Marx had been confident that the bourgeoisie would clearly identify itself as a class 'for itself' and seize control of the state, but the aforementioned events undermined this confidence in their ability to see their own interests clearly, which necessarily included 'bourgeois freedoms' such as universal suffrage. The options were, as Engels put it, 'an oligarchy ... capable of taking over, for good pay, the management of state and society in the interests of the bourgeoisie, or the "normal form" of a Bonapartist semi-dictatorship'.[29]

Marx's analysis of France and Germany is concerned with an interregnum between the collapse of the old order and establishment of the new. As a state is going to contain agents with an interest in the maintenance of the old order, Marx needs to identify agents who can take control of the state in order to enforce legislation in favour of the newly emerging order. The fact that the bourgeoisie in 1848 in France and Germany failed to do this, or that the state failed to respond in the required way to the needs of the new order, suggests a degree of autonomy. As Marx argues 'only under the second Bonaparte does the state seem to have made itself completely independent'.[30] The bourgeoisie failed to recognise their potential as a political force. Maguire argues that Marx's ideas on political action still make economic motivation critical in the last instance. '[P]eople act on motivations which can be related to the economic situation in which they arose and ... that in political crises classes will realise the dependence of their way of life on their economic position, and will act to preserve or further that position.'[31] Marx does acknowledge that before and after the event, choices could have gone other ways. The point is that even in a crisis when the state may appear to act autonomously, political decisions will have a material explanation. As McLellan argues, 'Marx ... considered this correlation between economic substructure and political formations to be a very loose one'.[32]

Even if one accepts that Marx was prepared to give greater significance to the political sphere of the state in his later work, especially in his analysis of transition, he nevertheless confined his analysis to legal and military procedures. As a result there is a tendency to represent the state as a tool, which the bourgeoisie either uses or does not. This places the proactive emphasis on the bourgeoisie as the agents in the mode of production and denies a vision of the state in a proactive role.

Despite the obvious closeness of Chomsky's analysis to Marx's, there is a distinct shift of emphasis. Not only does Chomsky state the explicit links between business interest and state action, his whole analysis of current events in society revolves around the state and its proactive character. The state is the key player that makes it all possible. Marx insists on economic imperatives that shape state decisions, i.e., material interests. But in Chomsky's view, were it not for this institution the economic system would self-destruct.

If we look at Rudolf Rocker's analysis of the development of capitalism, and accept that Chomsky regards his ideas as of a similar tradition,[33] then again we see a similar shift in emphasis. 'Later, when absolutism had victoriously overcome all opposition to national unification, by *its* furthering of mercantilism and economic monopoly it gave the whole social evolution a direction which could only lead to capitalism ...' (my emphasis).[34] In other words capitalism was not an outcome in the development of the productive forces but an outcome of the impact of centralised power on productive forces. According to Rocker and Chomsky, were it not for concentrated state power, capitalism would not have been possible. Indeed, Rocker is deeply critical of the view subscribed to by the historical materialist version of history that connects the rise of the national state with necessary progress. As far as Rocker is concerned '[t]he rise of the nationalist states not only did not further economic evolution in any way whatever, but the endless wars of that epoch and the senseless interference of despotism in the life of industry created that condition of cultural barbarism in which many of the best achievements of industrial technique were wholly or partly lost and had to be rediscovered later on.'[35] In a discussion of the development of European industry, Rocker talks of 'unbridled favouritism ... convert[ing] entire industrial lines into monopolies'.

This places a very different emphasis on the development of industry towards monopoly from that put forward by, for example, Lenin. In *Imperialism, the Highest Stage of Capitalism*, Lenin derides Kautsky for suggesting that capitalism would develop more rapidly without monopoly. Lenin says:

> Let us assume that free competition, without any sort of monopoly, would have developed capitalism and trade more rapidly. But the more rapidly trade and capitalism develop, the greater is the concentration of production and capital which gives rise to monopoly. And monopolies have already arisen – precisely out of free competition! Even if monopolies have now begun to retard the progress, it is not an argument in favour of free competition, which has become impossible after it has given rise to monopoly.[36]

Monopoly and its concomitant, imperialism, are necessary outcomes of capitalist accumulation rather than policy 'favouritism'. Lenin, writing in 1916, argues that capitalism has reached a state whereby the feature of free competition is being superseded by a new form characterised by monopoly. Crucial to this process is the role of banks, as these credit institutions become completely involved in decisions of industry, to such a degree that the industrial capitalist becomes wholly dependent upon the bank. This stage of finance capital enhances the concentration of capital and monopoly and means 'the predominance of the rentier and of the financial oligarchy'.[37] This in turn results in the export of capital or imperialism and hence the 'rentier state' – 'it means the singling out of a small number of financially powerful states from among all the rest'.[38]

Lenin's treatment of imperialism tends to regard the export of capital and the setting up of debtors who are tied to the creditor, as evolutionary. While the state is mentioned, it is only to note its rentier status and to recognise that imperialist state will be pitted against imperialist state in the race for the division of the world. There is no sense in which the state is regarded as having facilitated either concentration or export of capital.

That Chomsky accepts Rocker's line of analysis is suggested by the following comment Chomsky made in *Year 501*. Chomsky is discussing the formation of the Dutch East India Company. This company he argues had virtual state powers but was controlled by Dutch merchants and financiers. He says: '[i]n highly simplified form, we see already something of the structure of the modern political economy, dominated by a network of transnational financial and industrial institutions with internally managed investment and trade, their wealth and influence *established* and maintained by the state power that they mobilize and largely control' (my emphasis).[39]

The state and force

If the state's role, both at the birth of capitalism and during its mature imperialistic phase, is given only very scant attention, then it is possible to miss the important issue of the state's use of force. If, however, we give the state a more central and integral part to play in these devleopments then it is imperative to address this issue, given, as Weber pointed out, that the state claims a monopoly of the use of legitimate force over a given territory. Maguire argues that Marx accepts that force is a necessary accompaniment to the separation of 'independent producers' from their property, thereby making them property-less and hence suitable as waged workers. 'Force is the midwife of every old society pregnant with a new one.'[40] However, once the process is complete the 'dull compulsion' sets in. As Marx says in *Capital III*: 'The direct producer is driven rather by force of circumstances than by direct coercion, through legal enactment rather than the whip, to perform it on his own responsibility.'[41] And if we turn to Lenin's account of imperial expansion then we do get an account of war perpetrated by states, but the emphasis is on the resort to force by industrial competitors who are in the business of dividing the world in search of markets and resources. What we do not get in these accounts is a picture of those subjected peoples/countries that are 'plundered' or acquired, resisting and so necessitating force. This is because for Lenin the economic metabolic dynamic of finance capital brings about unproblematic subjection. 'Finance capital is such a great, it may be said, such a decisive force in all economic and in all international relations, that it is capable of subjecting and actually does subject to itself even states enjoying the fullest political independence.'[42]

Chomsky would not contemplate such a conclusion. He graphically demonstrates that countries unwilling to be subjected to the power of capital and who attempt some sort of independent development are instead subjected to the most violent reprisals by state force, and in particular American state force. Chomsky, then, is challenging the image of the iron grip of capital unproblematically rolling out to the satellites to incorporate the world under its global hegemony. Of course one could argue that Chomsky's focus is on 'developing' countries and that they are simply in a period of interregnum necessitating greater state prominence, in the same way as western Europe did during the period Marx was studying. The difference in Chomsky's analysis is that the state force, if not directly carried out by the metropolis state, as is sometimes the case, is encouraged and certainly facilitated by the metropolis state in other words by the state of a society no longer in a period of interregnum.

The state and international relations

This brings us to a key contribution of Chomsky's to the study of political theory in general, and state theory in particular. Chomsky's work is principally concerned with American foreign policy, in other words with the American state and its relations with other states and populations. This sounds narrowly focused, but he broadens his analysis by pointing out that the American state is supported and assisted in its policy by other 'advanced' (Chomsky would prefer to have them called simply 'wealthy') industrial states. These other states he points out are western, originally European and therefore white, that is except the Japanese who are regarded by western elites as 'honorary whites'.[43] However, Chomsky focuses on America not only because America is the most powerful state in the 'alliance' but also because he is himself American. He regards himself, along with every other citizen, as having responsibility for the policies of his own country, before those of other states.[44]

Very simply, Chomsky's thesis is that the American state actively pursues policies that are in the interest of American business both at home and abroad. A key feature then of foreign policy is to secure favourable conditions for American business. Broadly speaking business interests derive from the need capital has to invest abroad. This need arises, as Lenin made clear, from the very dynamic of capital itself. However, Chomsky holds that capital cannot achieve this on its own. Its development has to be facilitated by the state. So, the American state with the assistance of other advanced western states, which have similar interests, must ensure that less developed countries keep their doors open to foreign investment. This does not mean that there will not be tensions between those countries of the 'first world'. As well as having many similar interests internationally, these wealthy nation states are also in competition with one another. They are not monolithic, just as elites within a nation are not.

The tools by which the American state and its 'allies' can secure these interests, are not dissimilar to those employed by the state on its own population. These tools include legislation,[45] police enforcement and military intervention, and also, it is important to note, an economic role. Chomsky gives graphic accounts not only of military missions carried out by the American state but also of its capabilities in the arena of economic warfare. That the American state has to pursue such means illustrates the degree of resistance, and the overwhelming evidence put forward by Chomsky of its grotesque effects stands to question the theory that capital has some sort of automatic effect on anyone who comes into contact with it.

So the state is not only in the business of controlling its own population, among the wealthier nations it is also crucially concerned with controlling populations and states of less developed countries. This control is necessary because of resistance. Lenin says '[t]he creditor is more firmly attached to the debtor than the seller is to the buyer'.[46] This may be so but it would not itself preclude a debtor nation closing its doors and finding a solution to its own debts, except that this is not allowed because of the creditor's need to remain a creditor. And the institution that ensures that it is not allowed is the *state* of the creditor nation. That states have an international face does not, it seems to me, warrant separate study. The internal and external roles of states are inextricably linked. To study the state without consideration of its international role is to misrepresent it. Chomsky's thesis emphatically compels this conclusion.[47]

Why is it so important to incorporate questions concerning international relations into a theoretical analysis of the state? One of the central questions asked when studying a state concerns the nature of its relationship to its population. An answer to this is generally taken to identify the nature of the state in question. If we say a society today is 'liberal democratic', we mean its population enjoys universal suffrage and electoral equality in the form of one person, one vote. Individuals may elect representatives to form a government that in turn directs the state; and in this process there is freedom of speech and opinion and discussion. It also means that the state protects and enforces property rights. If property rights are enforced this means that individuals and corporations can run businesses independently from the state, as long as they observe the law. In other words there is a separation of the public and private domains. That a society is described as democratic is no longer regarded with the suspicion that it once was.[48] It is a positive feature that implies it is responsive to the will of the people, or rather, significantly, to the will of the people under its jurisdiction. In other words it is a term used to describe its internal relations. Its virtues are generally extolled when it is compared with totalitarianism, where a government and the state monopolistically control all economic institutions, media and military, often with the help of repression from a secret police.

Before addressing the central question about the incorporation of international relations into state theory, it is worthwhile to question the relative virtue of liberal democracy. For example, some commentators have argued that the chief problem of liberal democracy is that democracy can be illiberal – majorities can oppress minorities. Nevertheless this is no argument for totalitarianism. On the whole the political label of a democracy is worn with pride. Keane, in a discussion on democracy, argues that there is a case for the extension of democracy. However, in his view there are inherent weaknesses in democracy. He argues, for example, that it necessitates relativism and/or 'philosophical insecurity'. It is also a problem because of the possibility that it might fail to protect elements beyond man such as nature. In other words, Keane argues, democracy must know its limits. Nevertheless he concludes by saying '[a] bad democracy is . . . always better than a good dictatorship'.[49] But for whom is a bad democracy better than a good dictatorship? As Chomsky argues about a period prior to the collapse of 'actually existing socialism' '[f]or three-quarters of the population [in Brazil] . . . the conditions of Eastern Europe are dreams beyond reach'.[50] Similarly '[t]he UN Economic Commission for Latin America and the Caribbean (CEPAL) reports that the percentage of the Guatemalan population living in extreme poverty increased rapidly after the establishment of democracy in 1985: from 45% in that year to 76% in 1988'.[51] During an interview with David Barsamian, when Barsamian said 'I recall your saying that if a peasant in El Salvador were to fall asleep and wake up in Poland, he would think he were in heaven', Chomsky replied, 'Not much doubt about that'.[52]

Putting aside the problems of economic equality under a liberal democracy, the question must be asked. Can a liberal democracy retain its progressive claims, when representatives chosen by the people of a community can use their power internationally to secure favourable conditions for those people of that community at home, and in the process not only pursue economically undemocratic ends but also employ profoundly undemocratic means?

America, as Chomsky freely admits, 'is a free society, much more so than any other.[53] Nevertheless, the state, seeking to secure the interests of American business, attempts (often successfully) through its foreign policy to secure access to cheap resources and labour, as well as investment opportunities for American capital within less developed countries (LDCs) (including the Middle East). It does this, Chomsky argues, by building up alliances with local elites who use American aid to maintain a military and/or police force which can brutally suppress labour and overcome political organisations pressing for wealth redistribution. The process is not always smooth. In some instances an unsuitable elite is democratically elected (Chile), or a nation attempts some form of independent development (Nicaragua), or a local elite starts to step on the toes of American interests (Panama). In such instances the US responds with economic sanctions and may also engineer a CIA coup, as in Chile 1973, clandestinely fund contras who use terror to destabilise development (Nicaragua 1980s), or directly invade (Panama 1989) in order to restore suitable conditions. In a close analysis of events, Chomsky also finds that as the proportion of US aid increases, so too does the level of human rights abuses,[54] and that the US state engages in state terrorism,[55] all in the cause of 'deterring democracy'.[56]

Chomsky's contribution to state theory

That a country does not exist in a vacuum is obvious. This is most obviously understood at an economic level. The international character of capital can be seen in transnational corporations and in the international finance markets. No one doubts that if the Bundesbank cuts interest rates this will have some impact in England. But the sphere of politics at the level of the state is strangely resistant to such analysis. Taking the American state as an example and given the degree of power that it has internationally, which as Chomsky demonstrates, it is prepared to use, we must ask two questions: (1) to what degree can a state with such a repressive autocratic international tendency be regarded as representative of the democratic ideal, indeed the leader of the 'free world' (ignoring for the moment the known weaknesses of liberal democracy at the national level); and (2) is the very real freedom enjoyed under a liberal democracy dependent upon the maintenance of certain economic and/or political conditions internationally?

On the first question, Chomsky's work methodically exposes evidence about not only the degree and nature, but also the purpose, of American state intervention in the affairs of other countries. In order to do this he questions the official or hegemonic interpretation of events. A method Chomsky commonly employs to do this is to draw parallels. He does this either by comparing America's reaction to two separate events such as Iraq's invasion of Kuwait and Indonesia's invasion of East Timor, or he uses language which serves the same purpose. So, for example, he describes a Latin American dictator as 'fascist', elaborates on the nature of the regime and describes the unequivocal and supportive links the American state has with that regime, be it aid, arms or training for military personnel.

He does not then need to go on and describe Mussolini's Italy. The use of the term 'fascist' suffices. The problem with this, as Chomsky's critics are quick to point out, is whether the term 'fascism' can be applied to a dictator who is open to American support and domination, since a salient feature of fascism in the 1920/30s was its extreme nationalism.[57] Again Chomsky makes no attempt to defend his use of the term, but it could be argued that such a critique can be shown to have implicit within it a very narrow understanding of a state's nature, i.e. as concerned primarily with the state's relation to its own population. It is precisely the failure to recognise a state's international character that is constraining.

Fascism has a number of other important characteristics. For example opposition to the 'ideals of the Enlightenment', in other words opposition to 'the idea that people had natural rights, that they were fundamentally equal, that it was an infringement of essential human rights if systems of authority subordinated some to others.'[58] For Chomsky this opposition, and a resort to violent repression, are characteristics of Latin American dictatorships, and it is not enough to give them the more benign label 'dictator', which is compatible with their being despotisms of the benevolent variety. To conclude, as David Robertson does, that 'the word has very little place in our set of political categories',[59] is to suggest that language and meaning is static. Clearly they are not; words also have histories. As David McLellan points out, for example, 'the word "dictatorship" did not have quite the same connotation for Marx that it does for us'.[60]

Chomsky's work compels us to think that it is misguided to suppose a national state's character is determined solely by its mode of governance over its own territory. Similarly his related work on the way the elite has the power and opportunity to frame agendas and define issues, gives us a way of understanding why, as in this case, nationalism is still taken to be a defining characteristic of fascism. Agreeing with Orwell and his conception of 'newspeak', Chomsky seeks to expose the constraints language imposes on thought, in particular limiting the possibilities of radical dissent. So when Chomsky controversially uses the term 'fascism', it is possible to argue that because political concepts used for the labelling of a state concentrate upon those characteristics that concern the state's relationships internally, this encourages us to focus specifically upon those characteristics that are national. So as fascism has had a strongly nationalistic character it is assumed, as it was for example by Morris, that this is thereby a defining characteristic. Thus we cannot call a Latin American dictator 'fascist'. Similarly, because the government of America is elected by universal suffrage, it is therefore democratic. If a state is democratic it strains the imagination to connect it internationally with violent repression in support of fascist regimes, despite the now obvious reality.

Chomsky never actually argues that America is fascist even though he often alludes to certain similar characteristics. For example, he notes a piece of research carried out on the US Army manuals of the 1950s which finds a 'disturbing similarity between the Nazi's view of the world and the American stance in the Cold War'.[61] He is unwilling to collapse the differences between a liberal democratic state and a fascist state in the same way that Poulantzas (1979) does, but he does allude to certain similarities, internally, to totalitarianism. Gramsci (1976) observed that governments of the east relied upon force, whereas governments of the west had achieved hegemonic control. What Chomsky's work demonstrates is that the American state engages in force (abroad) and hegemonic control (at home), although Chomsky would prefer to refer to the latter as 'fraud' or 'propaganda'. The need for 'fraud', Chomsky argues, is to obscure the degree to which the state is involved in maintaining the system of private profit, and especially the very violent manifestations of this policy abroad. Fraud is principally achieved through the media, whereby the 'free market' in ideas pretty comprehensively filters out dissident ideas. This is not a particularly new concept. Curran and Seaton, for example, have tracked the dire effect the introduction of advertising had on 'left-wing' newspapers.[62] But again, Chomsky is unwilling to claim that the fate of the left-wing press was due to 'market forces'. The state also had a hand, because as he argues, media conglomerates, anxious for a regular supply of 'news-worthy' stories that can be presumed credible, so reducing the need to check and investigate, have a tendency to go to the government. This allows the government to feed out 'propaganda' and 'lies'. With reference to its success he says '[i]n a Free Society, *all* must goose-step on command, or keep silent' (original emphasis).[63]

Given the degree and nature of American state involvement abroad, as well as its attempts to obscure such action, it fits the fascist label quite well, as long as we are allowed to drop the 'nationalist' stricture.

Returning to Miliband and his debate with Poulantzas,[64] Miliband's critique helps us to see where Chomsky's contributions solve many of the problems Poulantzas was having. In his critique of Poulantzas, Miliband argues that Poulantzas sets out to establish the relative autonomy of the state but ultimately fails to distinguish between class and state power. Miliband, having unpicked Poulantzas's argument to establish that there are important differences between state, party and class rule, argues that Poulantzas is 'not really ... interested in the bourgeois-democratic form of state at all'.[65] This is because, he says, Poulantzas believed that 'Marx and Engels *systematically conceive* Bonapartism not simply as a concrete form of the capitalist state, *but as a constitutive theoretical characteristic of the very type of capitalist state*' (original emphasis).[66] Miliband argues that 'Poulantzas lays great emphasis on Engels's reference to Bonapartism as "the religion of the bourgeoisie"'[67] but he rejects Poulantzas's attempts to substantiate such a claim, beyond this single reference. Miliband concludes that 'Engels was wrong', that 'Bonapartism is not the religion of the bourgeoisie at all – it is its last *resort* during conditions of political instability so great as to present a threat to the maintenance of the existing social order'.[68] With the international perspective that Chomsky gives us, it is possible to see that the American state and its 'first world' allies do regard the international context as one of extreme 'political instability', especially in the conditions of the Cold War, but even without that pretext. Bonapartism is then perhaps more apparent in the capitalist state than Miliband is prepared to concede.

The tension between state 'forms', resolved by Louis Napoleon's *coup d'etat* showed to Marx that '[p]olitical liberties appeared irrelevant to the bourgeoisie, so long as business was good and social order maintained'.[69] Nevertheless, as Evans argues, Marx ultimately maintained that '[p]ure, undisguised class rule is always a danger to the ruling class, as it attracts rather than diverts the antagonism of the subject classes'.[70] The powerful modern state with its international features demonstrates that the choice of state form need not be an either/or choice.

Returning now to my second question: to what extent is the very real freedom enjoyed under a liberal democracy dependent upon the maintenance of certain economic and/or political conditions internationally? As we have seen Chomsky's work suggests that in an analysis of the state an international perspective is useful for understanding a state's character. It may be thought from this that what is being suggested is that the state has a benign and a nefarious face, and that these two are separate halves. This however is not Chomsky's position. The national democratic and international terroristic are two sides of the same coin. The faces may take different forms, but they belong to one coin. For Chomsky this coin is one that is ultimately profoundly anti-democratic. By this Chomsky means that the capitalist state is in opposition to 'the concept of democracy . . . as a system in which citizens may play some meaningful part in the management of public affairs'.[71] Elites across the world and throughout history, 'the gentry of industrialists, or the vanguard Party or the Central Committee', and those 'who qualify as "experts" because they articulate the consensus of the powerful (to paraphrase one of Henry Kissinger's insights)' find that the people are 'not to be trusted'.[72] Quoting 'experts' from seventeenth century England, to government officials of first world war America,[73] to the mentors of the intellectuals in the Kennedy era,[74] Chomsky finds references to the 'rascal multitude', 'beasts in men's shapes', the 'bewildered herd', the 'ignorant and mentally deficient', whereas 'rationality belongs to the cool observers'. In light of this, democracy has had to have a particular 'form'. The form taken is 'a political system with regular elections but no serious challenge to business rule',[75] whereby '[t]he public is granted an opportunity to ratify decisions made elsewhere'.[76] This 'form' has been most successfully achieved in the west and as such '[i]n the stable business-dominated western democracies, we would not expect the US to carry out programs of subversion, terror, or military assault as has been common in the Third World'.[77] Clearly Chomsky is arguing that western liberal democracy *is* qualitatively different from fascist or totalitarian regimes, but also from the 'fledgling' democracies of the 'south'. However, its relatively benign stability is principally due to the success business has had in having its interests met. With the new 'democracies' of the south, the populations are still learning that those 'government policies that private power finds unwelcome will lead to capital flight, disinvestment, and social decline until business confidence is restored with the abandonment of the threat to privilege . . . [so] unless the rich and powerful are satisfied, everyone will suffer'.[78] The south is learning this with the aid of a good deal of repression.

However, defining business interests is not a clear-cut issue, so the liberal western form of democracy gives rise to a range of possible positions or a plurality between the so-called Doves and Hawks. Nevertheless, Chomsky argues, '[t]here is essentially one political party, the business party, with two factions'.[79] Within such a system ideas/people become marginalised if they fall outside of 'the prevailing consensus'. But it is useful for there to be disagreements within the prevailing consensus between the Doves and the Hawks, because this serves to promote the idea that people do have choice and freedom. Also, and more importantly, '[t]here are differences between the Hawks and the Doves. Given the scale of American power, even small differences translate into large effects for the victims'.[80] Nevertheless '[t]he pragmatic criterion dictates that violence is in order only when the rascal multitude cannot be controlled in other ways'.[81]

The 'form' of democracy manifested in the state corresponds then to the degree to which business needs are met. However, it is also commonly observed that systems of government, even totalitarian ones, require a degree of legitimation, and do not rely totally upon terror. Neil Harding makes this point about the pre-1990s Soviet state.[82] He argues that it is one thing to explain its irrationality and another to explain, beyond the period of terror, its enormous stability. He maintains that the system could not have survived upon egalitarianism because it depended upon state allocation of 'graduated rewards' (or denial), and promises to out-perform all competitor systems. In this sense it enjoyed 'complicit legitimation'. It was not only its failure to out-perform but also, and related to this, the degree of its corruption which so discredited the system, that finally the regime became de-legitimated – crucially in the eyes of the elite.

Harding's argument is that despite the seeming 'irrationality' of a system, legitimation can be achieved through satisfaction of material needs. Western liberal democracies have been successful at meeting material needs and the concentration of wealth internationally has facilitated the degree of stability and legitimation. Chomsky himself often refers to 'welfare for the rich' and the 'poor subsidising the wealthy' but this is always in reference to western taxpayers subsidising the rich through state intervention. Nevertheless it seems that this is also an international phenomenon, i.e. that western economies are dependent upon 'third world' resources. For example, referring to 'British and indeed western interests in the Persian Gulf', Chomsky quotes official declassified documentation which states that, among other things, '[a]n assured source of oil is essential to the continued economic viability of western Europe'.[83] Stability and legitimation are closely connected to economic viability. Engels made a similar observation. In a letter to Kautsky he wrote: '[y]ou ask me what the English workers think about colonial policy? Well, exactly the same as they think about politics in general. There is no workers' party here, there are only Conservatives and Liberal Radicals, and the workers merrily share the feast of England's monopoly of the colonies and the world market.'[84] Lenin agreed: '[t]here is first the habit of economic parasitism, by which the ruling state has used its provinces, colonies and dependencies in order to enrich its ruling class and to bribe its lower classes.'[85]

On this matter Chomsky is never as explicit as Engels and Lenin, but certainly it is hard not to draw such conclusions from his arguments and ideas. The American state's control over weaker states and populations – in other words its pattern of international relations – is a necessary condition of its own internal stability. Even if economic 'realities' make the claim that the west is economically dependent upon the third world questionable, there is, as Chomsky also points out, the 'threat of a good example'. In other words western legitimation is more easily achieved if a more attractive and viable alternative can be ensured not to arise.

Given the degree of political and economic instability among the 'third world' countries, which indicates the extent of dissatisfaction among their populations with the current arrangements, the appropriate conditions for continued capital accumulation with its attendant excesses are by no means certain. Luckily for the rich and wealthy there is *the state* to ensure the system's maintenance. State aggression becomes *ipso facto* defence; defence of the *status quo*.

Conclusion

This chapter has sought to consider the defining features of a state, as exemplified by Chomsky's close scrutiny of the American state. Given Chomsky's assertion that the state operates in the interests of national business (recognising that the interpretation of these interests is far from obvious), this chapter has considered the international manifestation of this interest in the light of Marx's analysis of the state in capitalist society. We find that Chomsky's analysis not only considers the political manifestations of the state's role in the support of business, he also shows that it has a necessary economic role. Potential investors, sceptical about taking risks or not drawn by the level of profit, need to be tempted to invest and the state plays a crucial role in subsidising industry as well as purchasing its products. Recognition of the state's role as an economic agent is missing in Marx's analysis of the state.

Because Marx's early work fails to focus on the state's proactive role, there is a tendency to characterise it as a mere reflection of the seemingly self-sustaining metabolism of the economy. In other words there is implicit here the idea that structural processes massively influence and operate independently of agents within society. Nevertheless, Marx is forced to revise his analysis with the failure of capital's agents – the bourgeoisie in France and Germany – to take up the challenge of capital and submit the state to its command. This revision leads Marx to claim that the state and its agents assume a 'pretentious' form during crisis.[86] Marx, however still maintains that political action in the last instance is economically motivated. So despite this 'pretension' the state is still conceived of as subsumed to the dynamics of the market, in other words to structural conditions. Chomsky's shift of emphasis enforces a view of the state as having a more proactive role, as he refuses to reify the economy. Reification of the economy raises problems for an understanding of the way in which we are to understand the spread of capitalism's relations of production around the world.

In a similar vein to Marx, Lenin argues that monopoly and imperialism are inherent features of capital, which suggests that export of capital happens relatively unproblematically. But with Chomsky's emphasis on the role of the state, we see that its role is essential in providing the necessary conditions for export. Such a focus on the state's active role compels us to consider the role of force in the establishment and maintenance of business interests abroad, bringing into question any implied structurally determined allure of capital. The state, in pursuing business interests, seeks to secure conditions born out of capital's quest for markets and resources. The methods by which it achieves such conditions vary from economic to politically repressive, and the degree to which the state intervenes in the process indicates the degree of resistance to capital's international appetite.

The chapter concludes by arguing that if we keep in mind Chomsky's analysis of the American state's international activities then this very feature becomes enlightening in any attempt to identify the nature of a state. In other words, if representatives of the American state use their power repressively in the international arena, this must qualify the democratic credentials not only of that representative, but also of the state itself. That political analysis has been resistant to such a point is suggestive of the extent to which structural analysis has captivated political thought. Structural features and categories characterise the actions of agents, not the other way around. We can see this when we look at the reaction of critics to Chomsky's use of the term 'fascism' to describe dictatorships open to American domination. States are standardly defined by reference to their relationship with their own citizens, and because the first form of fascism was nationalistic this is taken to be a defining characteristic, despite the fact that fascism has other more durable features –

such rigidity in state theory acts to constrain thought. America is taken to be democratic, despite its international links with fascism and even its totalitarian features at home. Marx argues that the state is likely to become Bonapartist in nature during times of crisis and instability. When the international picture is included in an analysis of the state then the system looks much less stable than an analysis narrowly focused upon a state's internal characteristics. This suggests a Bonapartist form of state is more 'normal' than is often supposed.

It is not being suggested that the freedom enjoyed in 'first world' democracies is not real, even though this freedom is more attainable for some than for others. However, the question is raised whether its democratic form is not somehow dependent upon repression abroad. Any system of government requires a degree of legitimation, even under benign totalitarianism (i.e. totalitarianism not relying upon terror), and this is closely linked with the degree to which a system satisfies the population's material needs, and captures the 'hearts and minds'. Concentration of wealth internationally, made possible by the violent and repressive actions of the state, contributes to the degree of stability and legitimation enjoyed by the 'first world'.

It might be thought that concentrating on the American state is too narrow a focus, but Chomsky often seeks to demonstrate the complicity of other 'first world' states in its actions. That the American state seeks to secure *American* business interests does not lend Chomsky's views to particularism. Other state capitalist liberal democracies, having similar domestic structures to America's, exhibit the same tendencies in international relations as America, requiring foreign markets for investment, etc. Although this involves them in competition with America it also gives these states common interests in, for example, keeping third world countries open to foreign exploitation. So there is competition within an international alliance whose general function is the international expansion and global domination of private interests. As America has the strongest economy in the world it is not surprising that it leads the alliance. It is interesting that over 150 years ago Marx observed America's potential power because of the purity of the (American) state's relationship with its bourgeoisie. McLellan points out that for Marx America was 'the most perfect example of a modern state'[87] and 'that the state simply as an instrument of class domination was to be found only in North America'.[88] It seems it is still to be credited with such purity in its ability to recognise most clearly and ruthlessly its business interests.

It has been established that there is a discernible difference between Marx and Chomsky in terms of the emphasis placed on the role of the state in capitalist society, to the extent that Chomsky always refers to 'state capitalism', rather than simply capitalism. We see by this emphasis that Chomsky is keen to highlight the role of agency in social and political affairs, but in a way which recognises the influence of non-reified structural characteristics of society. The question that may now be raised is what effect does this shift of emphasis have on state theory, which has of course been massively influenced by Marx's nascent ideas? In other words, the question is whether Chomsky's observations and claims offer anything distinctive to debates on state theory and in so doing thereby constitute a theory of the state.

Notes

1 Morris, S. (1981) 'Chomsky on US Foreign Policy' in *Harvard International Review*, December–January vol. 3, no. 4. Morris accuses Chomsky of 'conceptually sloppy analysis', p. 5.

2 Skillen, T. (1972) 'The Statist Conception of Politics', in *Radical Philosophy*, 2, Summer. Also see Skillen, T. (1977) *Ruling Illusions Philosophy and The Social Order*, Brighton, Harvester.

3 Chomsky, N. (1992) *Deterring Democracy*, London: Vintage, p. 59.

4 Chomsky, N. (1973) *For Reasons of State*, New York: Vintage, p. 18.

5 See for example Chomsky, N. (1969) *American Power and the New Mandarins*, Harmondsworth: Penguin; and Chomsky, N. (1973) *op. cit.*

6 Chomsky, N. (1993) *Year 501 The Conquest Continues*, London: Verso. For example see p. 99.

7 Chomsky, N. (1992) *Chronicles of Dissent: Interviews by David Barsamian*, A.K. Press, p. 103.

8 '[T]hose interests that are particularly concerned with foreign policy are well represented in its formulation', Chomsky, N. (1973) *op. cit.*, p. 63.

9 Chomsky, N. (1993) *op. cit.*, p. 275.

10 Chomsky, N. (1992) *op. cit.*, p. 135.

11 Chomsky, N. (1973) *op. cit.*, pp. 62–63.

12 Chomsky, N. (1973) *op. cit.*, p. 63.

13 Chomsky, N. (1992) *op. cit.*, p. 144.

14 Lenin, V. I. (1975) *Imperialism, the Highest Stage of Capitalism*, Peking: Foreign Languages Press.

15 Chomsky, N. (1992) *op. cit.*, p. 108.

16 Chomsky, N. in Barsamian, D. (1992) *Noam Chomsky: Chronicles of Dissent*, Stirling, A. K. Press, p. 182.

17 Olin-Wright, E. (1978) *Class Crisis and the State* London: New Left Books; Offe, C., (1984) *Contradictions of the Welfare State* London: Hutchinson; Offe, C. 'The Theory of the Capitalist State and the Problems of Policy Formation' in Lindberg, L.N., *et al.* (eds) (1975) *Stress and Contradiction in Modern Capitalism*, Lexington, Mass: D.C. Heath.

18 Chomsky, N. (1992) *op. cit.*, p. 21.

19 Chomsky, N. (1992) *op. cit.*, p. 81. Also 'The Reaganites initiated a Pentagon-based consortium for semi-conductor research and development, and increasingly gave the Pentagon the task of functioning in the manner of Japan's state–corporate planner, organising R&D in chip and computer design, super-conductivity, high definition television, and other areas of advanced technology', p. 82.

20 Maguire, J. M. (1978) *Marx's Theory of Politics*, Cambridge: Cambridge University Press.

21 Marx, K. and Engels, F. (1848: 1935) *The Communist Manifesto*, Moscow: Lawrence and Wishart.

22 Miliband, R. (1973) 'Poulantzas and the Capitalist State' in *New Left Review*, November–December, 82, p. 85, n. 4.

23 Skillen, T. (1977) *op. cit.*, p. 4.
24 Maguire, J. M., *op. cit.*, p. 20.
25 Marx, K., *Capital I*, ch. 28, p. 737, cited in Skillen, T., *op. cit.*, p. 4.
26 Maguire, J. M., *op. cit.*, pp. 21–3.
27 Maguire, J. M., *op. cit.*, p. 23.
28 Lenin, V. I., *op. cit.*
29 Engels, F. (1975) in *Marx Engels: Selected Correspondence*, Moscow, cited in Maguire, J.M., *op. cit.*, p. 137.
30 Marx, K,. 'The 18th Brumaire of Louis Napoleon' in McLellan, D. (ed.) (1977) *Karl Marx: Selected Writings*, Milton Keynes: Open University Press.
31 Maguire, J. M., *op. cit.*, p. 121.
32 McLellan, D. (1971b) *The Thought of Karl Marx*, London: Macmillan, p. 219.
33 Obviously it is accepted that this does not mean Chomsky would agree. But it indicates a similar emphasis. See Otero, C. P. (ed.) (1981) *Noam Chomsky: Radical Priorities*, London: Black Rose Books, p. 34.
34 Rocker, R. (1937) *Nationalism and Culture*, Los Angeles, California: Rocker Publications Committee, p. 117.
35 Rocker, R., *op. cit.*, p. 116.
36 Lenin, V. I., *op. cit.*, p. 137.
37 Lenin, V. I., *op. cit.*, p. 69.
38 Lenin, V. I., *op. cit.*, p. 69.
39 Chomsky, N. (1993) *op. cit.*, p. 6.
40 Cited in Maguire, J. M., *op. cit.*, p. 149.
41 Cited in Maguire, J. M., *op. cit.*, p. 149.
42 Lenin, V. I., *op. cit.*, p. 97.
43 Chomsky, N. (1993) *op. cit.*, p. 3.
44 Chomsky, N. (1979) *Language and Responsibility*, Brighton: Harvester, p. 3.
45 Such as legislative bodies that are international in character but have heavy American representation, e.g. GATT.
46 Lenin, V. I., *op. cit.*, p. 122.
47 Skocpol, T. (1984) *State and Social Revolutions*, Cambridge: Cambridge University Press. Skocpol argues that international relations were decisive to understanding the shift of power from the state to civil society during a revolution.
48 See Arblaster, A. (1994) *Democracy*, Buckingham: Open University Press.
49 Keane, J. in McLellan, D. and Sayers, S. (eds) (1991) *Socialism and Democracy*, London: Macmillan, p. 15.
50 Chomsky, N. (1992) *op. cit.*, p. 228.
51 Chomsky, N. (1992) *op. cit.*, p. 218.
52 Chomsky, N. (1993) *op. cit.*, p. 192.
53 Chomsky, N. (1993) *op. cit.*, p. 182.
54 Chomsky, N. and Herman, E.S. (1979b) *The Political Economy of Human Rights*, vols I and II, Nottingham: Spokesman.
55 Chomsky, N. (1988) *The Culture of Terrorism*, London: Pluto Press.
56 Chomsky, N. (1992) *op. cit.*
57 Morris, S., *op. cit.*, p. 5.
58 Chomsky, N. (1993) *op. cit.*, p. 144.
59 Robertson, D. (1986) *Dictionary of Politics*, Harmondsworth: Penguin, p. 122.
60 McLellan, D. (1971b) *op. cit.*, p. 229.
61 McLintock, M. in Chomsky, N. (1992) *op. cit.*, p. 241.
62 Curran J. and Seaton, J. (1981) *Power without Responsibility*, London: Fontana, p. 241.
63 Chomsky, N. (1992) *op. cit.*, p. 317.
64 Miliband, R. (1973) *op. cit.*

65 Miliband, R. (1973) *op. cit.*, p. 89.
66 Poulantzas, N. in Miliband, R. (1973) *op. cit.*, p. 90.
67 Miliband, R. (1973) *op. cit.*, p. 91.
68 Miliband, R. (1973) *op. cit.*, p. 91.
69 Evans, M. (1975) *Karl Marx*, Political Thinkers no. 3, Parry G. (General Editor), London: George Allen and Unwin, p. 117.
70 Evans, M., *op. cit.*, p. 116.
71 Chomsky, N. (1992) *op. cit.*, p. 331.
72 Chomsky, N. (1992) *op. cit.*, p. 359.
73 Chomsky, N. (1993) *op. cit.*, p. 18.
74 Chomsky, N. (1992) *op. cit.*, p. 366.
75 Chomsky, N. (1992) *op. cit.*, p. 331.
76 Chomsky, N. (1992) *op. cit.*, p. 374.
77 Chomsky, N. (1992) *op. cit.*, p. 332.
78 Chomsky, N. (1992) *op. cit.*, pp. 375–6.
79 Chomsky, N. (1992) *op. cit.*, p. 373.
80 Chomsky, N. (1992) *op. cit.*, p. 272.
81 Chomsky, N. (1992) *op. cit.*, p. 385.
82 Harding, N. (ed.) (1984) *The State in Socialist Society*, London: Macmillan.
83 Chomsky, N. (1992) *op. cit.*, p. 184.
84 Lenin, V.I., *op. cit.*, p. 129.
85 Lenin, V. I., *op. cit.*, p. 123.
86 Maguire's term.
87 Marx in McLellan, D. (1971b) *op. cit.*, p. 207.
88 McLellan, D. (1971b) *op. cit.*, p. 210.

4 State theory

Chomsky's views on the state are notoriously scattered and untheorised throughout his voluminous works. Reference to the state is often general and to obtain a more accurate interpretation requires an appreciation of other threads prevalent in his works. Pulling together his ideas within the context of an existing debate on a particular subject is a good way of assessing the coherence of his position in order to establish whether in fact his ideas can be said to be constitutive of a theory.

Having compared Chomsky's views on the state with those of Marx's, I plan now to look at Chomsky's work in relation to contemporary state theorists such as Block, Carnoy, Skocpol and particularly Jessop. I am interested in those who have attempted to develop Marx's ideas into a coherent theoretical position because, as the last chapter established, Chomsky's work is close to this tradition, but he nevertheless demonstrates a distinctive shift of emphasis. The question is what relationship, if any, this shift of emphasis has with theories of the state. With this in mind, Jessop's work is of particular interest because in order to develop his own ideas within the Marxist tradition, he comprehensively engages with the main strands in contemporary schools of thought.

I begin by considering the three general positions within the Marxist tradition as identified by Jessop: capital-theoretical; class-theoretical; and strategic-theoretical, this last being Jessop's own position. I briefly consider other developments within state theory but on the whole do not find them relevant for considering Chomsky's views. I then examine a further development in state theory, namely the 'statist' position. This is relevant because it gives great prominence to the autonomous power of the state, and seems therefore to have some common ground with Chomsky's position.

In the light of these various strands of thought I turn to Chomsky's own position. The position most compatible with Chomsky's seems to be that offered by the class-theoretical approach, but again Chomsky's particular version contains significant modifications which have implications suggestive of a distinctive position.

Connections in Chomsky's work to the capital-theoretical or capital-logic approach are more difficult to ascertain. On the one hand Chomsky

refers to capitalism and capitalists, which suggests an economy susceptible to a certain capital dynamic, and on the other hand he is at pains
not to accord this dynamic or logic any conceptual primacy. Instead, in
his view, capitalism is a shadow of its theoretical self, given the extent
to which distortions are effected through the state by and on behalf of
elite groups.

Despite the fact that Chomsky's ideas on the state do incorporate
some of the criticisms made by Jessop of these two schools, Chomsky's
position is incompatible with Jessop's own strategic-theoretical approach,
which emphasises a degree of democratic participation as being constitutive and so necessary to any state theory under capitalism. Chomsky is
sceptical of the extent to which the democratic form of state capitalism
offers a real channel for popular intervention and participation. However, despite the fact that Chomsky does present the capitalist state as
offering a purer form of class rule than the presentations of Jessop
and others, he nevertheless does not argue that this is an unchanging
position. He points out that states and their elite are themselves subject
to competitive forces at the *international* level which alter the balance of
power between states. An international capital-logic (or capital-logics),
does then stalk the international environment because there is no international state to distort and manipulate capital's dynamic, in the way that
occurs within the national environment. In these ways, Chomsky's work
embodies a variation upon a long tradition of well-established theories of
the state.

Theories of the state

Bob Jessop in *State Theory*[1] seeks not only to explicate developments in
state theory over the last twenty years, but also to draw out from these
developments his own distinct views on the subject. As a Marxist he is
concerned, given the power and logic of capital, to work out and make
clear the extent and conditions of state autonomy. In particular he is
unwilling to concede that the developments, geographically and historically, of different state forms are simply differences in appearance, and
that 'in the last instance' they all function in the interests of capital.

Jessop identifies three general positions within the Marxist tradition
that can be taken on this question of 'relative autonomy':[2] (1) capital-
theoretical, (2) class-theoretical, and (3) strategic-theoretical. The debate
between the first two positions concerns the question of whether it is the
logic of capital or the nature of class composition that determines the
nature of, or more specifically the autonomy of, the state in the first
or last instance. On the first position Jessop argues that there are two
strands. Firstly, there are those who claim that the logic of capital generates the need for a state form which functions as the 'ideal total capitalist'.
As Mandel argues:

Capitalist competition thus inevitably determines a tendency towards an autonomization of the State apparatus, so that it can function as an 'ideal total capitalist' serving the interests of the protection, consolidation and expansion of the capitalist mode of production as a whole, over and against the conflicting interests of the 'real total capitalist' that is composed of 'many capitals' in the actual world.[3]

The state mediates and is therefore autonomous in relation to the interests of particular capitals, but is subordinate to the interests of capital in general. The other strand, having more historical specificity, stresses that the competition between particular capitals generates a need for a state under 'normal' conditions of laissez-faire capitalism but also the *increasing* need for the 'primacy of the political',[4] given the imperfections of the system which generates monopolistic rivalries and crises. In other words the relations of capital and their inherent contradictions give rise to a transitional nature of state form, which has apparent autonomy from the economy which is nevertheless illusory. It is illusory because of the state's 'function [. . .] to secure the cohesion of a class-divided society so that accumulation can proceed in stable social order'.[5] Holloway and Picciotto coined the term 'separation-in-unity'[6] to attempt to capture the unplanned chaotic character of capital accumulation, whereby the state has little direct effect on the process, except that periodic crisis triggers the 'steering mechanism of state intervention', thereby altering the form of the state itself. Holloway and Picciotto argue that '[t]his approach, which takes as its starting point the antagonistic relations between capital and labour in the process of accumulation, thus provides us with a framework for an historical and materialist analysis of the state'.[7]

The second approach, the class-theoretical approach, also has two strands. The first 'instrumentalist' approach finds that the state's role corresponds to the changing balance of class forces. The state and its managers have no autonomy, and class interests are unproblematically interpreted into policy. The state, then, is an instrument or tool in the hands of the ruling class. It simply transmits the interests of the dominant group, who are able to clearly articulate their interests.[8] The ease of this transmission is largely due, as Miliband pointed out, to the fact that the state is manned by personnel with social backgrounds and personal ties which give them values shared with the economic elites.[9] At certain points, perhaps during equilibrium of forces, or even an overall weakness of class forces, state managers are able to acquire an exceptional independence (Bonapartism). The second strand, sometimes referred to as 'structuralist', is associated with Gramsci's ideas and Poulantzas' work, and finds the state actively shaping class forces, rather than simply responding to them.[10] In shaping class forces, a process that depends upon the forms of organisation and representation, or structure, the state modifies the balance between them. Thus, the state is not simply an instrument but rather it actively organises the bourgeoisie's political and ideological domination and ensures the disorganisation of the dominated class. In other words, the threat to the unity of competing capitals is achieved through the nature of ideological hegemony and this unity is dependent upon the form of the state. This hegemonic unity extends to the incorporation of forces beyond the dominant groups, and so requires a degree of sacrifice of short-term interests from both dominant and dominated. The effectiveness of particular forms of state such as parliamentarianism is considered in respect of the different degrees of bourgeois domination. Despite the seeming separation of the economic and the political, they are dialectically connected, because an economic crisis can lead to a restructuring of the political, which in turn will be a precondition for overcoming that crisis. Having set out this distinction between the instrumentalists and structuralists within the class-theoretical approach, both Jessop and Carnoy point out that it is unhelpful to label the debate between Poulantzas and Miliband in this way because in fact aspects of each appear in the work of both thinkers.[11]

The strategic-theoretical approach, favoured by Jessop, is an attempt to develop and transcend the difficulties of the capital- and class-theoretical models. Within the 'capital-logic' approach, it is not clear exactly how the state functions as an ideal capitalist since it is assumed that in the last instance intervention is always in the interests of capital. In other words it is not clear how the interests of capital are to be determined, given, as Jessop argues, that capital accumulation is itself inherently contradictory.[12] The implicit argument of the capital-theoretical position seems to be that there is one logic of capital, and therefore only one strategy for its accumulation. Also absent from such an analysis are the non-economic variables of class struggle. Internal critiques attempting to address these shortcomings, by conceding the influence of class struggle and thereby recognising that state intervention may not correspond directly with the needs of capital, are nevertheless constrained, in Jessop's view, by a restrictive conceptual approach to class struggle. In other words, class struggle is not itself seen in turn as being influenced by the historical nature of political and ideological relations. In contrast, the class-theoretical approach which does address this latter point, tends to overestimate the autonomy of politics and ideology, failing to recognise the constraints of the economy, and therefore the dynamic of capital accumulation. It also takes for granted the unity of a class, without explaining this unity.

Jessop argues that it is not good enough to simply combine the two approaches, rather he argues it is necessary to make clear how the concepts and principles of the two approaches relate to one another. Firstly, he argues, it is useful to consider the contributions of the 'regulation approach' which, rather than postulating one universal logic of capital, postulates that there are various ways for accumulation to occur and that accumulation is influenced by institutional forms, social forces, and compromise.

In other words, capital accumulation needs to be regulated – it is not automatic and law-like. Equally, regimes of accumulation and regulation vary temporally and spatially and can be contingently influenced, making laws and predictions impossible. Secondly, using Poulantzas' later work, Jessop argues that the social forces or class struggle acts within and through the state and thereby gives the state power. The state in itself has no power, rather it gains power via the social forces that act through the state, making the state a social relation. However, the institutional form or structure of the state nevertheless contains a particular class bias. Jessop argues that how this emerges is the weak point, because it is not made clear in Poulantzas' work.[13] Even so the contradictory nature of class interests precludes the possibility of there being *a* simple 'logic' of capital and so a crude bias in the state. Jessop develops Poulantzas's position by arguing that the state becomes the site where the strategies for accumulation are developed. Such strategies are themselves always in part influenced by past patterns of strategic selectivity. He employs Foucault's idea that the way in which a strategy codifies power relations explains the unity of a system of domination, and that this itself is not the product of one person or group, it is simply the outcome of micro-power clashes.[14] The bias or domination then is intentional, but has no subject. The unity imposed upon the state's activities and the strategies of the moment, is achieved via a hegemonic project. There is, Jessop argues, a complex dialectic between social forces and economic and political structures.

There have been other developments within state theory. One is the post-Marxist work of Laclau and Mouffe,[15] who argue that the basic assumptions of Marxism are subverted by the new logic of hegemony which entails social compromise and thus contingency, thereby radically undermining the logic of capital. Discourses (social practices) fix social relations with meaning, but only in relation to other discourses, making it impossible to totally fix the meaning, so that social relations can only become relatively fixed moments. Society and thus the state become impossible to refer to as fixed social relations, requiring rather that in analysis their respective moments be deconstructed. A second development has been the 'autopoiesis' position. This position contends that some systems, the state being one, have within them the property of radical autonomy. In other words as a system the state 'defines its own boundaries relative to its environment, develops its own unifying operational codes, implements its own programmes, reproduces its own elements in a closed circuit, obeys its own laws of motion'.[16] However, neither of these two developments is particularly relevant to the question of Chomksy's position, partly because, as should become clear, he would question their underlying premises.

The state-theoretical or statist approach is a further development identified by Jessop within the recent body of work on the state that is relevant to establishing Chomsky's ideas on the subject. Such an approach either begins with an analysis of the state as an institutional structure with the power to penetrate society, or focuses on the independent power exercised by state functionaries. Within this position Skocpol argues to 'bring the state back in',[17] as she is concerned to move the debate away from the so-called 'society-centred' approach (a term Jessop is expressly critical of, given the amount of work Marxists have devoted to the influence, effects and autonomy of the state). The 'society-centred' approach it is argued, finds the state responding to and possibly subsequently affecting societal forces, be they the forces of class struggle or the laws of capital. For Skocpol the state itself is to be recognised as an independent source of power, separate from society, having its own special interests, as a result of its unique infrastructural capacities both in terms of its connection with international relations, and because of its mandate to maintain social order. As Skocpol argues 'the political crises that have launched social revolutions have not at all been epiphenomenal reflections of societal strains or class contradictions. Rather they have been direct expressions of contradictions centred in the structures of old-regime states'.[18] The state's autonomy, however, is not simply a static feature of all governmental systems, but rather its scope and the manager's willingness for autonomous action does vary. In Jessop's view this approach reflects a 'nostalgic desire to return to a strong state at the very moment when various trends in international organization, interstate security, and civil society are all undermining the typical features of the sovereign nation-state'.[19] Skocpol's position does seem to emphasise the view that the state has got a progressive character to it.

This approach is not dissimilar to that identified by Hall and Ikenberry[20] as the realist position, although the emphasis here is on the relationship of sovereign nation states within the international system. Nevertheless the state in this view, operating within an international relations capacity, is endowed with independent power, having no higher authority than itself. The point for realists is a Hobbesian one, namely that the prevention of anarchy and invasion and the maintenance of order are supremely important and that the state is the institution best able to secure peace and prosperity. 'The search for security by a state means that, in a system of states, it will seek to play balance of power politics.'[21] International trade rivalry can degenerate into war, or as in the post-world war two period, a 'hegemonic stability' can be negotiated giving one state a recognised leadership role, carrying with it certain functional obligations for the system as a whole. Realists also contend that for reasons of military security the state provides the impetus for industrialisation, highlighting a link between a state's power and its wealth.

Block's empirical work,[22] also in the statist tradition, claims to undermine the Marxist notion that the ruling class is class conscious and is a 'class for itself'. He seeks to demonstrate the degree of conflict and disagreement between managers and capitalists. Indeed he argues that the 'class-theoretical' or 'business dominance' approach, as he calls it, tends to 'understate the short sightedness and irrationality of the business community'.[23] But, as Domhoff has argued, the evidence of antagonism within the upper class 'does not contradict the evidence that the upper class is a governing class: there may be disagreements and even conflict over long-range strategies and short-run tactics, but the primary goal of that class to protect the private property system as a whole and to reproduce its own control over major institutions of society remains intact'.[24] Domhoff also wants to question where the autonomous state, characteristic of both the statist and realist positions, begins and ends.[25] As Levine has argued, Skocpol 'assumes the separation of the state from social and economic forces, analyses the state in its own right, and then claims that the state influences and directs change in both the economic and social spheres'.[26] What, she asks, are the origins behind the existing state structures?

Having briefly reviewed the various positions taken by those state theorists relevant to drawing out Chomsky's position, this chapter now turns to look at Chomsky's views on the state to establish the framework with which he works.

Chomsky on the state

How then do Chomsky's ideas fit in with these contemporary debates on the state? The principal focus of Chomsky's work concerns the United States and its foreign policy. This means that a key part of his analysis concerns the state. He combs state documents, quotes state managers and records state activities along with their effects. He considers the American state's relations with the rest of the west, with the east and with the so-called 'third world'. The state is found actively affecting the course of events both between states and other states, and between states and their populations. His more recent work is also concerned with the American state's activities in relation to its own population. Whether it is through 'aid', economic sanctions or military intervention, the state is found to have an enormous influence on world affairs.

It might be thought from this that Chomsky's analysis is compatible with the 'statist' position and, given his international focus, its 'realist' counterpart. However, this is far from the case. Chomsky is quite clear about his reasons for focusing upon the state, and the American state in particular, and it is certainly not because he sees it as an independent, or even *the* independent, root of social dynamics. Neither does he regard the power that states exercise as progressive, 'necessary' or inevitable. His reasons are political. As discussed in the last chapter he focuses upon the state, the American state in particular, because by exposing the often horrifying effects of foreign policy he hopes he can modify and put pressure upon the government. Because of the American state's form (democratic), it is relatively susceptible to domestic public opinion. He is concerned with the human consequences of his analysis. As he argues:

> It is, for example, easy enough for an American intellectual to write critical analyses of the behaviour of the Soviet Union in Afghanistan and Eastern Europe (or in supporting the Argentine generals) but such efforts have little if any effect in modifying or reversing the actions of the U.S.S.R. ... Suppose, for example, that some German intellectual chose in 1943 to write articles on terrible things done by Britain, or the U.S., or Jews. What he [sic] wrote might be correct, but we would not be very much impressed.[27]

Chomsky's own political position determines the particular focus that his work takes, and it is perhaps for this reason that the complexity and nuances of his work are often missed. This point is worth dwelling upon even though it involves a slight deviation, because it is the source of much misunderstanding of Chomsky's work. Chomsky's critics often accuse him of focusing solely upon the crimes of the US state (and its allies) to the exclusion of the crimes of other states. Steven Lukes, for example, accuses him of 'contributing to deceit and distortion surrounding Pol Pot's regime in Cambodia'.[28] Chomsky would make four points here. First, his work does not exclude criticism of so-called 'communist' regimes. Second, as with the point above: '[t]he crimes of Pol Pot could be denounced, but no one had any suggestion as to how to stop them. The comparable crimes in Timor at the same time could have been stopped by an aroused public opinion, since the US and its allies bore prime responsibility for them.'[29] He makes this a general point – that criticising one's own state or society is more effective than criticising others. Third, his work on Cambodia sought to illustrate his 'propaganda model' which demonstrates the media's biased handling of the affair which, based upon the available evidence *at the time* exaggerated atrocities. And fourth, atrocities of states that are so-called 'communist' or 'extreme nationalist' are in part a response to US pressure. Again, however, he qualifies this:

> Since gross distortion of these remarks is predictable, let me reiterate the obvious: this is not the sole factor leading to repressive and brutal practice in the regimes called 'socialist', but it is the one factor we can influence, and therefore will be the factor that will primarily concern those whose concern is to help suffering people rather than improve their image or contribute to imperial violence.[30]

So time and again he explains that the reason for his particular emphasis is the result of political calculation, but that this should not be taken as pointing to a particular priority theoretically.

The statist theory then would not encompass Chomsky's view of the state. He would go along even less with the international relations 'realist' stance, particularly the Hobbesian view that states are a means for peace. He carefully documents the extent to which states are perpetrators of violence and not even violence of the self-defensive sort. In Chomsky's view the state fails miserably to secure peace, even if one was to concede that Hobbes could conceive of state violence being a necessary means for peace. For Chomsky that end is never to be reached through those means. The state, in his view, is not some all-powerful, determining and self-determining entity, rather it is a 'centralised structure', which is governed by a 'branch of the ruling class'.[31]

This puts Chomsky firmly on the society side, if one is to accept Skocpol's state/society dichotomy. Chomsky's position is not however to be taken as some form of crude class-theoretical instrumentalism, whereby the ruling class simply utilises the state as a tool and had its interests unproblematically interpreted by state managers. His position is more complex for two reasons. First, he argues that the state itself does enjoy partial independence or autonomy; that 'independent interests' can be detected 'in some of the particular directions that state capitalism takes'.[32] Here he is thinking of military interests that in the US have acquired enormous assets and have considerable decision-making power. Nevertheless, he argues these could be 'liquidated by the ruling class at any moment by simply withdrawing its [the Pentagon's] resources'.[33] That this does not happen is a result of their 'interpenetration'.[34] It might be assumed that by 'interpenetration' here he means interpenetration in terms of personnel, that Pentagon officials have business interests in the military sphere, etc. But he means more than this, as I shall come back to.

The second point that gives Chomsky's arguments a more complex quality is that despite referring to ruling class interests he also emphasises that 'the ruling class itself has internal conflicts'.[35] This point that the ruling class itself is in conflict, and the difference between the particular interests of capital and the general interests of capital, are issues which Jessop is particularly keen to resolve because at the theoretical level they pose certain problems. However, Chomsky argues that at the practical level conflicts of interests are often only marginally damaging: '[Usually,] elements of the ruling class that have a particular interest in one or another sphere of governmental activity will probably tend to dominate them. What they do may be in conflict with class interests of others, but the others do not care that much; it's not a major thing with them, so they let it go. [Conflicts] sometimes . . . can break out into real conflicts – serious conflicts.'[36] But such contradictions of private accumulation are never enough to undermine the whole system. Chomsky does however want to take this point concerning ruling class conflicts a step further, because he argues that in important ways these conflicts of interests contribute to the illusion that there is a plurality of interests being represented in public life and that there is genuine debate and choice. He argues:

> Debate cannot be stilled, and indeed in a properly functioning system of propaganda, it should not be, because it has a system-reinforcing character if constrained within the proper bounds. What is essential is to set the bounds firmly. Controversy may rage as long as it adheres to the presuppositions that define the consensus of elites, and it should furthermore be encouraged within these bounds, thus helping to establish these doctrines as the very condition of thinkable thought while reinforcing the belief that freedom reigns.[37]

Chomsky, then, recognises that there are conflicts of interest within the ruling class that therefore undermine any simplistic view of the state acting at the behest of some monolithic ruling class. However, he also argues that in practice these conflicts do not on the whole damage certain interests enough to put into question the whole system or throw it into crisis. Presumably if a section of particular interests were to be severely threatened it is unlikely that these interests could acquire the necessary support to put enough pressure upon the state, precisely because their interests are particular – other particular interests 'do not care that much'. As long as conflict does not go beyond certain bounds it is a useful feature of a properly functioning capitalist democracy.

Chomsky's relationship to the ideas of the capital-logic school is more complex. On the one hand he clearly views the state as having a complex interdependent relationship with capitalists, or to be more accurate, using his terminology, with the corporate elite. This presupposes the notion of capital and therefore capitalism. He also quite clearly finds a class analysis compelling for considering 'how patterns of choice are influenced by material interests and other interests that are defined in class terms'.[38] However, on the other hand, he veers away from referring to, or enunciating, an economic law or logic of capital. Instead he argues that there are tendencies, but that as it is individuals who are in control it is conceivable that they could behave differently.[39] This last point is important because, as he repeatedly documents, certain people have more control than others. Indeed, some have so much control they are able to strongly influence the rules of the game. Agency then is crucial to any analysis of social and political organisation.

It seems fair to interpret the point that Chomsky seems to be making by claiming that to discuss the dynamic of capital and the nature of capitalism is to reify the processes. Chomsky takes capitalism to mean a system of free markets, but as he often argues we have only an approximation to capitalism. The market is subject to all sorts of distortions – distortions that benefit those who effect them.[40] In a sense he is less interested in the finer dynamics of the economic system, with its tendency for crisis, its ability for self-regeneration, and the state's role in these processes. He begins from the other end of the equation, so to speak, by acknowledging the ever-present interventions and extent of the distortions, which seriously undermine any notion of the economic system having direct determinist effects. Though a capital-logic theory may be more defensible if understood as the identification not of events but of tendencies, nevertheless to start from the premise of *a* capital-logic is to underestimate the constant presence of a further variable: a political power exercised in and through the state. The criticism of the capital-logic school being made here is similar to that made by Jessop.

Obviously this is not to say that contemporary work on political economy that employs concepts of capital and capitalism are not themselves sensitive to the impact and distortions of state intervention. From this perspective, however, it seems that the virtues or otherwise of intervention are considered in terms of their effects on the economic system and its stability or otherwise. Chomsky, on the other hand, takes intervention for granted, and asks rather how different forms of intervention affect the relationships of power between elites and the population. In fact he goes a step further. Rather than treating intervention as a novelty in the functioning of the system, perhaps during times of crisis, he regards it as a prevailing feature. 'The Great Depression had put an end to any lingering beliefs that capitalism was a viable system. It was generally taken for granted that state intervention was necessary in order to maintain private power – as, indeed, had been the case throughout the development process'.[41]

This shift of focus illustrating that Chomsky does not attribute any necessary priority to the logic of capital or the nature of capitalism, in his analysis of the state or of any other feature of society, can be demonstrated by looking at his ideas on Keynesianism and specifically military Keynesianism.

Chomsky regularly refers to military Keynesianism. This is the system whereby the state stimulates demand, in this case for military hardware. The need to stimulate demand arises because the economy has the tendency to spiral into recession as a result of investors withdrawing investment when the return is too low. Keynes argued that if the government stepped in and boosted demand, investors would be given the incentive to invest.[42] Under the military form of Keynesianism, the government not only subsidises production costs but is also the consumer. Keynes' model, however, sought for governments to intervene in the arena of welfare, with housing, hospitals and social welfare generally. Keynes recognised that workers are not just workers, they are also consumers, and that demand from them, and thus consumption, would be boosted if they had a higher standard of living. Hence creating a healthy productive economy. However, as Chomsky points out, these forms of state expenditure, when taken too far, interfere with the class-based nature of society, by giving ordinary people security and expectations which undermine the privileges of the wealthy.

Military Keynesianism is not dissimilar to Kidron's thesis on the 'Permanent Arms Economy'.[43] However, Chomsky shows a distinct shift of emphasis from Kidron's position. Kidron questions the effect of an inflated arms budget on the economy. Using Marx's theory concerning the tendency for the rate of profit to fall, Kidron finds that arms production serves as a leakage in the system because it is production of waste. In other words arms spending keeps up the rate of profit. As Kidron argues, in Marx's view there would be a tendency for the rate of profit to fall provided there were no leakages from a closed system where 'all output flows back into the system as productive inputs through either workers' or capitalists' productive consumption'.[44] The luxury consumption of capitalists was the only existing leak Marx could identify but he felt this was not sufficiently important to undermine the tendency for the rate of profit to fall. Leakages then keep the rate of profit from falling, but Marx did not think there were any of any significance. Given this logical claim derived from his analysis of capitalism, his theory was able to predict the crisis and therefore the likely collapse of capitalism. Kidron however, in the necessary attempt to identify a leakage, in order to explain the tenacity of capitalism, identifies arms spending as being sufficient to arrest the fall in the rate of profit.

Chomsky's focus is quite different. Again he will not reify the economic system. Instead he asks what effect a permanently inflated arms budget has on the respective classes. Chomsky finds that the effect is one of public subsidy for private profit. He uses several names for this system: military Keynesianism, the military industrial complex, and the Pentagon system.

> The 'military-industrial complex' – in essence, a welfare state for the rich with a national security ideology for population control (to borrow some counterinsurgency jargon), following the prescriptions of NSC 68. The major institutional mechanism is a system of state corporate industrial management to sustain high-technology industry, relying on the taxpayer to fund research and development and provide a guaranteed market for waste production, with the private sector taking over when there are profits to be made. This crucial gift to the corporate manager has been the domestic function of the Pentagon system (including NASA and the Department of Energy, which control nuclear weapons production); benefits extend to the computer industry, electronics generally, and other sectors of the advanced industrial economy.[45]

In short the system enhances the control by both state managers and the corporate elite over the production process. At the same time it weakens the position of ordinary people who are compelled to contribute, and not just through their labour, to the profits of the wealthy. Military Keynesianism is not the only market distorting intervention of this type, which makes the private enterprise system *appear* efficient. Others include the manipulation of energy costs,[46] the subsidisation of transportation, not to mention externalities like pollution. As Chomsky argues '[i]f the real cost of trade were to be calculated, the apparent efficiency of trade would certainly drop substantially'.[47]

Again then, we see that although Chomsky and Marxists employ similar terms and concepts, Chomsky is keen that the role of agency should not be removed by implication from the analysis. Kidron's thesis of a 'permanent arms economy' places the focus of this intervention entirely upon the function it has for the economy, thus removing the very political character of intervention.

The extent to which the capitalist system is taken as a given, and assumed to be the guiding light for capitalists (and hence by some theorists of capitalist states), can be seen in Block's work. He is unhappy with the Marxist arguments that there is a correspondence between capitalist interests and state activity. He argues that during some research on US international monetary policy, one of the 'most interesting aspects of the study was the discovery that the American policymakers who originally designed the International Monetary Fund did not share the vision of an open world economy that dominated the State Department and American foreign policy in the post-world war two period'.[48] He takes this as evidence not only of conflicting priorities between different government departments, but also as evidence of diverging priorities between the state and business interests. The problem with this conclusion is that it assumes that capitalists have an interest in the free market. As Chomsky argues:

> To the public they [the state] made free market talk, but in front of the business community they talked differently, and so James Baker the State Secretary announced with great pride to the business convention that the Reagan administration had offered more protection to US manufacturers than any of the preceding post war administrations, which was true, but a little modest. It was in fact offering more protection than all of them combined.[49]

Neither is it surprising that foreign policy departments talk about an open world economy. *Other* economies must remain open to foreign investment: 'there's a lot of passionate rhetoric about free markets, and of course that's free markets for the poor at home and abroad'.[50]

The economy then is, and always has been managed. Free markets are ideological tools, and in Chomsky's view intellectuals have fallen for the story.

Something like a capital-logic?

In Chomsky's view, the state managers and the corporate elite together can, on the whole, manipulate things to their advantage. However, as they operate within a parliamentary democracy their manipulations have to be obscured. The extent to which they can manipulate things is in part determined by their ability to control the rest of the population, or at least deny them access to elite decision-making processes. Capitalist democracy offers 'a symbolic pageant or, at most, a device whereby the public can select among competing elite groups and ratify their decisions, playing the role assigned them'.[51] Some direct state manipulations fail and then it becomes convenient to allow what are often concentrated private interests to keep non-elite interests at bay. Chomsky uses such an analysis in his account of the media. Here he finds that the concentrated private interests are a useful controlling factor in the battle to retain positions of privilege. In other words this is an example of (loaded) markets leading to control in favour of privilege.

This is particularly clear in his analysis of the media, where he employs what he calls the 'propaganda model'. He argues that there are a number of filters that operate to preclude the possibility of dissident opinions or ideas receiving a voice within the media. Two of these filters are particularly significant in that they demonstrate the powerful part secured by private interest. The first he calls 'the size, concentrated ownership, owner wealth, and profit orientation of the dominant mass-media firms'.[52] Here he is pointing to the enormous amount of capital required to set up a newspaper, making such a venture prohibitive to just anyone with an interest in such a venture. However, the degree of concentration is, Chomsky argues, a result of the successful effects of the market, but crucially not a free market. Chomsky uses the work of Curran and Seaton[53] who argue that during the early nineteenth century a thriving radical press was seen as a thorn in the side of the ruling elites. The government tried to respond to this directly by introducing taxes to put up costs in the hope of squeezing out radical newspapers. However, '[t]hese coercive efforts were not effective, and by mid-century they had been abandoned in favor of the liberal view that the market would enforce responsibility'.[54] Chomsky also notes the way in which the deregulation of the media market has loosened restrictions on concentration and cross ownership, making take-overs easy, and contributing to the need for such enterprises to be unequivocally aggressive concerning profitability.

The second filter that demonstrates the 'benefits of the free market as a means of controlling dissident opinion'[55] concerns the role of advertising. Prior to advertising having the role it has today, the price of a newspaper had to cover the costs of production. This ensured that the customer's choice influenced the success of the paper. However, with the introduction of advertising as a critical form of revenue for the survival of media, it became a powerful mechanism to ensure that views not generally consonant with business interests are denied access. 'With advertising, the free market does not yield a neutral system in which final buyer choice decides. The *advertisers*' choices influence media prosperity and survival' (original emphasis).[56]

Chomsky is thus invoking the machinations of the market, but only to highlight that it is far from 'free', being rather the avenue by which private interests can exercise power. It is notable that in Chomsky its invocation is concerned with the non-direct control of ordinary people.

It seems then that Chomsky is saying that the two filters are important for demonstrating the logic of heavily loaded markets where private interests are concentrated, but significantly only for the control of the general population. By contrast it cannot be said to be determining of state activity. The economic system in place is a mere approximation of its abstract ideal type, principally because of the degree of manipulation afforded to those state and corporate elites. And so capital's logic is a useful mechanism for disciplining the 'bewildered herd' (the elite view of ordinary people). 'In general invocation of market forces as if they were laws of nature, has a large element of fraud associated with it. It's a kind of ideological warfare with its inherent class interests.'[57]

Hence, we see that Chomsky's position provides a shift of emphasis on the state in capitalist society from the positions offered by the capital – and class-theoretical models. In particular he is reluctant to accord special priority to any economic logic, given the possibilities for manipulation and distortion afforded the state/corporate elites. The latter, however, cannot be said to represent a monolithic unity, and conflicts of interest abound between them, but are rarely serious enough to affect the system of production for private accumulation.

There is, however, a major problem with the story so far. If the elite have it so well sewn up how are differences in state form explained geographically and historically? How, in other words, do we account for change? Or, to put it another way, how do we account for the waxing and waning of national fortunes within a climate of what we might want to call aggressive 'competition'. Certainly there is a tendency in Chomsky's work to emphasise the similarities and continuities rather than to draw out the intricacies of difference. This is because at the political level there remains, in his view, an 'elite hostility to ... a functioning democracy ... responsive to appeals from the masses of the population'[58] no matter what the nuances of policy or party are. This point holds for both western forms of government and also so-called Communist forms. So, for example, it is Chomsky's view that despite the end of the so-called Cold War, US policy will be 'more of the same'.[59] There will continue to be opposition to nationalist development with any form of meaningful redistribution of resources. It may no longer be possible to blame such developments on Soviet expansionism or to call intervention 'self defence'. But this simply means new pretexts will have to be devised.

Before addressing this question of change to national fortunes some of the parallels between Chomsky's view of the state and Jessop's strategic-theoretical approach are worth considering. Both reject the notion of a logic of capital having a determining effect on the state. Without this it becomes necessary to identify a mechanism or mechanisms to account for state activity. Jessop employs the notion of 'strategy', arguing that the state is the site that brings together dialectically past strategies with the present balance of forces, which generates new strategies and hegemonic projects. Jessop clearly wants to reject notions of instrumentalism and agency, but it is difficult to see how, using the notion of strategy, these can be avoided. Even given the conception of dialectical forces converging on the state, if one uses the notion of strategy it suggests intentional, subjective articulation of direction to determine ways and means. Chomsky meanwhile would accept the claim that his analysis involves issues of intentionality. As he argues:

> business, state, and cultural managers, and articulate sectors gener-ally ... must internalize the values of the system and share the necessary illusions that permit it to function in the interests of concen-trated power and privilege ... But they must also have a certain grasp of the realities of the world, or they will be unable to perform their tasks effectively.[60]

Chomsky also concedes a dialectical relationship between such intention-ality and social structures. In other words he claims that intentions not only affect social and economic structures but are formed in and by them. He argues: 'Acting as individuals, most people are not gangsters. Matters are often different when they subordinate themselves to institutional struc-tures of various sorts, such as corporations or the national state.'[61]

It has been argued that Chomsky regards elites as having a significant amount of power over and above any capital-logic, power which they wield to ensure that the accumulation process functions largely in their favour. But there is yet another level to Chomsky's position, a deeper underlying set of arguments. It is possible to bring these out by turning now to the divergencies between the positions of Jessop and Chomsky.

In Jessop's model, the democracy is a system constituting meaningful working-class participation. But by Chomsky's view, this is given far too much conceptual weight. The so-called compromises made by business within a capitalist democracy are not treated by Chomsky as representing sufficiently working-class interests, for the agenda is always pre-set and characteristically narrow. Chomsky agrees that there are rare times when the population can exert significant pressure on the state. The decade of the 1960s was such a time, with the civil rights movement and opposition to the Vietnam war. The parliamentary system, however, does not, in Chomsky's view, indicate meaningful working-class or popular participation. Neither, for that matter, does corporatism, another state form which Jessop puts much store by as evidence of a state not wholly responsive to business interests: in other words as evidence of a relatively autonomous state. Chomsky is much more sceptical of the degree to which participation is open to ordinary people (although he does not deny that there is some), and he often refers to the population as being treated like an audience or as mere bystanders. 'The public are to be observers, not participants ...'[62] Indeed he is so convinced of the degree to which decisions have been, and are being, removed from public scrutiny and participation that he no longer regards the concept of hegemony as a useful one.[63] He speaks of the 'de facto world government' that is appearing in the form of the World Bank, the IMF, GATT and other trade organisations, which are increasingly removing power from parliamentary institutions.[64] He also studies opinion polls and regularly notes the discrepancy between claimed support for government activity and actual support. For example:

> In the 1980 elections, 4 percent of the electorate voted for Reagan because they regarded him as a 'real conservative'. In 1984, this dropped to 1 percent. That is what is called 'a landslide victory for conservatism' in political rhetoric.[65]

Chomsky's ideas then are wholly at odds with those rational choice theorists such as Adam Przeworski who argues that at certain points under capitalist democracy workers' and capitalists' interests may not be completely irreconcilable.[66] Indeed, in Przeworski's view, it may even be the case that it is rational for workers to choose capitalism for both material and political reasons. For Chomsky such choices exist only within certain narrow bounds and, as careful analysis of opinion polls can show, what represents a 'choice' is often wildly misrepresented.

The weight put on the effectiveness of democratic institutions in Jessop's work serves in part as a powerful counter to the idea of pure class rule or at least to an obvious bias. Jessop would reject the possibility of outright bias or class rule given the contradictions within ruling class interests. In other words, for Jessop, the nature of democratic institutions and the possibility for a shift in the balance of class forces are significant in accounting for change. Chomsky on the other hand seems to be arguing that there is a much purer class rule than Jessop and others allow for. In his view the elites, by virtue of their wealth and power, can manipulate the system for their own ends, and it does not matter that these ends are sometimes in conflict. But this leaves the question of how change comes about. How does Chomsky's work account for historical and geographical differences?

Central to Chomsky's work is the view that elites are organised within the nation state. It is through the nation state (although not exclusively) that many important victories and market distortions are achieved for elite interests. This emphasis on the nation state in a sense concentrates on and emphasises the competition between capitalists internationally. In other words capitalists are brought into international competition with one another in a very specific manner, through their respective nation state. It is the emphasis on this point in Chomsky's work that indicates a deeper underlying logic to his views on political economy. Here we find an economic logic at work that has the power to subvert and undermine national elite power by virtue of the dilution of the states' influence internationally. To illustrate the point being made it is useful to consider an example in Chomsky's work. Elsewhere it has been shown that in Chomsky's view the military Keynesian system operates in favour of national elites by securing public subsidy for private profit. There are, however, dangerous implications in the longer term at the international level, as Chomsky argues:

> Japan has been remarkably successful economically. It's by no means weak from a military point of view, but its military strength is not commensurate with its economic power. In fact, the United States has been trying to get Japan and Europe to re-arm, to increase their armaments, partly because our industrial planning system, which is so militarily oriented is very inefficient. It means you are producing waste and our competitors are doing the work on different grounds. Japan also has an industrial planning system, but it's not producing waste, it's producing computers and cameras and tape-recorders and so on. That's driving the United States out of world markets, so we want them to create an inefficient system like ours through armament.[67]

The point then is that elite manipulations through the state at a national level have effects that cannot be controlled so easily at an international level. Rather, an economic logic is at work in the competition between nation states and their elites, that no one set of national elites can control for any length of time. It is not being argued that capitalists and elites are in any way nationalist in the usual sense of the word. It is recognised that they do not normally demonstrate any loyalty to a particular piece of land, or the maintenance of a cultural form, and so this gives them an internationalist character. Nevertheless it *is* being argued that attachment to a national state is of paramount importance to the maintenance and entrenchment of their privileges. Neither is it being argued that national elites and their states do not have *any* power or influence internationally. As Chomsky's work amply demonstrates, the American state has exerted enormous influence internationally, and particularly in the 'third world'. In this sense the American state has attempted to pose as an international state and manipulate the international economy for its own ends, suggesting that any international dynamic is itself subject to distortions. But one state among many, no matter how powerful, is not capable of enough manipulative power. After all, there is a real contradiction. On the one hand, there is the requirement that other nations have healthy open economies with which to do trade (for example economies actively created by the USA through the Marshall Plan). On the other hand, there is the possible danger that these same national economies can become real and ruthless competitors. Without an international state, the elites are forced to nation state allegiance, generating a special type of competition and conflict between them. It is at the international level that something like a capital-logic comes into play.

Conclusion

The theory of the state that is implicit within Chomsky' work demonstrates a characteristic combination of complexity and simplicity. By comparing his work with that of other theorists, in particular Jessop, it is possible to draw out the subtle points of difference in Chomsky's work. Like Jessop, Chomsky rejects any simplistic notion of ruling class interests, interpreted as some monolithic unity. However, Chomsky does not consider their disunity to be system-threatening or an insoluble contradiction leading to inevitable crisis, characteristic of the capitalist mode of production. This is because he regards the so-called free-market system as recognisably (by capitalists and state managers alike) unworkable. Instead the state intervenes (not unproblematically), as it always has, bringing distortions to the market in an effort to maintain and/or entrench divisions in wealth, power and privilege. In this sense Chomsky offers what might be called a complex instrumentalist view of the state. Complex in the sense that Chomsky's theory distances itself from any economic determinist view of the state, yet does not ignore that structural advantages exist and are in a constant state of flux and re-negotiation through state manipulations of the national political economy. In other words, his theory recognises that the direction and momentum of the economy's metabolism is far from self-sustaining, but requires constant regulation. This view clearly divides Chomsky from the 'capital-logic' school of Marxist thought.

Chomsky is also less convinced than Jessop and others that democratic state forms offer effective channels for the working class to have any meaningful influence in the flux and negotiation of power and privilege. He in no sense wishes to underrate the differences between democratic capitalist society and totalitarian regimes. Indeed he argues that the 'United States is probably the most open and freest society in the world.'[68] Such freedom however is largely formal and elusive to grasp for the bulk of the population, because of the lack of structural conditions for its exercise. Anyway, freedom is of course a relative concept, and to argue that America is 'the most free', is not to say it could not be freer. Capitalist democratic state forms then, are far from being an effective measure of popular participation. In general Chomsky finds that the population is successfully relegated to the safe confines of bystander status.

Though Chomsky does not think that a capital-logic has any significant overriding determining power at the national level, it does seem possible to infer from his works that in his view a capital-logic does have contradictions that can undermine a nation's private interests at the international level. That this is so is, its suggested, the result of the absence of a state to regulate matters for particular interests at the international level. While there is no international state, the most powerful elites will converge on national states in an effort to secure their continued privileges. This allows for the possibility that the success of one national economy can, under the dynamics of competition, undermine and constrain the power of another national economy. So, on the one hand, Chomsky can be interpreted as saying that at the national level elites can distort, circumvent and mitigate against the contradictions of capital accumulation, but that at the international level, because there is no corresponding state, a capital-logic can manifest itself in unpredictable ways.

Chomsky's arguments offer a distinctive and comprehensive set of views on the state. His emphasis upon the international dimension of state power is especially important. To claim, as Jessop does, that the international perspective does not require special attention is surely to miss something crucial.[69] Chomsky's views do meet the criteria of a theory, in the sense that they offer a coherent framework with which to critically analyse a disparate set of variables. While his theory is quite clear about the structural features of social and political organisation, he is, nevertheless, at pains to establish that these structural features are not static, law-like and inert, they are, rather, fluid, temporal and spatial. Although we are all agents of these structures, as well as subject to them, some are more responsible for their maintenance than others. So his theory is positing a capacity for prediction, and yet always with the proviso that things could be different.

If we are to accept Chomsky's theory on the state, then we can see that those who act in and through the state are actively engaged in manufacturing and securing the 'national interest', however narrowly conceived this interest may be. His theory, like those of Marxists, acknowledges that private business interests are constitutive of the 'national interest'. However, his theory places emphasis on this 'national interest' within the international arena. The international context forces us to consider the implications for our understanding of nationalism. In other words, if agents acting in the 'national interest' mean that state behaviour is constitutive of nationalism, then those nations with significant international power must be particularly successful in ensuring their 'national interest'. America is a case in point, even though its nationalism goes largely untheorised and even unremarked. This raises questions about the way in which nationalism is theorised. These questions form the focus of the next chapter.

Notes

1 Jessop, B. (1990), *State Theory: Putting Capitalist States in their Place*, Cambridge: Polity Press.
2 These positions do not exhaust Jessop's coverage of arguments on the state for there are also the arguments of post-Marxists like Laclau and Mouffe and the autopoiesis positions. However, these positions are far removed from the tradition from which we might say Chomsky belongs, and so consideration of these views raise a different set of questions, from the ones under consideration in this chapter.
3 Mandel, E. (1978) *Late Capitalism*, London: Verso, p. 479.
4 Jessop, B., *op. cit.*, p. 86.
5 Jessop, B., *op. cit.*, p. 87.
6 In Jessop, B., *op. cit.*, p. 86.
7 Holloway, J., and Picciotto, S. 'Towards a Materialist Theory of the State' in Holloway, J. and Picciotto, S. (eds) (1978) *State and Capital: A Marxist Debate*, London: Edward Arnold, p. 26.
8 This strand is illustrated by Lukes' conception of both the one dimensional and the two dimensional view of power. Lukes, S., *Power: A Radical View*, London: Macmillan.
9 Miliband, R. (1986) *The State in Capitalist Society*, London: Weidenfeld and Nicolson.
10 Gramsci, A. in Hoare, Q. and Nowell Smith, G. (trans. and eds) (1971) *Selections from the Prison Notebooks*, London: Lawrence and Wishart. Poulantzas, N. in O'Hagan T. (trans. and ed.) (1973) *Political Power and Social Class*, London: New Left Books.
11 Jessop, B., *op. cit.*, p. 250; and Carnoy, M. (1984) *The State and Political Theory*, Princeton, NJ: Princeton University Press, p. 214.
12 Jessop, B., *op. cit.*, pp. 150–5.
13 Jessop, B., *op. cit.*, pp. 256–7.
14 Foucault, M. (1981) *The History of Sexuality, Volume 1: An Introduction*, London: Penguin.
15 Jessop, B., *op. cit.*, pp. 288–304.
16 Jessop, B., *op. cit.*, p. 320.
17 Skocpol, T. 'Bringing the State Back In: Strategies of Analysis in Current Research' in Evans, P. R., Rueschemeyer, D. and Skocpol, T. (eds) (1985) *Bringing the State Back In*, Cambridge: Cambridge University Press.
18 Skocpol, T. (1979) *States and Social Revolutions*, Cambridge: Cambridge University Press, p. 29.
19 Jessop, B., *op. cit.*, p. 286.
20 Hall, J. A., and Ikenberry, J. G. (1989) *The State*, Milton Keynes: Open University Press.
21 Hall, J. A., and Ikenberry, J. G., *op. cit.*, p. 11.
22 Block, F. (1987) *Revising State Theory*, Philadelphia: Temple University Press.
23 Block, F., *op. cit.*, p. 9.
24 Domhoff, G. W. in Carnoy, M., *op. cit.*, p. 212.
25 Domhoff, G. W. in Carnoy, M., *op. cit.*, p. 285.
26 Levine, R. F. in Jessop, B., *op. cit.*, p. 285.
27 Chomsky, N. in Otero, C. P. (ed.) (1988) *Noam Chomsky: Language and Politics*, Montreal: Black Rose Books, p. 369. See also Chomsky, N. (1969) 'the responsibility of intellectuals' in *American Power and the New Mandarins*, Harmondsworth: Penguin.
28 Lukes, S. 'Chomsky's betrayal of truths' in *Times Higher Education Supplement*, 7 November 1980.

29 Chomsky, N. in Otero, C. P. (ed.) (1988) *op. cit.*, p. 319.
30 Chomsky, N. in Otero, C. P. (ed.) (1988) *op. cit.*, p. 322.
31 Chomsky, N. in Otero, C. P. (ed.) (1988) *op. cit.*, p. 185.
32 Chomsky, N. in Otero, C. P. (ed.) (1988) *op. cit.*, p. 185.
33 Chomsky, N. in Otero, C. P. (ed.) (1988) *op. cit.*, p. 185.
34 Chomsky, N. in Otero, C. P. (ed.) (1988) *op. cit.*, p. 185.
35 Chomsky, N. in Otero, C. P. (ed.) (1988) *op. cit.*, p. 184.
36 Chomsky, N. in Otero, C. P. (ed.) (1988) *op. cit.*, pp. 184–5.
37 Chomsky, N. (1989) *Necessary Illusions*, London: Pluto Press, p. 48.
38 Chomsky, N. in Otero, C. P. (ed.) (1988) *op. cit.*, p. 190.
39 Chomsky, N. in Otero, C. P. (ed.) (1988) *op. cit.*, p. 191.
40 Chomsky, N., *World Orders: Old and New*, Lecture at Conway Hall, Red Lion Square, 22 May 1994.
41 Chomsky, N. (1992a) *Deterring Democracy*, London: Verso, p. 21.
42 Keynes, J. M. (1936) *The General Theory of Employment, Interest and Money*, London: Macmillan.
43 Kidron, M. (1967) 'A Permanent Arms Economy' in *International Socialism*, Reprints: 2, 1:28 (Spring); republished 1989, London: Socialist Workers Party.
44 Kidron, M., *op. cit.*, p. 7.
45 Chomsky, N. (1992a) *op. cit.*, p. 21. NSC 68 refers to a National Security Council resolution which Chomsky refers to as the US Cold War document, which argues that US policy has been containment and deterrence. By contrast the USSR is said to be the aggressor, demanding total power and authority over the rest of the world. See p. 10.
46 Chomsky, N. in Otero, C. P. (ed.) (1988) *op. cit.*, p. 217.
47 Chomsky, N. (1994) Lecture, *op. cit.*
48 Block, F., *op. cit.*, p. 16.
49 Chomsky, N. (1994) Lecture, *op. cit.*
50 Chomsky, N. (1994) Lecture, *op. cit.*
51 Chomsky, N. (1992a) *op. cit.*, p. 348.
52 Chomsky, N. and Herman, E. S. (1988) *Manufacturing Consent: The Political Economy of the Mass Media*, New York: Pantheon Books, p. 2.
53 Curran, J., and Seaton, J. (1981) *Power without Responsibility*, London: Fontana.
54 Chomsky, N., and Herman, E. S. (1988) *op. cit.*, p. 2.
55 Chomsky, N. and Herman, E. S. (1988) *op. cit.*, p. 14.
56 Chomsky, N. and Herman, E. S. (1988) *op. cit.*, p. 14.
57 Chomsky, N. (1994) Lecture, *op. cit.*
58 Chomsky, N. (1992a) *op. cit.*, p. 58.
59 Chomsky, N. (1992a) *op. cit.*, p. 59.
60 Chomsky, N. (1992a) *op. cit.*, p. 370.
61 Chomsky, N. in Otero, C. P. (ed.) (1988) *op. cit.*, p. 303.
62 Chomsky, N. (1992a) *op. cit.*, p. 370.
63 Personal conversation with Chomsky, London: 23 May 1994.
64 Chomsky, N. (1994) Lecture, *op. cit.*
65 Chomsky, N. (1992a) *op. cit.*, p. 374.
66 Przeworski, A. (1979) *Economic Conditions of Class Compromise*, Chicago: University of Chicago, mimeo.
67 Chomsky, N. in Otero, C. P. (ed.) (1988) *op. cit.*, p. 573.
68 Chomsky, N. in Otero, C. P. (ed.) (1988) *op. cit.*, p. 599.
69 Jessop, B., *op. cit.*, p. 15.

5 Nationalism

Chomsky's work on the subject of state theory raises certain questions about the nature of nationalism. Indeed his work throws into question the way in which nationalism is usually conceived. In particular, political thought on nationalism, like state theory, pays too little attention to the impact of the international environment on nations. The international environment is treated as having an inevitable dynamic of its own, instead of being seen as the product of the 'national' agenda setting possibilities afforded to those more powerful nations.

It is common when discussing nationalism to distinguish between nation and state. This is because some commentators object to equating nation with state on the grounds that some nationalist movements seek recognition of a people (often using notions of ethnicity) who have no single unified territory and therefore state (for example pan-Turk). Equally there is the desire to keep apart notions of nationalism and nation, because some nationalisms are nations of intent. In other words some nationalisms seek the establishment of a nation. In reality, what might be described as successful nationalisms are those that achieve establishment of the nation, recognition of which requires a state; hence the tendency to collapse the two terms into one. If, as Alter argues, a nation is a goal rather than an actuality and consequently the nation is 'synthetic',[1] and given that the state relies upon notions of the nation, then any so-called 'nation', even the most accepted and established ones, must constantly seek acceptance and recognition. Nationalism is that process. As Michael Walzer has said of the state, the nation is invisible, 'it must be personified before it can be seen, symbolized before it can be loved, and imagined before it can be conceived'.[2]

In this chapter I begin by looking at some of the conditions commonly said to be necessary for nationalism to arise. For many it is associated with the modern period and, in particular, is seen to arise in the transitory process to modernity and progress. In other words it is a feature of a society in interregnum. A further consideration concerns that of the role played by the intelligentsia. The intelligentsia is regarded as pivotal in finding a way of unifying a people that, in the context of Enlightenment ideals, finds sovereignty lies with it. Herder,[3] for example, finds that common ethnicity and culture are an important social cement and that, through the survival of these distinctive characteristics, the national will can be ascertained. In the spirit of the Enlightenment he is careful not to attribute superior value to certain ethnic or cultural attributes. However, whatever his intentions, it is hardly surprising that the use of ethnicity, when linked to notions of modernity and progress, should lead to the idea of superior cultures and even the concept of a master race.

Having considered these common features, I then look at several dichotomies that are used as a way of theoretically distinguishing between the various manifestations of nationalism. In this section I look specifically at the work of three writers on nationalism: Kamenka, Plamenatz and Smith.[4] I find that the way in which they take nationalism as having polar forms is characteristic of much work on the subject of nationalism. The work of Alter and Schwarzmantel,[5] for example, also makes similar reference to two polar positions as a way of comprehending the different forms of nationalism. The difference between the polar forms of nationalism lies in the distinction between those nationalisms seeking supremacy and those seeking liberation. Implicitly, and sometimes explicitly, this dichotomy carries normative claims: former, bad, latter, good. Plamenatz and Smith argue that early forms of nationalism tended to be tolerant and liberal whereas later forms prevalent in the 'third world' have tended to be separatist and intolerant. Smith meanwhile regards earlier forms of the supremacist type as 'special' while later forms are at least understandable, given the onslaught of modernism. The dichotomies also carry a temporal feature, suggesting perhaps the death of nationalism with the birth of the nation.

In the next section I look at the problems raised for such interpretations, given that none of the commentators consider the nature of the international political economy. All implicitly regard the direction in which this period of modernism is going as 'normal' or inevitable, and therefore fail to see that the character of modernism serves the interests of some peoples/nations more than others. Using Chomsky's insights into American foreign policy it is possible to recognise that international affairs are driven by the 'national interest'. This 'national interest' however, is actually the very narrow interests of business elites. The process by which elites attain consent, or at least lack of opposition, constitutes a form of nationalism: in fact a rather pernicious, intolerant form of nationalism, not made available for consideration by the uncontextualised temporally located dichotomies mentioned above. Since American nationalism seeks ends that are in many instances compatible with the nationalism of other nations who accept the international context, for example other nations in the west, American (and other western) nationalism appears both tolerant and invisible. I plan to look at the dichotomies employed by each of the three commentators in order to turn each on its head, using

Chomsky's work on American foreign policy as a case study for doing this.

In the last section I raise and answer possible objections to the argument that the behaviour of America and western nations generally constitutes an ignored form of nationalism. First, a possible objection may be that the trend towards internationalism is especially characteristic of the 'first world' and, connected with this, that the bourgeoisie are more internationalist than the working class might ever hope to be. A second possible objection is that America fails to exhibit the mass support characteristic of nationalism. Both criticisms, however, fail to recognise the importance to the bourgeoisie of the nation state. This can be seen first in the collection of national taxation, necessary to support the pursuit of profit through the provision of public subsidy; and second the role played by the state in propagating the myth of a distinctive American national trait of concern for principles. This, it can be argued, ensures the diversion of opposition, which serves for tacit consent – a form of mass support.

Conditions for nationalism

Nationalism is a concept that is applied to many different social and politico-economic movements and sets of circumstances. Indeed it is applied to movements with such different characters that most commentators on the subject feel it is necessary to construct binary oppositions as a way of distinguishing the good from the bad variety. So there are the democratic varieties versus the authoritarian varieties (Kamenka 1976), or the Western forms versus the Eastern forms (Plamenatz 1976), or the polycentric versus the enthnocentric nationalisms (Smith 1971). However, it is possible that such distinctions blur continuities and perhaps more damagingly preclude the possibility of seeing certain forms of national behaviour as nationalistic or as constituting nationalism.

For many, nationalism is essentially modern and it has even been claimed to be the 'gateway to modernity'.[6] For some, it dates more specifically from the French Revolution.[7] With the revolution came an attempt to embody ideals of the Enlightenment that sought to put ordinary people at the centre of things. Kedourie argues that Kant's ethical teaching helped to foster and encourage new behaviour and beliefs based upon self-determination. 'A good man is an autonomous man, and for him to realize his autonomy, he must be free. Self determination thus becomes the supreme political good.'[8] Kedourie goes on to argue that, as nationalism is essentially a doctrine of national self-determination, it found in Kant's writings a powerful source of vitality. Smith defines nationalism as 'an ideological movement for the attainment and maintenance of self-government and independence on behalf of a group, some of whose members conceive it to constitute an actual or potential 'nation'.[9]

Kedourie's verdict is, however, negative. Kedourie argues that with the influence of these ideas politics became a fight for principles. As such, conflicts become, he argues, less open to negotiable peace. This is because principles cannot be compromised in the same way that interests can be. Putting aside reservations about Kedourie's idealist stance and the question of why self-determination is a matter of principle rather than interest, Kedourie's main unease, it seems, lies in what he calls the elasticity in interpretation of the French Constitution of 1790. Two years after declaring it had renounced all wars of conquest, the French nation then decreed that it would seek to defend all peoples struggling in the cause of liberty. As such, Kedourie argues, a new style of politics came into being, making the expression of will the cornerstone by which to override treaties and compacts. With this '[t]errorism became the hallmark of purity'.[10] Smith rejects Kedourie's outright negative verdict. However, it is possible that Kedourie's sweeping appraisal has more insight than Smith gives him credit for, a point to which I shall return.

Linked to the arguments that nationalism is associated with, or to put it more strongly, provides the impetus for modernisation is another factor, which Smith (1971), Nairn (1977), Kedourie (1966) and Plamenatz (1976) all deem a necessary condition for nationalist movements. This concerns the role of the intelligentsia. Recognising the constraints of traditional society, the intelligentsia propagate a new education, of which nationalism is a product. Of course this raises the question of whether nationalism is a grass root sentiment or an elite construction, and this point distinguishes those who think it to be an ethnic movement from those who regard it as a statist construct. The latter argue that nationalism arises in those who seek self government within borders prescribed by colonisers, and the former argue that nationalism arises within those who consider themselves to be an 'ethnic' group, with common culture etc. and become politicised.[11] Both seem constraining. Smith argues that education, literacy and developments in communication generally, made possible the spread of nationalist ideas, and Anderson demonstrates the way in which the modern novel and the daily newspaper situates the reader within the 'national imagination'.[12] But, as Smith points out, the aspirations of the intelligentsia together with technological opportunity do not in themselves explain the doctrine's appeal.[13]

Nevertheless, nationalism is seen to be a necessary adjunct to modernisation. It 'arises in the course of stabilizing or making possible the transition from autocratic to democratic, or at least popular, government',[14] a transition which may be painful. As Nairn argues, nationalism became the 'historical construct' to make rapid development tolerable and to ensure the rejection of 'alien rule'.[15] The powerful French Napoleonic state was seen to embody notions of Enlightenment progress, and progress was something the western intelligentsia put great store by. As such the nation state came to symbolise progress, the way to preserve independence and to become modern. This, Plamenatz argues, is politicised nationalism, because he regards nationalism as a primarily cultural phenomenon.

What then is the link between those liberal and democratic ideas and nationalism that can then take illiberal and undemocratic forms? Enlightenment ideas, which preached the right to exercise individual free will, prompted a backlash by those who feared for the stability of the existing community. As Smith argues, recognising that individuals are not atomistic and isolated but rather are rooted in communities, which give rise to common characteristics, nationalism found in the 'national character' a channel through which to embody the ideas of Mill and Locke. Political freedom became the active retention of historically evolved habits and traits. Political freedom became promotion of Rousseau's 'General Will'. Following the French Revolution the people had come to be seen as the source of sovereignty, and the boundaries of their will became the national boundaries. Recognition of this general will would secure national self-determination, creating a potent combination, with its curious amalgamation of backward looking and forward looking characteristics. The promise is that the security of 'our' future lies in the autonomy of 'our' will (a will that it is 'our' right to defend), which evolves from 'our' traditions and past, ensuring that 'we' progress during uncertain times without interference from the 'other'. It is the interpretation of whose will belongs to the general will, 'us' and not 'them', which has led to some of the more obviously pernicious forms of nationalism. This is especially so because nationalism, in seeking a common identity, looks to identify common language, history and even blood.

To summarise, it is argued that nationalism is a feature of modernity and becomes prominent in those societies moving from premodern to modern forms of social, economic and political organisation; in other words societies in transition or in a period of interregnum. It is also said to embody Enlightenment concepts such as freedom and self-determination, but within the context of a national will. It is therefore resistant to any form of external control or encroachment. However, its attempts to identify commonality within a group based upon various interpretations of ethnicity also makes it open to notions of superiority and hierarchy which can give nationalism a supremacist and divisive tendency.

Dichotomies

The tension within nationalism between resistance and supremacy reflects the potential that nationalism has to take different forms and, as already stated, theorists attempt to categorise these polar forms. Kamenka, in discussing the conditions for the different manifestations of nationalism, argues that the reactionary form arises within nations with secure, longstanding states and national territories. By contrast, the more progressive form grows in nascent oppressed nations, which are not yet politically nations, and require the vehicle of nationalism to ensure progress.[16] Kamenka is more interested in making understandable the logic of the reactionary type, and has little to say about the progressive type except to raise the case of German nationalism. Early German nationalism was progressive because it sought unification, being well aware of its 'disunity and political backwardness'.[17] This it was thought contributed to its exclusion from world trade by the Swedes, Dutch and French. However, its later nationalist fervour, once it has become an established nation, Kamenka argues, was a 'rather special phenomenon'.[18] Reactionary nationalism, then, is treated as unusual. Similarly, Alter has argued that the German case was 'perverted nationalism'.[19] It was special not just because of certain specific historical circumstances, but because, he claims, it sought primacy among European nations, a tendency not generally associated with the early liberal modernisers. We are left wondering what gave rise to the more reactionary form and why Germany, presumably an example of this, is considered a special case.

Plamenatz goes some way to answering this question. He distinguishes between the eastern and western variety.[20] Within the western variety there are two sub-varieties: on the one hand, the liberal form, a feature of the last century, found amongst those peoples who had not achieved political union but aspired to it (Italy, Germany); and on the other hand, the frequently illiberal form apparent in the next century, epitomised by the fascist movements. Like Kamenka, Plamenatz obviously sympathises with self-determination, and seeing nationalism as essentially the embodiment of this, feels the need to explain the specific historical circumstances which gave rise to the illiberal form. As he explains: 'in the west this illiberal nationalism has been the nationalism of people defeated in war or disappointed in victory. It has been the nationalism of peoples already united politically and humiliated or disregarded in spite of this unity.'[21] Clearly it is treated, even in its most oppressive form, as essentially a reaction to something. But the question of what, exactly, is not raised except to refer vaguely to those 'defeated in war or disappointed in victory'.

Of the eastern variety, Slavic, Asian and African, Plamenatz regards this as being quite different. Here people, having had ideas and practices exported to them that they were unfamiliar with, then had to transform themselves. They had to 'reequip themselves culturally . . . if they were to raise themselves to the level of the peoples who, by the standards of civilization into which they were being drawn, were more advanced than they were'.[22] In other words, they have had to create national identities in order to 'assert themselves as equals'. Here then nationalism is emulative and competitive – necessary in order to 'catch up'. In these cases, Plamenatz argues '[t]his eastern nationalism is in some ways far removed from the spirit of Herder. It is both imitative and hostile to the models it imitates and is apt to be illiberal'.[23] Its distance from the ideals of Herder lies in the fact, according to Plamenatz, that 'eastern' nationalism often abandons its own cultural roots, seeing them as inadequate instead of having respect for what is 'native' as Herder had argued. So, in contrast to Kamenka, Plamenatz regards 'eastern' nationalism as usually illiberal, but both treat it as comprehensible in terms of a reaction to external stimuli.

When we turn to Smith, who contrasts ethnocentric with polycentric nationalism, it is notable that he regards nationalism as a feature not only of the modern period but also of the premodern and ancient period.[24] This is because Smith is troubled by the view that all accounts of nationalism associating it with the modern period account for its rise by reference to exogenous factors imposed on human beings. So variously thinkers have attributed its rise to industrialisation,[25] capitalism,[26] state and nation building,[27] political messianism[28] or intellectual invention and imagination.[29] Smith, in contrast, is of the view that nationalism's appeal can only be accounted for by reference to more enduring and perhaps endogenous features. For example the recognised power of appeal to 'symbols, myths, values and memories, attachments, customs and traditions, laws, institutions, routines and habits – all of which make up the complex community of the nation'.[30] These, he argues, are enduring features of human appeal that are tapped by nationalism. As such any explanation of nationalism that links it causally with modernity will fail to account for nationalism's enduring persistence.

Of ethnocentric nationalism, Smith argues that this form finds inherent in *its* people only, by the grace of God, power and value. Its culture and religion is the repository of truth and those beyond this culture are inferior and in ignorance. Smith argues that this category of nationalism characterised the ancient and medieval world, for example the Greeks. Anderson, who regards the development of nationalism as essentially an eighteenth-century phenomenon, also argues that the great global religions and sacred languages of the past generated communities that were as taken-for-granted and self-evident as nationality is today.[31] As Anderson argues, one notable and characteristic feature of these classical communities concerned their views on membership. 'Chinese mandarins looked with approval on barbarians who painfully learned to paint Middle Kingdom ideograms. These barbarians were already halfway to full absorption. Half-civilized was vastly better than barbarian.'[32]

By contrast, Smith's characterisation of polycentric nationalism accepts that there are many power centres and that other groups have value from which it is possible to learn. This nationalism seeks ' "[n]ormalisation", the idea of becoming a "nation" like others, in a condition of dignified equality', aiming to be one among equals, belonging to a 'family of nations'.[33] Of this type, Smith argues that there are no examples in the ancient world. It is a modern form of nationalism. However, he does want to assert that there are many examples of 'ethnocentric' nationalism in the modern world, although, as Anderson points out, rules of membership are slightly less tolerant than those associated with the great global religions. Here Smith is thinking of the nationalisms, if only incipient, of Africa, Asia and Latin America.

So, despite the need to distinguish between the different varieties, they all find that nationalism is an internal reaction to a set of external circumstances prompted by among other things (depending upon when nationalism is dated from) modernisation, which is succinctly put by Smith as 'collective resistance to foreign rule'.[34] Other common elements then draw out the distinctions between the polar positions.

Problems

What is missing from these accounts is an exploration of what the common characteristics or the nature of this 'foreign rule' might be – in other words what is constitutive of modernisation. The form modernisation assumes is usually taken for granted and it is, in a sense, treated as inevitable, necessary and agent-less. Alternatively, it is treated as a 'special' case and as representative of a peculiar set of circumstances. What is missing from these analyses of nationalism is a consideration of and linkage with the international political economy. Certainly the external trigger is associated with a period in the development of societies which is transitional and is to do with their painful passage to modernisation. Implicit within this idea is that once a society becomes a modern nation then, unless it has a problem with minorities, nationalism becomes a thing of the past. However, perhaps the virulent but seemingly invisible nationalism of some powerfully established nations within the international political community explains why certain groups seek the unifying umbrella of nationalism to resist. In other words the 'foreign rule' is itself a form of nationalism, but one which cannot be accounted for by the dualisms offered. It is peculiar that this is overlooked given that many commentators would accept that all contemporary states use nationalism in different forms and to different degrees to achieve cohesion.

If we turn to Chomsky, we find that he traces the inextricable links between the nation, the state and the international political economy. Looking at the US, he argues that 'policy is driven by the twin goals, of reinforcing the private interests that largely control the state, and maintaining an international environment in which they can prosper'.[35] If we accept that an aspect of nationalism is resistance to 'foreign rule', then, the fact that 'intervention in the Third World . . . [is] in part impelled by the goal of securing a hinterland for the state capitalist economies' surely requires consideration.[36] In other words what requires consideration is the dynamics of these capitalist economies in relation to their modern states. Chomsky contends that if we do look closely at the nature of, for example, the American political economy we will see that 'militancy abroad to assert US power, and military spending' are useful 'to revive a flagging economy at home'.[37] Concern about a flagging economy is principally a concern about flagging profits, but in this respect military spending is useful. Development in military technology, which then feeds into all sorts of other high technology industries is state subsidised – in other words, is funded by the taxpayer. Once these developments become profitable the private sector takes over, and in the military sector there is a guaranteed market. This ensures the maintenance of profits. In effect, military spending becomes a regular injection in the arm of the economy.

What the aforementioned theories about nationalism do, then, is preclude the possibility of seeing an established nation, like America for example, as a case study for nationalism. As Chomsky's work demonstrates, however, it would in fact serve as a very good case study. Of course, here it might be objected that what Chomsky describes is American neo-imperialism and that imperialism and nationalism should be kept conceptually distinct. This is true on both counts, but what Chomsky does make clear is that in order for America to act as it does internationally, it must ensure national support, or at least it must not attract opposition. It must, in other words, make sure that the state and its elected representatives are free to pursue policies and action that are in 'America's national interest'. Imperialism is the other side of the nationalist coin. To conclude as Kamenka does that 'nationalism as a political movement normally does not arise on a scale sufficient to make it a central issue in political life ... [because] ... [o]ne does not agitate for that which one already has'[38] suggests a static reified nation that, once established, exists within a vacuum, unquestioned and untroubled by competition or external threat, perceived or real. Or that it is just a case, as Winston Churchill put it, of 'rich men dwelling at peace within their habitations'.[39] It also assumes that once nations have established a state, the boundaries of 'their' territory, the relevant nature of 'their' cultures and history become unproblematically unified, without internal or class conflict. Again, as Chomsky shows, through the example of America, this is simply not the case. The American state employs nationalist techniques to seek support and suppress resistance internally and abroad.

Having critically assessed the main contentions that nationalism is essentially a transitory and passing phenomenon, characteristic of those societies being born into the modern world, I shall now look at the more specific boundaries drawn by Kamenka, Plamenatz and Smith to account for nationalism's different manifestations. I shall then consider these in the light of Chomsky's work.

Progressive versus reactionary nationalism

As we have seen, Kamenka treats progressive nationalism as a phenomenon characteristic of oppressed societies that use nationalism to modernise. While notions of modernisation and progress are open to question, the literature on nationalism seems to take, as a qualifying characteristic of the modern period, inclusion of the people within the political system: in other words the move away from absolutist monarchy to some form of democracy. The implication is that once a nation is born, as long as it does not suffer from the 'special' reactionary type of nationalism, it has by definition progressed, and so possesses the relevant modern characteristics. Any group of people seeking independence from an oppressor will find unification under a banner such as national self-determination a useful weapon. But in reality, a modernised nation having attained independence, a national identity, territory and state can become anything but democratic, and it need not thereby be suffering from a 'special case' of reactionary nationalism. Chomsky's work shows that countries officially designated as democratic are a long way from the ideals of the Enlightenment despite being labelled liberal democracies.

Rudolf Rocker is highly sceptical of the association of the development of nations and states with progress.[40] 'The [French] revolution did, indeed, free the people from the yoke of royal power, but in doing so it merely plunged them into deeper bondage to the national state. And this chain proved more effective than the straitjacket of the absolute monarchy because it was anchored, not to the person of the ruler, but to the abstract idea of the 'common will', which sought to fit all efforts of the people to a definite norm'.[41] Rocker counter-poses culture and nations, arguing that the former has become impoverished as political unity has become entrenched. Greece, he argues, 'brought forth a great culture and enriched mankind for thousands of years, not *in spite of* but *because* of its political and national disunion'.[42] Kamenka paints a quite different picture, seeing within the modern period the conditions for progress, consensus and harmony. 'Some nations had been fortunate and had gained their territorial and political status before the demand for popular sovereignty; they could settle down, needing little more than a modest glow of pride in their history and culture, to the task of economic and political progress and to friendly co-operation with other nations.' Chomsky, like Rocker, would be more than a little sceptical of Kamenka's harmonious impressions. He would also want to take issue with the image of 'friendly co-operation' between nations. As he argues, America views with increasing unease the development of the European Community, seeing it as an attempt for greater independence, which might interfere with US 'global interests'. Prior to 1989 he argued 'Europe and Japan pose a greater potential threat to US world power than the Soviet Union, if they move towards a more independent role', not however, that he thinks the likelihood of outright conflict likely.[43] Nevertheless he traces the contours of conflict within and between liberal political economies, rather than harmony.

Turning to Kamenka's notion of reactionary nationalism, this, Kamenka argues, is 'for the deprived, for the unfortunate, for those who still have to find or create the conditions for their own dignity'.[44] Nationalism that is reactionary, he argues, is that which reverts to primitive hates and chauvinism. It is difficult to know what he means by 'primitive', but it is likely that it is supposed to mean something that is not informed by reason, a hatred that is irrational. Kamenka does not give examples of reactionary nationalism, except to discuss the obvious case of Germany. But he wishes to argue that this is a special case. Chomsky's analysis of American foreign policy suggests that it is difficult to think of a more appropriate case of reactionary nationalism than American elite attitudes to so-called communists. These elites are hardly the unfortunate and the deprived.

Chomsky argues that any country which seeks a form of truly independent development, in other words a country that perhaps seeks land redistribution without any influence from America or the west, is automatically labelled 'communist' and as 'excessively nationalist'. The reasons for this are threefold. First, prior to the collapse of the Soviet Union, to label a country communist/nationalist was to automatically link it with the Soviet Union. This had the effect of creating the impression that the Soviet Union was on some sort of expansionary mission, ready to take on the world, which meant that the country accused of behaving nationalistically could be seen as being by implication aggressive. 'Throughout history, the standard device to mobilize a reluctant population has been the fear of an evil enemy'.[45] This excuse has of course been removed, with the collapse of the Soviet Union, and Chomsky notes the problem America has had since in finding a satisfactory cause to stimulate the 'primitive hatred'.[46] Second, this had the effect of obscuring things in order to allow for sufficient public support for continued maintenance of a large military budget, in case there needs to be 'defensive' action. Happily, military Keynesianism also stimulates the economy. Third, any 'defensive' action undertaken can then become, by implication, a freeing of the indigenous population from the terrors of totalitarian communism. This serves to stimulate and maintain the chauvinism embodied in the belief that America is the leader of the free world, bearer of progress and the embodiment of Enlightenment freedom. The 'primitive hatred' then, is far from 'irrational'. It is highly rational for those whose interests it serves.

Perhaps when Kamenka refers to reactionary nationalism, which he sees as being informed by irrational hatreds, he is thinking of Nicaragua or even Vietnam. But as Chomsky dryly comments: 'Westerners have often been baffled by what they call the "xenophobia" of Asian peasants and tribesmen, a phenomenon not yet explained by modern anthropology, which seems to arise among groups that are subjected to saturation bombing, forced population removal and other modes of "protection" designed by their foreign benefactors.'[47]

Eastern versus western nationalism

Unlike Kamenka, Plamenatz finds the liberal form of nationalism a dead breed. It was, he argues a feature of the west in the nineteenth century. Nationalism in this century, by contrast, has been primarily illiberal, both in its western and eastern forms – both comprehensible given the relative external pressures. Again, however, the nature of this external pressure is considered at a rather abstract level. Concerning the eastern variety, vague reference is made to the export of ideas from recognisably advanced nations, which prompts the desire to catch up and emulate. Plamenatz seems faintly critical of eastern nationalism for abandoning its cultural roots, but no room is made for seeing it as anything other than a necessary and chosen path. Taking the example of Vietnam again, in his first political book Chomsky looks at the way the mandarins of American power pondered the problem of exporting the idea of setting up certain institutional arrangements necessary to counteract instability. He argues, 'what is striking is the implicit assumption that we have a right to continue our efforts to restructure the South Vietnamese government, in the interests of what we determine to be Vietnamese nationalism'.[48] Then, when attempts to export the idea failed, the Americans resorted to force, because they perceived this to be *in their national interest*. America claimed that the South Vietnamese were puppets of the communists. They could not decide which communists – 'the American authorities persisted in the assumption, a point of rigid doctrine, that China was an agent of Moscow, the VietCong an agency of North Vietnam, which was in turn the puppet of Moscow or "Peiping" or both . . .'.[49] This allowed them to claim that they were assisting the South Vietnamese in their struggle for self-determination and democracy. But as Chomsky's study of the Pentagon papers shows, no link between Vietnam and China or Moscow was ever substantiated. Such an example illustrates the clear reactionary nationalism of American foreign policy, which as Chomsky documents, contributed to the development of the oft-labelled reactionary nationalism of the Vietcong.

But if, as argued by Kamenka and Plamenatz, the liberal or progressive brand of nationalism can be identified by its faith to the doctrines of the Enlightenment, as well as having respect for what is 'native', then the South Vietnam National Liberation Front should have qualified. As Chomsky argues:

> It organized 'the rural population through the instrument of self-control – victory by means of the organizational weapon', setting up a variety of self-help 'functional liberation associations' based on 'associational discipline' coupled with 'the right of freedom of discussion and secret vote at association meetings', and generating 'a sense of community, first, by developing a pattern of political thought and behaviour appropriate to the social problems of the rural Vietnamese

village in the midst of sharp social change and, second, by providing a basis for group action that allowed the individual villager to see that his own efforts could have meaning and effect'.[50]

It is possible to see from this example that Kedourie's concern about the French nation decreeing to defend all peoples struggling in the cause of liberty is perceptive, if not for the reasons that Kedourie gives. Kedourie's problem with it is that the doctrines of nationalism presuppose an idealistic state of perfection, based upon human reason and social justice. Kedourie takes a highly conservative stance, viewing such quests as unattainable and thus dangerous in an imperfect world. But Kedourie's concern might have been a concern about who does the interpreting of the decree. The question is who is the French nation? It seems to be assumed that if a society is deemed to have modernised then the state is accepted or assumed to be the embodiment of the general will. This is questionable and as the state operates within a wider environment, specifically the international political economy, this too needs to be taken into consideration. As Chomsky argues, for 'corporations and business generally ... their (special) interests are the national interest'.[51] That being so we must be suspicious of such state support for peoples struggling in the cause of liberty.

Ethnocentric versus polycentric nationalism

Smith's so-called ethnocentric nationalism is, as we have seen, a phenomenon not just of the modern world, specifically the 'third world', it is also something which has characterised ancient societies. Smith does want to argue that this type of nationalism is 'weak', at least not in the sense that the movement is less intense, but that it is weak because of the '"submergence" of the idea of the "nation" and its "independence" under that of the religious culture and the divinity'.[52] This form of nationalism is also characterised by attempts to export and extend its influence. It is fairly common to see in nationalist movements the same claim to absolute truth, together with the use of ritual and myth, as can be seen in religious movements. Indeed nationalism has been described as a 'secular religion'.[53] Now it may be, as Smith suggests, that some 'third world' nationalist movements do hold to the fore deference to certain religious ideals which are considered repositories of a greater 'truth' than that which can be supplied by the general will. But, in terms of the export of influence, again, as Chomsky's work shows, a better and more successful example of ideas being exported could not be found than in America and the west more generally. Not only this but American intellectuals are also shown to worship the secular religion of the state: '[W]orship of the state has become a secular religion for which the intellectuals serve as priesthood.'[54] Chomsky is referring to the way in which intellectuals accept, on faith, American state claims to act only for moral reasons and always in the defence of freedom, despite the historical record. When reality collides with the myth, as in the Vietnam war, the intentions are still regarded as high, but the consequences were merely mistaken. He goes on to say:

> The more primitive sectors of Western culture go further, fostering forms of idolatry in which such sacred symbols as the flag become an object of forced veneration, and the state is called upon to punish any insult to them and to compel children to pledge their devotion daily, while God and State are almost indissolubly linked in public ceremony and discourse . . .[55]

Quoting an American journalist who wrote '[d]emocracy has been our goal in Nicaragua, and to reach it we have sponsored the killing of thousands of Nicaraguans. But killing for democracy – even killing by proxy for democracy – is not a good enough reason to prosecute a war',[56] Chomsky notes that despite the critical tone, it is simply assumed that policy is guided by a 'yearning for democracy'. The official doctrine is that this 'yearning' is not equivalent to trying 'to convert anyone to a specific political, social or economic system'.[57] Rather it is simply, in the words of a *New York Times* diplomatic correspondent, the desire 'to see American-style democracy duplicated throughout the world'[58] – American-style democracy being conveniently designed to satisfy elite interests. However, the historical record shows that this is more than just a desire, as the example of Allende's Chile among others demonstrates. An ambassador, commenting on the use of sanctions, explained the need at the time to 'do all within our power to condemn Chile and the Chileans to utmost deprivation and poverty'.[59] When this failed, assassination proved decisive in realising the 'desire'. At one level the desire might be thought to have failed, given the nature of 'democracy' in, for example, Indo-China, the Dominican Republic, the Philippines, El Salvador and Guatemala. But as Chomsky argues, 'it makes little sense to attribute to the United States greater tolerance for "political ideological deviations" on the grounds that it does not insist on "the U.S. brand of democracy" and tolerates "authoritarian dictatorships" '.[60] Actually it can be deduced that the political form is largely irrelevant to the American 'desire' – what is really important is that the economic order is receptive to US interests. Nevertheless, Chomsky does notice that there is increasing convergence between the social conditions of the so-called 'third world' and the west. 'One thing you have to give Reagan credit for: he has to a certain extent broken down the distinction between the United States and the Third World. He's a real egalitarian. You now have Third World conditions in Kansas . . . There are more homeless in the streets of the United States than in Managua, per capita.'[61] America, it seems, provides an excellent example of Smith's depiction of ethnocentric nationalism, but is curiously absent from the discussed cases. It seems that attempts to theorise nationalism renders American nationalism invisible.

Returning to the use of dichotomies to classify the types of nationalism, Alter employs the term 'integral nationalism' to refer to a category of nationalism not unlike that referred to here by Smith as 'ethnocentric' nationalism. Speaking of the Italian, German and Jocobin examples he states:

> [e]xponents of integral nationalism are prepared unscrupulously to assert the interests of their own nation at the expense of others. ... What is now 'ethical' and morally justified is whatever serves the nation and its power; for that higher purpose injustice, even crime, is acceptable. Here lie the roots of relentless persecution and violation of the law, of expansionist foreign policy and the unbridled ambitions of a 'master race' . . .[62]

America comes to mind as a more contemporary candidate for this type of nationalism. In the arena of international law, the US is a regular offender, given, as Chomsky notes, that 'the U.S. government . . . consistently prefer[s] the arena of force to that of diplomacy',[63] resorting to blatantly illegal attacks and acts of terrorism. These offences are monitored and ruled upon by international bodies such as the UN, the International Court of Justice and the World Court. In 1986, for example, the World Court ruled that the US attack on Nicaragua constituted 'an unlawful use of force'. But such decisions have little influence it seems. 'The United States . . . vetoed a UN Security Council Resolution calling on all states to observe international law' and it also 'voted against a General Assembly resolution calling for compliance with the World Court ruling'.[64] Such decisions are defended in terms peppered with ethical rhetoric about the US requiring 'freedom to protect freedom', while the UN is slammed for 'trying to undermine the legitimacy of western ideas, institutions and interests'.[65] Meanwhile, argues Chomsky, the global conquest by Europeans, which is led by one of the European-settled colonies, America, goes on, a conquest which has lasted 500 years.[66] In the early years of this conquest, during the English colonisation of North America, Chomsky notes the frequent use of racial categories to distinguish the barbarians or 'savages' from the 'noble race'.[67] This usefully contributes to demonising the 'enemy', a necessary process before the job of 'felling trees and Indians'.[68] Even this century, Winston Churchill sought support for the use of poison gas against Kurds and Afghans, referring to them as 'uncivilized tribes', while Lloyd George argued for the 'right to bomb niggers'.[69] The master race it seems may no longer refer to a group bound by biology but rather a group bound by economic and political interests.

Chomsky does regard the 1960s as a turning point in terms of an 'improvement in the intellectual and moral climate'.[70] This period, he argues, saw an increase in awareness of and concern for oppressed sectors of the population. Such sentiments, however, came under heavy attack during the 1980s as they were in danger of threatening elite interests. As a result those who continued to draw attention to the issues of ethnocentrism started to be accused of 'political correctness'. As Chomsky argues 'what could be more natural than a propaganda campaign claiming that it is left-fascists who have taken the commanding heights and control the entire culture, imposing their harsh standards everywhere'.[71] Nevertheless, despite the backlash, and it still became less acceptable to refer to peoples in racist terms; that is with the exception of, as Chomsky argues, 'anti-Arab racism', the 'only kind of racism that can [still] be openly expressed'.[72]

In more ways than one, then (but not in every way as I shall argue), the United States can be described as conforming to the ethnocentric form of nationalism. One question that might be asked is whether polycentric nationalism is either a realistic characterisation of any nationalist movement or, even if nationalists themselves truly seek this, whether it is attainable. Smith argues that '(collective) autonomy, individuality and pluralism ... form the *sine qua non* of modern "polycentric" nationalism'.[73] However, it is doubtful in today's internationalised economy whether national aspirations of collective autonomy and individuality are realisable. Smith concedes that '[p]olitical independence is typically perceived to be insufficient without economic autarchy'.[74] Nevertheless it seems plausible to suggest that the issue is one of degree; some nations have more autonomy than others, so some nations can be more nationalist than others. If this is the case, then it calls into question the whole notion of plurality or pluralism. This defining characteristic of polycentric nationalism, conforming to Herder's ideals, presupposes an international order of nations having equal status, each able to express its own cultural character: a 'family of nations'. It seems that the realisation of such an ideal is what is sought when one considers the setting up of the United Nations. However, in reality to achieve any sort of common ground amongst nations that are essentially in competition with one another is a tall order. As Chomsky points out, in 1987 the United Nations, 'speaking for "the community of nations" voted a series of disarmament resolutions. It voted 154–1, with no abstentions, opposing the build-up of weapons in outer space (Reagan's Star Wars) and 135–1 against developing new weapons of mass destruction. The Assembly voted 143–2 for a comprehensive test ban, and 137–3 for a halt to all nuclear test explosions. The US voted against each resolution, joined in two cases by France and one by Britain.'[75] The failure of pluralism within a 'community of nations' is demonstrated by the impotence of the United Nations which is unable to enforce resolutions. This is particularly visible when one of the more powerful nations opposes a resolution, but suddenly

becomes less visible when, for example, the US seeks to use a UN resolution to cover for intimidatory tactics. In other words America uses the
concept of human rights abuses as a weapon against its enemies. The
enemies are those guilty of 'excessive nationalism' or 'ultranationalism'
or those who are 'fiercely nationalistic' because they seek reforms that
challenge privilege, and/or because they seek development that is independent of and does not recognise the needs of American interests:
American 'national interests'.[76] That this concern for human rights is mere
rhetoric is shown by the correlation Chomsky finds to exist between the
level of US aid and the level of human rights abuses.[77]

Using Chomsky's work, then, we can challenge the notion that some
nations engage in this benign form of polycentric nationalism. We can
challenge it, not just with the historical record that Chomsky provides,
but also on the grounds of logical consistency. In theory, the mouthpiece
for the nation is the state, but in practice the state serves the interests
of a narrow but wealthy business-orientated section of the population,
and it is this sector's interests that become the 'national interest'. This
sector's interests, as Chomsky vividly shows, are not merely internal
but external too. In other words the state, in the process of securing
the 'national interest', seeks not just certain internal conditions, but also
certain external or internationally conducive conditions. Such internationally conducive conditions might include securing production possibilities
in a tax free zone, or ensuring repatriation of profits, or having access to
an un-unionised, and therefore passive, cheap labour force. The uneven
nature of capitalist development has meant that nations do not meet on
a 'level playing field'. In other words, the pluralistic conditions necessary
for a 'benign' polycentric nationalism are simply not present. The national
interest of weaker nations may simply be to pursue an independent path
of development (or self-determination), and this decision will be taken as
a response to the national aspirations of stronger nations whose aspirations extend beyond their own national borders. It is this very prevalent
and contemporary form of nationalism associated with the stronger nations
of the west, which is strangely absent and invisible from attempts to theorise about nationalism.

Possible objections

The argument put forward so far is: first, that nationalism is not simply
a transitory phenomenon associated with the birth of a nation, but rather
is an ongoing dynamic of all nations within the modern climate of international capitalism. Acceptance of this premise allows us to see certain
forms of national behaviour as nationalistic or as constituting nationalism.
Second, given this premise, it is argued that attempts to theorise about
the different forms of nationalism become problematic. They become problematic because expansionary national behaviour of a society no longer

in a period of interregnum gets ignored which, in turn, leads us to miss the significance of this for understanding the defensive nature of nationalism in what are known as developing nations. Nationalism of 'third world' countries is typically treated in a reified way as though it is a reaction to some form of inevitable international development of the forces of production, industrialisation or modernism. In fact it is more realistic to recognise 'third world' nationalism as a reaction to the concrete experience of the intentional expansion of ruthless 'first world' nationalism. As such then, it is possible to see American behaviour as not only a form of nationalism, but as fitting more accurately the illiberal, reactionary ethnocentric conceptions usually reserved for describing the eastern, or third world nationalisms of today, or the so-called 'special', 'perverted' nationalisms of yesterday's Europe.

There are two possible objections that could be raised against such an argument. First, it may be asserted that the bourgeoisie are internationalists rather than nationalists. As Lowy points out, 'Marx stressed that "while the bourgeoisie of each nation still retained separate national interests, big industry created a class, which in all nations has the same interest and with which nationality is already dead"'.[78] Certainly, Marx saw a trend towards internationalisation suggesting the demise of nationalism. Second, it would be quite easy to show, especially using Chomsky's own work, that America is a class-ridden society and so does not display the mass support characteristic of nationalist movements.

On the first objection, what Marx's point fails to recognise is the extent to which 'big industry', despite being highly mobile and appearing to have no respect for national boundaries, still remains, as Chomsky's work makes clear, dependent to a large degree upon the support of a particular state. In other words, big business remains intimately linked with the nation state because of its need for subsidy, developments in technological know-how and guaranteed markets, or even simply to push its interests abroad. Elites, then, retain links with the nation and in particular the state, in order to benefit from, among other things, national taxation. Elites, interested in maintaining certain interests abroad are also dependent upon the state, as Chomsky makes graphically clear, when they require the use of force, in order to ensure the submission of those resistant to their interests.

Smith has argued that internationalism, rather than being a threat to the survival of nationalism, actually helps to fan the flames of nationalism. To a certain extent this is a similar point to those points already made above, although it would be more helpful to draw out the impetus behind the so-called internationalism and recognise it as another form of nationalism. Smith does go on to argue that 'internationalism is simply the mutual recognition and legitimation of other people's nationalisms, institutionalised in a global framework'.[79] But by not recognising that behind the apparent internationalism are certain nationalisms that set the agenda, he fails to note that the institutionalised global framework is not equally tolerant of other people's nationalisms. In other words the international framework favours some nationalisms over others rendering the favoured ones invisible. Smith's framework implicitly regards social organisation around global capitalism as normal. As Hobsbawm argues secessionist nationalisms are in fact useful to and can be encouraged by the more powerful nations as long as it is not secession from them.

> The optimal strategy for a neo-colonial transnational economy is precisely one in which the number of official sovereign states is maximized and their average size and strength – i.e. their power effectively to impose the conditions under which foreign powers and foreign capital will have to operate – is minimized. . . . [T]he US . . . and their corporations would prefer to deal with Alberta rather than Canada.[80]

All the while, if there is no international state to ensure the preservation of elite interests, elites will have to resort to allegiance with a particular nation state.

The second possible objection concerns the extent to which nationalism can be said to be a feature of America, given that there is no obvious mass support commonly found in nationalist movements. This is true although Chomsky would probably want to qualify this by arguing that a certain degree of idolatry towards the state and its national interests can be found among the intelligentsia. This is important because as Anderson has argued the intelligentsia is crucial for the development and promulgation of nationalist sentiment. For some, nationalism is not instinctive, as Zelinsky has argued – it is not genetically encoded, rather it is a doctrine that must be drilled into the hearts and minds of its adherents.[81] However, having argued that America does not display characteristics of mass support, Chomsky's work shows that the American state is extremely thorough in its attempts to divert internal opposition. So, although there is no mass support, successful attempts to divert attention mean that neither is there mass opposition. While it is possible to argue that the considerable degree of voter apathy in America is evidence of dissent, inaction actually has the effect of reinforcing the status quo, thereby acting as (mass) tacit consent. In other words in contrast to behaviourist claims a non-action is still an action.

The usual method by which attention is diverted is by the use of propaganda, another typical feature of nationalism. As the next chapter argues, Chomsky devotes much time to studying the media, which, because they are a business like any other, successfully filter out dissident ideas. Through the use of comparison Chomsky shows that American elites will use high moral rhetoric, spiced with misrepresentation and historical inaccuracy, in an effort to secure support (even if only tacit) for intervention or sanctions. Such actions are deemed necessary in order to secure the 'national interest', which is considered threatened even if that threat is simply the 'threat of a good example', as in Nicaragua.[82] However, the rhetoric will be that intervention is necessary to free people from a tyrannical leader guilty of human rights abuses or simply of being a communist. Meanwhile, the media keep quiet about events occurring elsewhere which are morally offensive, but which for a number of reasons, including sale of arms, may serve the American 'national interest' (e.g. East Timor).

All commentators agree that fear of an enemy is very useful in promoting national unity. Alter, writing of Germany, argues that 'images of a hostile world beyond Germany's borders, were evoked to whip up support at home for the nationalist cause; ongoing political tensions with other countries were artificially heightened to bolster national loyalty'.[83] Again this mirrors American anti-Communist policy. As Foley has argued, the Cold War 'was a war designed to produce the type of national anxiety upon which xenophobic and blind national solidarity could thrive'.[84] Another channel that, Chomsky argues, serves to divert attention is that of sport. National sport he argues is 'a way of building up irrational attitudes of submission to authority, and group cohesion behind leadership elements, in fact it's training in irrational jingoism'.[85] In concurrence, Zelinsky, who regards nationalism as a civic religion, argues that 'if nationalism or statism is the high church version of the new dispensation, then sport may be looked upon as its low church manifestation'.[86]

An important difference, then, lies between arguing that America does not exhibit the mass popular support characteristic of nationalism and arguing that the population does not actively oppose policies supposedly designed for the 'national interest'.

American nationalism

If America is taken as a case study for nationalism, what can be said about it? Zelinsky, in a study of American nationalism that fails to systematically highlight the problem this nationalism has for theories of nationalism, nevertheless argues that work on nationalism is 'eurocentric', according the US 'only a passing glance'. He argues that the 'American experience may tell us more about the essential nature of nationalism and statism than any other example'.[87] Foley argues that American nationalism rests upon a belief that the American people have a divinely-inspired historical purpose to set a moral example to the rest of the world: that, as Zelinsky puts it, 'divine providence is utilizing the US to achieve universal freedom'.[88] Early American political thinkers,[89] providing the necessary input from the intelligentsia for the development of national sentiment, but being unable to appeal to ethnicity, common history, common culture or even language, found, in rhetoric about democracy and liberty, the necessary glue for a national identity. Nye argues that 'American nationalism has always been connected not to place but to principles'.[90] As such it is infinitely more subtle, for expansionary purposes than, for example, Hitler's crude appeal to superior racial characteristics. In this sense, Foley argues that the American War of Independence and the American Civil War were two events concerned with liberty and civil rights, which shaped the American identity. Accordingly ministers from Kennedy's era to the present appeal to the population to recognise that 'the United States has responsibilities . . . [where] other nations have interests'.[91] Certainly, if one turns to Chomsky's work, we find him comparing official policy rhetoric concerning certain high moral ideals with the reality as gleaned from official records. Chomsky consistently finds the rhetoric wanting. The ideals that serve as national cement to American unity persistently remain just that, ideals.

Before concluding this chapter on nationalism, it is necessary to consider whether its findings leave it open to the charge of offering a conception of nationalism that locates nationalism only with conditions of modernity. Smith in his latest book on nationalism[92] argues that the tendency in much of the literature to locate nationalism with modernity fails to enable us to account for nationalism's enduring presence. He also argues that this literature implies a political instrumentalist approach, where 'culture is infinitely malleable and elites free to choose whatever aspect of a culture that can serve their political purposes or mobilise the masses'.[93] In his view

> . . . such a usage is unduly restrictive. It omits other important dimensions of 'nationalism' such as culture, identity and 'the homeland', and pays little attention to the character of the object of nationalist strivings, the 'nation'. The result is a serious underestimation of the scope and power of nationalism, and of its ethnic roots.[94]

While Smith may be correct to identify some forms of nationalism with real grass root sentiments for 'the homeland', this does not thereby need to exclude the political constructivist approach to nationalism. The two need not be mutually exclusive. Exclusive emphasis on the cultural roots of nationalism, emphasising common ethnicity, language and history may again serve to constrain our understanding of nationalism, rendering invisible American nationalism. As Nye argues, here we have a form of nationalism motivated less by place than by the foundation of a supposed universalist principle, the principle of freedom. In this sense, American nationalism mythically creates a closer loyalty to the ideals of the Enlightenment than could be imaged by Herder.

Conclusion

This chapter has sought to show that characteristics usually picked to define nationalism such as ethnicity, history, language and culture are inadequate. This is not to say that nationalist movements do not appeal to these features to build national sentiment, it is simply to say that focus upon them constricts a wider and more adequate appreciation of nationalism. By abandoning this constriction and another widely held belief that nationalism is a feature of societies in transition to the modern period, we get what promises to be a richer appreciation of nationalism and one that makes visible the nationalism of America. It seems that studies of nationalism, like state theory, also concentrate too much on internal characteristics of the nation and the state, and too little on the dynamics of the international character of the nation and state. Vague reference is made to reified notions of transition and modernity, without proper consideration of the concrete nature and workings of the international political economy. Indeed the international order in place is taken as 'normal' and as potentially desirable for all peoples and nations, especially if they want to 'catch up'. As a consequence of the lack of appreciation for the international environment, and depending on the degree of resistance to this international order, nationalisms get ranked on a linear scale of liberal versus illiberal types. This implicitly evaluates the nationalisms, the former being the better variety and the latter being the less attractive form, even if these latter are comprehensible, given that acceptance of the international order is likely to offend certain historically cherished cultural characteristics. Because the international order is taken as a given, separatist nationalism becomes by definition extreme, ethnocentric and reactionary, rather than a case of peoples simply seeking an alternative form of development, separate from the international order. Meanwhile, those cases with an extreme illiberal character that nevertheless accept the international order get labelled special or perverted.

By questioning the theoretical dichotomies, and by keeping in mind the nature of the international politico-economic environment in order for nationalism not to be treated as only a transitory phenomenon of modernising nations, it becomes possible to see the national behaviour of countries like America as deeply nationalist; further a nationalism of the reactionary, ethnocentric and illiberal variety. Indeed, it becomes possible to see nationalism as a feature of all contemporary state capitalist societies (as well as developing transitory ones). Instead of regarding expansionary tendencies as a 'perverted' form or as the 'offspring of "genuine" nationalism',[95] and typical of those struggling to modernise, this form should be seen as a corollary to the maintenance of state capitalist society, and as typical therefore of the more developed nations.

America and 'first world' nationalisms are, it seems, highly successful at disguising themselves, particularly from political theorists. Their invisibility is suggestive of the extent to which their manifestation is taken as the norm. As black writers and feminists have argued, one extremely significant characteristic of racism and sexism is the extent to which the white male is taken as normal so that everything else is 'other', different, pathology. This is also true for state and nationalist propaganda. For the invisible to remain invisible and for the norm to remain the norm, the possibility of the 'other' must be quieted, removed. This means information, knowledge and rhetoric must secure these requirements. Chomsky's social and political thought not only exposes this 'other' it also offers a theory, to which we now turn, about the 'manufacturing of consent'.

Notes

1 Alter, P. (1989) *Nationalism* London: Edward Arnold, p. 21.
2 Walzer, M. in Zelinsky, W. (1988) *Nation into State: The Shifting Symbolic Foundations of American Nationalism*, Chapel Hill, North Carolina: The University of North Carolina Press, p. 15.
3 See Plamenatz, J. 'Two Types of Nationalism' in Kamenka, E. (ed.) (1976) *The Nature and Evolution of an Idea*, London: Edward Arnold.
4 Kamenka, E. 'Political Nationalism – the Evolution of the Idea' in Kamenka, E. (ed.) *op. cit.*; Plamenatz, J. in Kamenka, E. (ed.) *op. cit.*; Smith, A. D. (1971) *Theories of Nationalism*, London: Duckworth; Smith, A. D. (1979) *Nationalism in the Twentieth Century*, Oxford: Robinson; Smith, A. D. (1991) *National Identity*, London: Penguin.
5 Alter, P. *op. cit.* Alter refers to Risogimento versus Integral nationalism, pp. 28–50; Schwarzmantel, J. (1991) *Socialism and the Idea of the Nation*, Hemel Hempstead: Harvester Wheatsheaf, p. 10.
6 Smith, A. D. (1991) *op. cit.*, p. 105. See also Smith, A. D. (1998) *Nationalism and Modernism*, London: Routledge. Here Smith considers those 'perennialists' who see nationalism as a more enduring quality associated with ethnicity.
7 Kedourie, E. (1966) *Nationalism*, London: Hutchinson.
8 Kedourie, E., *op. cit.*, p. 29.
9 Smith, A. D. (1998) *op. cit.*, p. 188.
10 Kedourie, E., *op. cit.*, p. 18.
11 Smith, A. D. (1971) *op. cit.*, p. 176.
12 Anderson, B. (1983) *Imagined Communities: Reflections on the Origin and Spread of Nationalism*, London: Verso.
13 Smith, A. D. (1971) *op. cit.*, p. 30.
14 Kamenka, E., *op. cit.*, p. 15.
15 Nairn, T. (1977) *The Break up of Britain*, London: New Left Books.
16 Kamenka, E., *op. cit.*, p. 16.
17 Kamenka, E., *op. cit.*, p. 10.
18 Kamenka, E., *op. cit.*, p. 11.
19 Alter, P. (1989) *op. cit.*, p. 27.
20 Plamenatz, J. (1976) *op. cit.*, uses these labels to point to their origins, wishing to include within eastern nationalism that form of nationalism found in Africa, Asia and Latin America. Gellner, E. (1983) *Nations and Nationalism*, Oxford: Basil Blackwell, this the 'Habsburg and points south and east' nationalism.
21 Plamenatz, J., *op. cit.*, p. 29.
22 Plamenatz, J., *op. cit.*, p. 30.
23 Plamenatz, J., *op. cit.*, p. 34.
24 Smith, A. D. (1998).
25 Gellner, E. (1983) *Nations and Nationalism*, Oxford: Basil Blackwell.
26 Nairn, T., *op. cit.*
27 Giddens, A. (1985) *The Nation-State and Violence*, Cambridge: Polity Press.
28 Kedourie, E., *op. cit.*

29 Hobsbawm, E. and Ranger, T. (eds) (1983) *The Invention of Tradition*, Cambridge: Cambridge University Press; Anderson, B. (1991) *Imagined Communities: Reflections on the Origins and Spread of Nationalism* (2nd edn), London: Verso.
30 Smith, A. D. (1998) *op. cit.*, p. 138.
31 Anderson, B. (1983) *op. cit.*
32 Anderson, B. (1983) *op. cit.*, p. 91.
33 Smith, A. D. (1971) *op. cit.*, p. 159.
34 Smith, A. D. (1971) *op. cit.*, p. 166.
35 Chomsky, N. (1992a) *Deterring Democracy*, London: Vintage, p. 24.
36 Chomsky, N. (1992a) *op. cit.*, p. 23.
37 Chomsky, N. (1992a) *op. cit.*, p. 21.
38 Kamenka, E., *op. cit.*, p. 14.
39 Churchill in Chomsky, N. (1992a) *op. cit.*, p. 45.
40 Rocker, R. (1937) *Nationalism and Culture*, Los Angeles, California: Rocker Publications Committee.
41 Rocker, R. (1937) *op. cit.*, p. 431.
42 Rocker, R. (1937) *op. cit.*, p. 409.
43 Chomsky, N. in Otero, C. P. (ed.) (1981) *Noam Chomsky: Radical Priorities*, Montreal: Black Rose Books, p. 134.
44 Kamenka, E., *op. cit.*, p. 16.
45 Chomsky, N. (1992a) *op. cit.*, p. 28.
46 Chomsky, N. (1992a) *op. cit.*, p. 114.
47 Chomsky, N. in Otero, C. P. (ed.) (1981) *op. cit.*, p. 92.
48 Chomsky, N. (1969) *American Power and the New Mandarins*, Harmondsworth: Penguin, p. 41.
49 Chomsky, N. (1973) *For Reasons of State*, New York: Vintage, p. 51.
50 Chomsky, N. (1969) *op. cit.*, p. 42.
51 Chomsky, N. (1992) *What Uncle Sam Really Wants*, Berkeley, California: Odonian, p. 89.
52 Smith, A. D. (1971) *op. cit.*, p. 160.
53 See Mosse, G. L. 'Mass Politics and the Political Liturgy of Nationalism' in Kamenka, E. (ed.) *op. cit.*
54 Chomsky, N. (1992a) *op. cit.*, p. 19.
55 Chomsky, N. (1992a) *op. cit.*, p. 19.
56 Chomsky, N. (1989) *Necessary Illusions*, London: Pluto Press, p. 51.
57 Chomsky, N. (1992a) *op. cit.*, p. 18.
58 Chomsky, N. (1989) *op. cit.*, p. 49.
59 Chomsky, N. (1993) *Year 501*, London: Verso, p. 36.
60 Chomsky, N. (1992a) *op. cit.*, p. 245.
61 Chomsky, N. in Otero, C. P. (ed.) (1988) *Noam Chomsky: Language and Politics*, Montreal: Black Rose Books, p. 740.
62 Alter, P. (1989) *Nationalism* London: Edward Arnold, p. 39.
63 Chomsky, N. (1988) *The Culture of Terrorism*, London: Pluto Press, p. 14.
64 Chomsky, N. (1988) *op. cit.*, p. 68.
65 Chomsky, N. (1988) *op. cit.*, p. 80.
66 Chomsky, N. (1993) *op. cit.*
67 Chomsky, N. (1993) *op. cit.*, p. 26.
68 Chomsky, N. (1993) *op. cit.*, p. 21.
69 Chomsky, N. (1993) *op. cit.*, p. 23.
70 Chomsky, N. (1988) *op. cit.*, p. 257.
71 Chomsky, N. (1993) *op. cit.*, p. 54.
72 Chomsky, N. in Otero, C. P. (ed.) (1988) *op. cit.*, p. 691. He also notes: 'You

don't put caricatures of blacks in the newspapers anymore; you do put caricatures of Arabs.'

73 Smith, A. D. (1971) *op. cit.*, p. 170.
74 Smith, A. D. (1971) *op. cit.*, p. 172.
75 Chomsky, N. (1992a) *op. cit.*, p. 96.
76 Chomsky, N. (1992a) *op. cit.*, pp. 273, 51 and 202 respectively.
77 Chomsky, N. and Herman, E. S. (1979c) *The Washington Connection and Third World Fascism*, Nottingham: Spokesman, p. 43; Chomsky, N. (1993) *op. cit.*, p. 120.
78 Lowy, M., 'Marxists and the National Question' in *New Left Review*, 96, April–May 1976, p. 82.
79 Smith, A. D. (1979) *op. cit.*, p. 192.
80 Hobsbawm, E. (1977) *op. cit.*, p. 8.
81 Zelinsky, W. (1988) *op. cit.*, p. 6.
82 Chomsky, N. (1988) *op. cit.*, p. 217.
83 Alter, P. (1988) *op. cit.*, p. 42.
84 Foley, M. (1991) *American Political Ideas: Traditions and Usages*, Manchester: Manchester University Press, p. 179.
85 Chomsky, N. in Wintonick, P. and Achbar, M. (eds) (1994) *Manufacturing Consent: Noam Chomsky and the Media*, Montreal: Black Rose Books, p. 92.
86 Zelinsky, W. (1988) *op. cit.*, p. 285.
87 Zelinsky, W. (1988) *op. cit.*, p. 15.
88 Zelinsky, W. (1988)(*op. cit.*, p. 285, n. 11.
89 See Reimer, N. (1967) *American Political Theory: The Democratic Experience*, vol. 1, New York: D. Van Nostrand.
90 Nye in Zelinsky, W. (1988) *op. cit.*, p. 18.
91 Foley, M. (1991) *op. cit.*, p. 186.
92 Smith, A. D. (1998) *op. cit.*
93 Smith, A. D. (1988) *op. cit.*, p. 155.
94 Smith, A. D. (1988) *op. cit.*, p. 177.
95 Alter, P., *op. cit.*, p. 40.

6 Politics and the media

The media is a key area in the political analysis of Noam Chomsky. The term 'media' here is used to refer to forms of mass communication. As Inglis argues, '[m]edia are the instruments of [the] strange, taken-for-granted transformation ... [that occurs when] we learn to ... match blobs of coloured pigment on canvas to our expectation of a landscape ... [or] see runic squiggles as letters making sounds'.[1] Many of the frameworks that inform Chomsky's interpretation of events are implicit within his more general critique of American foreign policy. This is not so of his view of the media. Here he and Edward Herman set out a systematic framework or theory, which they call the 'propaganda model'. They then proceed to test this model. However, despite Chomsky's explicit attempt to set out his theory in this area it is useful to place his framework within the wider context of his social and political thought.

This chapter does two things. First, the central theoretical traditions within media theory are set out. Then Chomsky's propaganda model is described. To complement this model other ideas of Chomsky's are drawn in. Second, Chomsky's theory is examined in the light of this large tradition of media theory. Apart from the social science discipline of international relations, media theory is the only social science discipline that makes any sort of regular reference to Chomsky's political thought. What is of interest is the way in which many media theorists use and interpret his work (largely incorrectly, I would argue).

Studies of the media can usually be divided into three general areas: analysis of the conditions of ownership and control; analysis of the nature of media content; and analysis of audience reception or the effects of the media. Approaches to these questions are, on the whole, polarised between those who employ a Marxist framework of analysis and those who employ a liberal pluralist perspective. Within both perspectives are tensions between those who regard the media as an instrument or tool of some group or individual, for example the owner/s, or perhaps the editor, and those who regard the media as a structured institution within the wider structure of society. Here individuals within these institutions are agents whose actions are determined by these structures, for example the structure of ownership or patterns of consumption.

In looking at the general theoretical debates on the media, it is interesting to discern where Chomsky is positioned by those who attempt to draw together the enormous body of work in this area in order to place research within the various available frameworks and perspectives. There seems to be universal agreement among media theorists that Chomsky's work belongs within the instrumentalist Marxist tradition. This 'labelling' involves important implications for the assessment and usefulness of his work. In an attempt to unravel the debates, I shall consider whether Chomsky's label is appropriate.

It is usually argued that those who adopt a Marxist perspective focus their research on the questions of ownership and control, or content analysis. Conversely, those who adopt a liberal pluralist perspective favour research into audience reception and effects. As a result, criticism has been levelled at work in both traditions for failing to address the full picture. It is suggested that the focus of analysis leaves open implications about whichever part remains unresearched. In other words, the findings that Marxists make about ownership, control and content are said to imply certain characteristics about, among other things, the audience. By labelling Chomsky's work as instrumentalist Marxist, there is implicit criticism that his work is lacking in two respects: that it does not take sufficient account of structures; and that it fails to offer an analysis into audience reception and effects. It is probably for these reasons that there is little serious attempt to offer a more comprehensive analysis of his work. I shall be considering then not only whether Chomsky is appropriately described as an instrumentalist, therefore implying lack of structural analysis, but also whether he does indeed fail to offer an insight into the media's effects on its audiences.

Apart from questioning other interpretations of Chomsky's works, this chapter seeks therefore to elicit Chomsky's views on the media in terms of the three areas in which questions about the media are usually raised: ownership and control; content analysis; and audience and effects. In order to do this it is imperative to look at his work with Herman within the wider context of his ideas in social and political thought.

Media theory

How do we understand the role of the mass media in our society today? This question has exercised social and political theorists since the early days of newspaper production, but particularly since the rise of fascism.[2] Questions one might ask about the media and its place in our society can be said to fall into three areas. What implications, if any, are there to be drawn from the nature of media ownership and control? Can any conclusions be drawn from the form and content of the media? Lastly, what, if any, are the effects that media messages have on audiences and thus society more generally. Attempts to provide a theoretical framework within which to answer these questions have, largely speaking, fallen into two distinct and mutually exclusive positions.

In the literature that tracks the history of ideas contained within these two theoretical traditions, the two positions are usually labelled liberal pluralist and Marxist.[3] Broadly speaking the former position finds that media institutions, personnel working within the industry, and audiences, are largely autonomous. They are autonomous in the sense that their behaviour and decision-making patterns cannot be said to be determined systematically by, respectively, other institutions (e.g. the state), by 'bosses' or, in the case of audiences, by media messages. Such a framework implies certain characteristics about the nature of modern industrial society generally, namely that no one group in society can be said to be systematically dominant, that power is pluralistically distributed, and that people are capable of articulating and exercising their individual and group interests. One consequence of working within such a framework is that questions concerning the character of ownership have a reduced importance, since owners are only one of many interest groups in our pluralist society. Such conclusions are supported by evidence of the apparent (but perhaps relative) demise of the old press baron and the rise of the 'faceless' shareholder. Indeed as the many studies looking at editorial decision-making processes will bear witness, there is often tacit support for Burnham's 'managerial revolution thesis'.[4] Research within this tradition, then, has focused upon, for example, 'agenda setting' conventions or (and this has been particularly so of American work) research into audience reception/effects.[5]

By contrast Marxist work in the field has begun from the premise that media institutions work within and are subject to the constraints of the wider economic, political and social framework of capitalism. As this economic system significantly privileges a minority group, who might loosely be described as 'owners of the means of production', then it seems logical to conclude that the ideas and messages put out by media institutions operating within this system will avoid undermining these privileges. This is perhaps to put the argument too carefully, for many from this tradition have been more pointed in their interpretation of such messages, finding them positively supporting the status quo. To this end, then, theorists from this tradition have concerned themselves with two sorts of questions. On the one hand, there are matters of political economy. For example it is argued that the rise of the shareholder has not significantly altered structural relations between the powerful minority and the majority, even if the minority are less easy to identify.[6] And it has also been argued that the minority are not as 'faceless' as might at first be thought, indeed that there are significant individuals/families whose names repeatedly appear within the category of 'owner'.[7] On the other hand, there has also been considerable work done analysing media content, which claims to find demonstrable bias in favour of the status quo.[8] Just as the pluralist position is said to carry with it implicit assumptions about the nature of society, so too does the Marxist position. The implicit assumption behind such a framework is that audiences are an undifferentiated mass who unproblematically 'read' messages in the 'required' way. In other words, messages flow in one direction from top down, hence the oft-quoted analogy with a 'hypodermic needle'.

Within both traditions, there are varieties of nuance and differences of emphasis and there have been attempts within each perspective to address criticisms levelled from without. Within the pluralist tradition there has been a readiness to acknowledge certain structural constraints such as those placed upon a media institution and hence its managers by, for example, consumers. This position thus recognises limits to autonomy.[9] Marxist analysis has, however, sought to address the 'polysemic' nature of messages, seeking to identify the 'preferred meaning', but recognising that encoding and decoding are separate moments in discourse. Such work, taking its lead from Gramsci (1971) rejects the implicit analogy of audiences with sponges, finding instead that meanings are negotiated. Notions of bias are dropped in favour of terms like 'inferential structures'.[10]

Within both perspectives an important tension, already alluded to, concerns the extent to which practices, outcomes or events can be attributed to intentional action rather than structural constraint or vice versa. It is often around this question that commentators bring in the contributions of Chomsky, or rather, to be more precise, Herman and Chomsky, as an example of work in the Marxist tradition that is also instrumentalist. Golding and Murdock argue that: '[i]nstrumentalists focus on the ways that capitalists use their economic power with [sic] a commercial market system to ensure that the flow of public information is consonant with their interests. They see privately owned media as instruments of class domination'.[11] Instrumentalists are contrasted with structuralists who are said to be 'concerned with the ways the options open to allocative controllers are constrained and limited by the general economic and political environment in which the corporation operates'.[12] Golding and Murdock argue that the instrumentalist case is 'vigorously argued' for in Herman and Chomsky's *Manufacturing Consent*.

Ownership and control: the propaganda model

This is a good point at which to begin an analysis of Chomsky's contributions to this debate on the media's role in society. Before doing this, however, it is worth commenting upon the focus of *Manufacturing Consent*, given that Chomsky co-authored the book with Edward Herman. Being co-authored, the book cannot be taken as a pure representation of Chomsky's ideas. In the light of this, having set out the propaganda model, I shall attempt to tease out differences or similarities between Chomsky and Herman by looking at this work in the light of Chomsky's other writings that are not co-authored. In setting out the propaganda model I shall also consider Golding and Murdock's charge (or perhaps it is an attribution?) of instrumentalism.

As Chapter 1 has shown, Chomsky maintains that he does not have a political theory. 'Is there anything in the social sciences that even merits the term "theory"? That is, some explanatory system involving hidden structures with non-trivial principles that provide understanding of phenomena? If so, I've missed it.'[13] However, looking at his work with Herman on the media, in *Manufacturing Consent*, their 'propaganda model' certainly looks like some sort of theory, and one with strong structuralist elements at that. The 'propaganda model' suggests that there are five filters through which the 'raw material of news must pass' before an event is deemed newsworthy.[14] Three of these five filters are unquestionably structural in flavour; all suggesting that there can be tests of the model as a whole.

The first notes the necessary large investment required which precludes the majority from 'ownership of media with any substantial outreach'. In the case of the press, the application of the free market and the drive for profit led to an 'increased stress on reaching large audiences', and this, together with technological improvements, meant an increase in capital costs, which drove out the working-class press.[15] In other words such structural constraints preclude all but the wealthy from setting up in the media business. From the time of media entry into the market, processes of concentration and conglomeration mean 'the pressures of stockholders, directors, and bankers to focus on the bottom line are powerful'.[16] This also means that media institutions lose 'some of their limited autonomy to bankers, institutional investors, and large individual investors'.[17] The point is, then, that the 'media giants are ... brought into close relationships with the mainstream of the corporate community'[18] through directorships and outside investment in media stock. At this point Herman and Chomsky bring in the possibilities for instrumental action, when they argue that '[t]hese holdings, individually and collectively, do not convey control, but these large investors can make themselves heard, and their actions can affect the welfare of the companies and their managers'.[19] They go on to argue that '[a]nother structural relationship of importance is the media companies' dependence on and ties with the government'.[20] Note that they even use the term 'structural'. Here they are referring to the fact that the government grants franchises and licenses, and so presumably has the possibility of exerting pressure, of requiring companies to conform to regulations that bear some relation to the interests of the government.

The second filter identifies the media's dependence upon advertising as a source of revenue, which means that the advertisers' choices affect media prosperity and thus survival.

With the growth of advertising, papers that attracted ads could afford a copy price well below production costs. ... For this reason, an advertising-based system will tend to drive out of existence or into marginality the media companies and types that depend on revenue from sales alone. With advertising, the free market does not yield a neutral system in which final buyer choice decides.[21]

This has two effects. First, the lion's share of advertising revenue will tend to gravitate towards media forms attracting the affluent audience. Chomsky notes the sophisticated techniques media companies use in selling 'space' according to audience profile. In other words, at the extreme, little support could be found from advertisers for television programmes attracting audiences without buying power. In the case of the British press, Raymond Williams has noted the sharp polarisation that has occurred since the introduction of advertising between the tabloid and broadsheet press, so that there are no longer any national newspapers of what he calls the 'old "middle" weight' type. Furthermore, despite the fact that 'society ... has been becoming significantly better educated and informed', the popular press has 'moved back towards older cultural styles' using '[a]ll the devices of sensational simplification and spurious personalisation'.[22]

So '[w]orking-class and radical media ... suffer from the political discrimination of advertisers. Political discrimination is *structured* into advertising allocations by the stress on people with money to buy. But many firms will always refuse to patronize ... those whom they perceive as damaging their interests'[23] (my emphasis). Again, as with the first filter, this is clearly a structural claim. Nevertheless, as with the first filter, Herman and Chomsky inject intentionality into the structural framework, and this point constitutes the second effect: that advertisers have the possibility of withdrawing their patronage from 'unfriendly media institutions'.[24]

The third filter in the 'propaganda model' concerns the media's requirement for a regular and credible supply of stories to meet news schedules, which leads them to rely heavily upon the government and business corporations. Economic criteria are highly influential here:

> They cannot afford to have reporters and cameras at all places where important stories may break. Economics dictates that they concentrate their resources where significant news often occurs, where important rumours and leaks abound, and where regular press conferences are held.[25]

This makes governments and corporations obvious choices for attention. Such sourcing satisfies two media institutional needs, first that government and corporate sources are deemed credible, allowing the media to maintain an air of objectivity, and secondly that this in turn reduces the need for costly investigative checking for credibility.

Again, such economic criteria are structural. However, Herman and Chomsky are not satisfied to leave the argument at a purely structural level. The relationship between the media and the government and business they argue is 'symbiotic', and they go on to document the size and sophistication of the various public relations operations within government departments and corporate businesses that seek to have their interpretation of events and agendas publicised. 'In effect, the large bureaucracies of the powerful *subsidize* the mass media, and gain special access by their contribution to reducing the media's costs of acquiring the raw materials of, and producing, news' (original emphasis).[26]

As indicated above, while the last two filters are less obviously purely structural in character, they clearly have structural elements to them.

The fourth filter Herman and Chomsky identify is 'flak and the enforcers'. This refers to the ability and substantial resources that government and big business have to mobilise complaints and pressure which 'can be both uncomfortable and costly to the media'. As they argue, '[i]f certain kinds of fact, position, or program are thought likely to elicit flak, this prospect can be a deterrent'.[27] Herman and Chomsky go on to document the various bodies in the United States that are mainly funded by large corporations which seek to redress a perceived liberal bias in the media. The possibility of doing this 'reflects the power of the sponsors'.[28]

Herman and Chomsky call the last filter the 'ideology of anticommunism'. This refers to the tendency (which is due to the first three structural filters) for the media to interpret any policies at home and abroad which threaten property interests, but particularly American property interests, as 'communist' or 'pro-communist' and therefore as representing a threat. As they show, however, the concept of communism is 'fuzzy' and can refer to anything from countries that seek an independent nationalist development path, to policies that promote some kind of land or property distribution. The term becomes an emotive, catch-all phrase to refer to anyone not committed to the economic and power distribution of the status quo. As such 'issues tend to be framed in terms of a dichotomized world of Communist and anti-Communist powers, with gains and losses allocated to contesting sides, and rooting for "our side" considered an entirely legitimate news practice'.[29] Since their work on *Manufacturing Consent*, Chomsky has noted the quest for some new threat to replace the 'Communist threat' now that the Soviet Union has collapsed.[30] Drug wars (Noriega) and totalitarian monsters (Hussein) have proved useful alternatives, but are ultimately less effective than the threat of the 'evil empire'. The fall of that empire may have brought about changes in the terminology and the targets, but the point remains that alternative views are demonised. These last two filters are clearly more instrumental than structural.

These findings could suggest one of two things. They could suggest that the blanket charge of instrumentalism be misplaced. Certainly in terms of the ideas contained within *Manufacturing Consent*, it is inappropriate to label them instrumentalist and therefore not structural. In 1980 Murdock argued that the dichotomy between instrumentalism and structuralism is a false dichotomy, and that for an analysis to be effective it ought to incorporate both. It seems that in his later work with Golding, when he finds *Manufacturing Consent* to be instrumentalist, Murdock fails to see that Chomsky and Herman do indeed 'look at the complex interplay *between* intentional action and structural constraint' (original emphasis).[31] Indeed, Herman and Chomsky baldly state that to 'see the pattern of manipulation and systematic bias' . . . 'requires a macro, alongside a micro- (story-by-story), view of media operations'.[32]

Alternatively, such findings could suggest that the instrumentalist elements of the propaganda model are peculiar to *Manufacturing Consent*, and are not therefore characteristic of Chomsky's work generally (in which case the charge of instrumentalism would be more appropriately directed at Herman and Chomsky, not Chomsky). If we look at the rest of Chomsky's writing, we do indeed find that setting out the 'propaganda model' as a framework with which to understand the workings of the media is unique. Nowhere else does he explicitly formulate a framework or theory, with which to make sense of events.[33] The clues to the framework with which he works lie scattered about within his empirical observations. This seems to suggest that perhaps the charge of instrumentalism is appropriate to Chomsky's work, but the same cannot be said of his work with Herman. Certainly Milan Rai seems to think that he can detect 'an interesting difference of emphasis between the two Propaganda Model theorists': 'Herman, as befits an economist, stresses the corporate power of the media enterprises and the mergers and other forms of economic concentration which have enhanced monopoly or oligopoly power.' In other words, Herman focuses on the structural aspects, whereas: 'Chomsky, in contrast, tends to emphasize the individual surrender of each intellectual to the dominant ideology.'[34] This point made by Rai is extremely persuasive. Chomsky does argue that '[a]cting as indi- viduals, most people are not gangsters. Matters are often different *when they subordinate themselves* to institutional structures of various sorts' (my emphasis).[35] Unlike other researchers into the media, who may simply refer to 'the journalist' Chomsky always names individuals. However, Rai is also correct to employ the term 'emphasize'. Although Chomsky's work does not set aside special and discrete space to developing struc- tural models with which to make sense of events, as previous chapters have attempted to establish, it cannot therefore be concluded that such structural aspects are absent from his work.

Structuralism in Chomsky

It has been established that the propaganda model does place consider- able emphasis upon structural features at work within the production of media output. But this is not just peculiar to Chomsky's work with Herman. Chomsky's analysis of the Cold War, for example, is unremittingly informed by underlying structural considerations. As we shall see, his content analysis of the media shows that it is the intellectuals and the media that fail to draw upon these structural considerations. Chomsky has argued that the conventional explanation of the Cold War, both within the media and amongst intellectuals, is in terms of a superpower conflict. There are variations, but essentially the argument suggests that there are two superpowers, one, essentially totalitarian in structure, is aggressive and expansionist, while the other is democratic, seeking to safeguard democratic tolerance in the world and therefore acting defensively. An alternative explanation, according to Chomsky, requires reference to the facts, for it is his contention that 'the facts are irrelevant' to the conventional view.[36] However, as Chomsky himself contends '[a]n understanding of the Cold War era requires an account not only of the actual events, but also of the factors that lie behind them'.[37] Here he is arguing that 'if you want to understand foreign policy you begin by looking at domestic structures', and that it is important to look at the historical record.[38] Again we see Chomsky referring to structures. To this end he seeks to establish 'how far policy was determined by specific features of the Cold War era, and how far it merely adapted persistent institutional demands to new conditions'.[39] He finds a high degree of continuity between pre- and post-Cold War, as well as during, which suggests that it is the 'persistent institutional demands' that are dominating. In light of this he questions the thesis that the Cold War is now over, given the collapse of the Soviet Union. To paint the picture simplistically, when he refers to the 'domestic structures', in the case of American society, he is referring to a society which is polarised between the rich and the poor. The rich control the production process, and in seeking to maintain their economic and political power build up a formidable military might, which has intimate links with other aspects of industrial production. Chomsky refers to this using Eisenhower's description of the 'military-industrial complex'.[40] The elite seek to extract taxes from the population, in order to subsidise the process and as a way of stimulating demand in the economy. The system amounts to military Keynesianism, which Chomsky translates to mean public subsidy to underwrite private profit. The taxpayer pays for costly technological research and development, and then when there is profit to be made, the private sector steps in. Further, for private companies producing military equipment, the state is able to provide a guaranteed market. In order for the public to support this system they need to be led to believe that they have a fearful enemy. As he argues:

> it is not an easy matter to sell to the general public a domestic program based on impoverishing a large part of the population for the benefit of the wealthy, destroying the environment, eliminating health and

safety standards, and subsidizing the production of high-technology waste. There is a classic means of achieving this end: heightening international tensions and creating a war scare.[41]

Chomsky is at pains to point out that this system of 'national security ideology for population control (to borrow some counter-insurgency jargon)' was equally useful for the Soviet Union.[42] 'The rulers of the Soviet Union march along a parallel path'.[43] Meanwhile, for the United States, apart from the enemy at home, the real enemy has been any country (although typically it has been the so-called third world) which attempts an independent course of development.[44] In other words the real threat is the threat of nationalism.[45] This fear of nationalism is due to America's concern to protect its access to cheap labour and resources,[46] while at the same time precluding others from gaining access.[47] It is also concerned to avoid the 'threat of a good example'[48] which rivals capitalism in its struggle to win and maintain the 'hearts and minds' of the people. In all these senses, of course, the Soviet Union was in conflict with America, but the conflict also served as a convenient front.[49]

> In crucial respects, then, the Cold War was a kind of tacit arrange-ment between the Soviet Union and the United States under which the US conducted its wars against the Third World and controlled its allies in Europe, while the Soviet rulers kept an iron grip on their own internal empire and their satellites in Eastern Europe – each side using the other to justify repression and violence in its own domains.[50]

It is for structural reasons, then, that Chomsky is sceptical about heralding the end of the Cold War (or its beginning for that matter), because what remains are 'the guiding geopolitical conceptions, which are essentially invariant, since they are rooted in the unchanging institutional structure of ownership and domination in our own society'.[51]

As can be seen from this example, Chomsky employs structural analysis alongside the more apparent focus upon intentional action. His work demonstrates that the two are not incompatible. Those that claim his work is instrumentalist intend this as a criticism, implying a failure to use a structuralist approach. A close reading of his work suggests not only that the claim is inappropriate, but also that Chomsky himself would not accept the pejorative implications usually associated with the term 'instru-mentalism'.

The crucial point about Chomsky's analysis, however, is his recogni-tion that structures exist only because certain powerful people intentionally uphold them. 'These are not laws of nature, and we need not merely watch as events unfold in their inexorable progression. Human decisions are made within human institutions; alternatives exist and can be pursued.'[52] As an alternative to instrumentalism, structuralism is usually taken to imply that people's actions are determined unintentionally by social structures. This suggests immutability. As Golding and Murdock argue, some 'forms of structuralism ... conceive of structures as building-like edifices, solid, permanent and immovable'.[53] It is curious that 'instrumentalism' is used pejoratively because people do intentionally act through institutions, although it is also true that institutional or social structures do limit the ranges of alternative actions and make some possibilities more difficult, and therefore less likely, than others. As we've seen, Chomsky accept this dialectical relationship when he argues that: '[a]cting as individuals, most people are not gangsters. Matters are often different when they subordinate themselves to institutional structures of various sorts, such as corporations or the national state.'[54] Nevertheless his work implies that the room for manoeuvre for those at the top is much greater than for those at lower levels. Chomsky is absolutely clear about the levels of intentionality among the powerful and is unceasing in his documentation of this, together with its consequences. It is plausible to argue that he places the emphasis here (and it is an emphasis) for strong political and scientific reasons.

The responsibility of intellectuals

This point relates to a piece of Chomsky's early writing, 'The Responsibility of Intellectuals'.[55] Here he argues that '[i]t is the responsibility of intellectuals to speak the truth and to expose lies', and he seems to include journalists as well as academics within the term 'intellectuals'.[56] He adds that they should do this in the hope that by so doing the liar will be forced to reconsider his or her action. His choice of emphasis then is determined by its moral value, 'where the moral value of an action is judged in terms of its human consequences'.[57] So, for example, when asked why he focuses on and gives priority in his political writings to US foreign policy, Chomsky gives three reasons. First:

> I find it in general horrifying, and that I think that it is possible for me to do something to modify it, at least to mitigate some of its most dangerous and destructive aspects. In the concrete circumstances of my own society, where I live and work, there are various ways to do this: speaking, writing, organising, demonstrating, resisting, and others.[58]

Second:

> In part it reflects a judgement as to relative importance: the impact of US foreign policy on millions of people throughout the world is enormous, and furthermore these policies substantially increase the probability of superpower conflict and global catastrophe.[59]

And third that:

> In part, it reflects my feeling that while many people here do excellent and important work concerning crucial domestic issues, very few concerned themselves in the same way and with the same depth of commitment to foreign policy issues.[60]

The point is that while important structural elements are present in Chomsky's work, for him the more important emphasis is to focus upon the way in which such structures facilitate, encourage and therefore tend to produce intentional action, intentional action which can have crucial consequences. For many this constitutes the rising spectre of 'conspiracy theory'. But as Herman and Chomsky argue in their preface to *Manufacturing Consent* '[w]e do not use any kind of "conspiracy" hypothesis to explain mass-media performance. In fact, our treatment is much closer to a "free market" analysis, with the results largely an outcome of the workings of market forces'; market forces which, nevertheless, allow and encourage a 'guided market system'.[61] However, lengthy analysis of the various structural conjunctures that are possible at any particular historical point in time merely raises the debate to a level of abstraction that is of 'monstrous irrelevance' given the ongoing character (despite the variety of structural possibilities) and nature of inequality experienced by so many.[62]

Chomsky's content analysis

Having established that there seems to be only a marginal difference of emphasis between Herman and Chomsky, *Manufacturing Consent* can serve as an appropriate source for establishing Chomsky's views on the subject of the media.

The propaganda model is concerned with setting out the character of ownership and control of the media within capitalist society. Herman and Chomsky, and Chomsky in his other work, then set out to test the model, using the hypothesis that the character of ownership does influence media content. Indeed, Chomsky finds the media regularly guilty of bias in the failure to highlight contradictions in rhetoric. Unlike most other analysts of media content, Chomsky focuses his attention on the coverage of foreign affairs, and in particular the treatment of such coverage by newspaper journalists. His analysis covers both the quantitative and qualitative character of reporting. Having said this he does confine his analysis to what might be described as the more easily empirically verifiable aspects of media choices such as their agenda-setting role, the frames of reference used and the language employed. In other words, unlike the Glasgow Media Group, he does not get involved in any sort of semiotic analysis of picture content.[63] Their emphasis however, in part, reflects the fact that the Glasgow Media Group use television coverage, in which significant aspects of the storyline are conveyed through film footage. Newspapers use photographs, but they are less central to conveying meaning. It is a choice, however, that also seems to reflect the desire of a committed 'scientist' to make his work strictly verifiable. As picture content relies heavily upon connotation rather than denotation, this stricture cannot be met.

The bias Chomsky identifies is that 'the media serve the interests of state and corporate power, that are closely interlinked, framing their reporting and analysis in a manner supportive of established privilege and limiting debate and discussion accordingly'.[64] This sort of argument usually elicits some of the familiar objections addressed in Chapter 3. How can the media be said to serve interests that are often conflictual? Implicit in such a criticism is the view that Chomsky's contention presents interests as monolithic. This is certainly the form that Harrison's critique of the Glasgow Media Group's work takes.[65] And Schudson, for example, argues '[it is] a problem ... to understand why, if the large corporations and the media work hand-in-glove, the corporations in the early 1970s should have been so vehemently and sincerely aghast at media coverage of politics, the environment, and business'.[66] However, it is certainly an over-simplification of Chomsky's position to suggest that media/corporate/state interests are homogenous. Because Chomsky is far from content to leave his argument at the level of abstraction, but rather concentrates upon empirically verifying the 'propaganda model', careful reading in conjunction with such generalised contentions (as quoted at the beginning of this paragraph), provide an infinitely more nuanced position. It is Chomsky's contention that the business sector is hierarchically structured in terms of size and respective power. The most powerful sectors recognise the state's general utility in terms of its necessary role in aiding the processes of private accumulation.[67] Such aid includes the costly business of research and development into new technology, maintaining general law and order at home and protecting or enhancing foreign investment. The government's viability rests upon its ability to provide such aid, while at the same time presenting itself as representing the general national interest. The government (as distinct from the state), the personnel within the state, and corporate elites, however, can and do disagree about the best policy to achieve these aims. Here is where the conflict can and does arise. The recognition of such potential for differences in opinion in no way conflicts with the contention that none of these players question the utility of state involvement in general or the principle of private accumulation.

Like everything else under state capitalism, the media are also hierarchically structured. Chomsky's charge of bias is principally directed at what he calls the 'elite media'. This is because they have the largest circulation, so the potential of impact is large, they are also agenda setters for the smaller outlets, and because the elite media become part of the historical record. In other words their interpretation becomes history. As we have seen above in the five filters of the 'propaganda model', Chomsky argues that the media has strong personnel and structural links with the state and corporate sectors. '[T]he political class and the cultural managers typically associate themselves with the sectors that dominate the private economy; they are either drawn directly from those sectors or expect to join them.'[68] Such association, together with the knowledge of possible sanctions (filters three and four), mean that the media are unlikely to question the underlying assumption regarding the utility of the state and the private accumulation process. But, as Chomsky wants to emphasise, this does not mean they cannot.

The question though is how can this view of the media be reconciled with the view that the media are 'too liberal' and 'cantankerous'? Indeed, as Chomsky notes, the American media are often portrayed as having too much irresponsible power – power that they are said to wield with significant outcomes. In the case of the Vietnam war, for example, the media are said to have turned the American public against the war, leading to America's defeat; or, in the case of Watergate, they are said to have brought the downfall of Nixon. Both these cases are held up as examples that serve to refute the proposition that the media can be said to be in any way subservient to state-corporate interests.[69] On the contrary, however, Chomsky argues that '[t]he spectrum of discussion reflects what a propaganda model would predict: condemnation of "liberal bias" and defence against this charge, but no recognition of the possibility that "liberal bias" might simply be an expression of one variant of the narrow state-corporate ideology – as, demonstrably, it is'.[70] In the case of Vietnam, Chomsky argues, the media wholly accepted the view that American intervention constituted defence against Communist aggression. Nowhere in the American media is it admitted that America attacked Vietnam. Nor is there any question that America had the right to intervene, although in time some concede that its intentions were misguided. As it became plain that the Americans were not going to get a quick victory, opposition mounted. However, among the Doves, both in government and the media, opposition to the war was couched purely in terms of the ineffectiveness of American intervention and the growing costs, both economically and in terms of American body bags.[71] In the case of Watergate, the media displayed much outrage when the Nixon administration was found to have broken into the Democratic Party headquarters. But Chomsky argues there was no outrage 'over the far more serious crimes of the Nixon and earlier administrations, exposed at exactly the same time, including the use of the national political police to undermine the Socialist Workers Party by repeated burglaries and other illegal acts from the early 1960s'.[72] As he suggests, the media obviously recognised '[t]he Democratic Party represents domestic power, the Socialist Workers Party – a legal political party – does not'.[73]

The media, then, do become adversarial, but only when certain sectors of the elite make their power too transparent. Periodically the media are threatened with some form of regulation, but as Chomsky points out all this serves the useful purpose of maintaining the image that the media do function as a 'fourth estate'. The cry comes up that the press must remain free from the state to protect democracy, and most accept that this is a laudable objective. Chomsky argues that no one raises the possibility that they also be set free from private power. So not only do the media keep the discussion within tight bounds, they also do not themselves raise the possibility that they are not adversarial. The accusation of bias bears 'the implicit message: thus far, and no further'.[74] In other words it delimits the 'bounds of the expressible'.[75]

One method Chomsky employs to test his 'propaganda model' is to use 'systematically selected examples that are as closely paired as history allows'.[76] For example he looks at the media's treatment of Cambodia under Pol Pot and compares it to the coverage (or lack of coverage) of East Timor. Chomsky's research directly calls into question the findings of those media researchers who, by watching journalists at work in setting the agenda, attempt to identify the *general* 'codes and conventions' employed in the 'gate keeping' role. Galtung and Ruge argue that a key decision, for example, about whether an event is worthy for selection or not is whether it can be offered as perceptually intelligible to the audience. In other words consideration is given to whether an event is interpretable within the cultural framework of the receiver.[77] On these grounds it might be claimed that East Timor did not fit the convention of perceptual intelligibility, thereby explaining the paucity of coverage. Chomsky would find such a claim highly questionable. His works leads to a thorough questioning of the hypothesis that journalists do work to such general codes and conventions. In contrast to the findings of Galtung and Ruge his contention is that 'the US mass media's practical definitions of worth are political in the extreme'.[78]

Chomsky's alternative contention is that 'the US business community has been warm toward regimes that profess fervent anti-communism, encourage foreign investment, repress unions, and loyally support US foreign policy'.[79] In other words, such countries can be fairly easily identified as being friends or foe.[80] Those that are victims of regimes that are identified as foe become worthy victims, whereas the victims of friends are seen as unworthy. Chomsky compares the treatment in the media of the Polish priest Jerzy Popieluszko, who was murdered by the Polish police in October 1984, with that of one hundred religious workers who were murdered, with strong evidence of official involvement, in different areas of Latin America between 1980 and 1985. It needs to be born in mind that Popieluszko was murdered by what was at the time an 'enemy state', in the sense that Poland was said to be communist. Chomsky finds that the relative coverage in terms of number of articles/news items, column inches, front pages and editorials for Popieluszko far outweighs the number of articles etc. for *all* the Latin American victims put together. He also finds that the coverage of the religious workers in Latin America 'displayed considerably less outrage and passion than that of Popieluszko'.[81] Rather, Chomsky argues, coverage 'was low-keyed, designed to keep the lid on emotions and evoking regretful and philosophical generalities on the omnipresence of violence and the inherent tragedy of human life'.[82] This is despite the fact that seven of the victims were themselves American citizens and four of these were women who were raped before being murdered. The one hundred also included the murder of Archbishop Oscar Romero. It is difficult to see how any one of these victims, but particularly the eight just mentioned, would not have satisfied journalistic criteria for newsworthiness, and particularly the criteria for cultural relevance. As Chomsky says '[t]he drama is there for the asking – only the press concern is missing'.[83] This case is not an isolated one.

Galtung and Ruge do concede that the 'codes and conventions' employed by journalists have a distorting effect on the character of news production. In particular they note that there is a tendency for news to be centred on elite nations and elite people. They go on to point out that this preference means that where possible events will be presented as the actions of particular people. This they argue means that there is a tendency not to present events as the outcome of 'social forces'. This is compounded in their view with a preference for events that unfold and acquire meaning quickly so that they are easily accessible to the audience, rather than events that take place over a long period of time. The latter they argue are unlikely to get recorded until a dramatic climax is reached. This tendency is strengthened, they suggest, by the nature of the medium (particularly television with its reliance on the sound bite). In other words the medium itself is partly responsible for an inability to deal with historical and social processes.[84]

Chomsky regularly comments not only that 'the study of institutions and how they function' is absent in news reports, but also that they 'must be scrupulously ignored'.[85] It is likely that he would find rather patronising the journalistic convention that prefers quickly unfolding events because it is thought that this aids the audience. He is noted for commenting in an interview with James Peck

[w]hen I'm driving, I sometimes turn on the radio and I find very often that what I'm listening to is a discussion of sports. These are telephone conversations. People call in and have long and intricate discussion, and its plain that quite a high degree of thought and analysis is going into that. People know a tremendous amount. They know all sorts of complicated details and enter into far-reaching discussion about whether the coach made the right decision yesterday and so on. These are ordinary people, not professionals, who are applying

their intelligence and analytic skills in these areas and accumulating quite a lot of knowledge and, for all I know understanding.[86]

He goes on to argue, 'I don't think that international affairs are harder', it is just that people are not given enough information which is easily accessible.[87] This last point about accessibility is important, because Chomsky's critics are keen to come up with occasions when newspapers can be found to say something challenging. But his point is not that such insights never appear, because as he argues '[a] diligent search through all the media would unearth an occasional exception to [the] pattern, but such exceptions are rare'.[88] Such exceptions are no good if they are isolated cases, or an obscure point buried in column seven of an article. Quantity of information is all important. To this end Chomsky counts column inches, and notes where within the newspaper or news bulletin an issue is raised. Governments are well aware 'that one of the best means of controlling news was flooding news channels with "facts", or what amounted to official information', to push things off the agenda or at least down it.[89] In this way '[b]y dint of endless repetition . . . the required doctrine . . . become[s] established truth'.[90] Harrison argues that the Glasgow Media Group's use of the term 'rare' or 'unusual' to draw attention to the frequency with which issues are raised is unacceptable because neither term is scientifically quantifiable. This however sounds as though he is suggesting that human behaviour must have the same degree of predictability as phenomena in the natural world, for the study of human behaviour to be regarded as scientific. Of course Chomsky would object to the study of human behaviour being called a science. But even if one were not to accept this claim, 'rarity' can have a social statistical basis.

Not only can it be demonstrated that the media do place enormous emphasis on certain issues, and very little on others, while at the same time using emotive language for some cases and not for others. Chomsky also argues that a cruder method of 'thought control' can be identified, namely the use of Orwellian newspeak, whereby 'language is abused, tortured, distorted, in a way, to enforce ideological goals'.[91] To illustrate this he gives the example of when, in 1947, the Pentagon stopped being the War Department and became the Defence Department. Others like 'the free world' and 'the national interest' are

designed, often very consciously, in order to try to block thought and understanding. For example, about the 1940s there was a decision, probably a conscious decision, made in public-relations circles to introduce terms like 'free enterprise' 'free world' and so on instead of the conventional descriptive terms like 'capitalism'. Part of the reason was to insinuate somehow that the systems of control and domination and aggression to which those with power were committed were in fact a kind of freedom. That's just vulgar propaganda exercises.[92]

It is also possible to see that since the collapse of the Soviet Union it has become common to refer to the west as having 'market economies', since it is reckoned that market distribution is better than state distribution.

It is Chomsky's contention that the combination of the endless repetition of certain views, together with the 'fostering [of] lively debate' strictly 'within the permitted bounds', as well as the use of questionable terminology, makes for an extremely 'well-functioning system of propaganda' which ensures that '[t]o escape [its] impact ... is remarkably difficult'.[93] This question of the media's effect is something to which I will return.

Chomsky's bias?

Before moving on from the methodology and form of Chomsky's content analysis, it is worth considering another common criticism that is made of his approach. Chomsky's criticism of the nature of the media's coverage of 'enemy states' is often taken as some sort of defence of the actions of those states. This criticism suggests to me that the critic has not properly read Chomsky's work, for Chomsky is always careful to point out his condemnation too. For example regarding the media's treatment of the Popieluszko case, he argues, '[t]he act was vicious and deserved the presentation it received'.[94] However, his interest is not in a lengthy repetition of such condemnation, but rather to look at the relative treatment of other equally objectionable, possibly worse actions, which in his view deserve equal or even greater publicity or condemnation. Some of Chomsky's critics come from the 'left'. Indeed, in his view a significant achievement of the propaganda system has been its ability to keep the left divided and on the defensive. He notes that 'western propaganda' was quick in 'identifying the dismantling of socialist forms as the establishment of socialism, so as to undermine left-libertarian ideals by associating them with the practices of the grim Red bureaucracy'.[95]

In 1979 Chomsky and Herman published *After the Cataclysm*. The book looks at 'the facts about postwar IndoChina insofar as they can be ascertained, but a major emphasis will be on the ways in which these facts have been interpreted, filtered, distorted or modified by the ideological institutions of the West'.[96] One chapter is devoted to Cambodia where they argue 'there is no difficulty in documenting major atrocities and oppression, primarily from the reports of refugees'.[97] They offer a lengthy discussion on the difficulties of ascertaining the credibility of reports generally, but particularly of refugee reports, and recommend caution. They then go on to argue that in fact their concern is less with the facts about events in Cambodia, and more to do with the lack of evidence provided to support 'the standard media picture: a centrally-controlled genocidal policy of mass execution'.[98] This is because

[w]hen the facts are in, it may turn out that the more extreme condem-
nations were in fact correct. But even if that turns out to be the case,
it will in no way alter the conclusions we have reached on the central
question addressed here: how the available facts were selected, modified, or sometimes invented to create a certain image offered to the
general population.[99]

They also consider the complete lack of consideration given to those
who suggested an alternative from the original interpretation of events.
For example that many of the reported deaths were 'not the result of
systematic slaughter and starvation by the state but attributable in large
measure to peasant revenge, undisciplined military units out of government control',[100] as well as starvation and disease which were a direct
consequence of the 'legacy of colonialism and more specifically, the US
attack on a defenceless society, [and] the United States withhold[ing]
desperately needed aid'.[101] The media failed to admit that reports from
the region were mixed, and some reports suggested 'that there was a
significant degree of peasant support for the Khumer Rouge and the
measures that they had instituted in the countryside'.[102] Another telling
silence, again occurring at the same time, was the complete lack of media
indignation expressed for the American-backed Indonesian invasion and
'apparent massacre of something like one-sixth of the population of East
Timor'.[103]

A year after the publication of this book Steven Lukes, a figure of the
left, published an article entitled 'Chomsky's betrayal of truths'. Lukes
accuses Chomsky of 'contributing to deceit and distortion surrounding
Pol Pot's regime in Cambodia'. He asks 'what responsible person, let alone
intellectual can doubt that Cambodia between 1975 and 1978 suffered a
regime of terror, with mass killings, brutal forced labour, the systematic
elimination of cultural life, the extraction of confessions, and tortures and
atrocities of all kinds?'[104] But as Chomsky points out in an unpublished
reply to Lukes, he was not disputing this conclusion. In a sense, Chomsky's
conclusions on the evidence concerning Cambodia are irrelevant to the
point he is trying to make. As he and Herman state in their book 'we
have not developed or expressed our views here'.[105] The point being made
by Herman and Chomsky was the lack of evidence, and the selective use
of what evidence there was, to support claims concerning (a) the purported
numbers involved and (b) the causes. It is a point of logic that a true
conclusion may be reached through bad argument and inadequate
evidence.[106]

Chomsky on effects and audiences

This issue raises another, which brings us on to the last type of question
that is commonly raised in connection with the media: namely, what, if

any, effect can the media be said to have on its audience? Clearly Chomsky regards one effect of the endless repetition of certain interpretations of events to be that it becomes enormously difficult to get heard and be understood when questioning the established interpretation. In other words, one effect that the media has, given the nature of ownership and control, is that anything but complete patriotic support for one's own state gets translated into an apologia for another state's atrocities.

Chomsky's contention on this point is that the endless repetition of narrowly bounded debate has the effect of making the accessibility of views such as his extremely difficult. This conclusion is not hypothetically deduced. It is, as we have seen, based upon experience. In a 'free' society, his questions and questions like them get silenced or misunderstood and derided. As he states in an interview with Barsamian, when referring to his work in *The Washington Connection, After the Cataclysm* and *Fateful Triangle,* '[i]n England and Australia, again countries very much like us, these books are reviewed, discussed, etc. Not in the United States, however'.[107] Of course these countries have 'essentially the same values, institutions, social organizations, etc.' but the books can be reviewed in these other capitalist countries because they are 'primarily concerned with American policy'.[108]

It was pointed out at the beginning of this chapter that Marxist perspectives on the media, which look at ownership structures and observe biased content, are accused by liberal pluralists of dealing with the effect on the audience of such media organisation by implication. The implication is that the audience simply absorbs media messages unproblematically.

Chomsky's views on the media's audience or the population at large are, like many of his ideas, more or less deeply embedded within his many works. His views are usually associated with the Marxist tradition, and by implication what is known as the 'mass society thesis'. The most influential theorist of this thesis is C. W. Mills in his work *The Power Elite*.[109] McQuail in reviewing this thesis argues that its central propositions put an emphasis on

> the interdependence of institutions that exercise power and thus the integration of the media into the sources of social power and authority. Content is likely to serve the interests of political and economic power-holders. The media cannot be expected to offer a critical or alternative definition of the world, and their tendency will be to assist in the accommodation of the dependent public to their fate.[110]

In other words the media are centralised and dominant, the public is an atomised mass, the direction of influence is from above and is one way – this view of things is described as pessimistic. By contrast the liberal pluralist perspective is said to view the audience as being 'fragmented', 'selective', 'reactive' and 'active'. Support for this view is provided by the many empirical studies that suggest audiences can be shown to come away with very different interpretations of what they have seen.[111]

Chomsky's views on the audience cannot be said to fit into either of these categories, for the simple reason that both these perspectives paradoxically view the individuals that make up 'the audience' as having the same degree of power as one another. In the 'mass society thesis' each individual within the audience as such has no power. The audience is a mass. In the pluralist thesis each individual within 'the audience' is deemed as such to have the power to be 'selective', 'reactive' and 'active'. Chomsky by contrast employs a type of class analysis and for him an individual's ability to be 'selective', 'reactive' and 'active' depends upon their class position. But what does it mean for individuals to be 'selective', 'reactive' and 'active'? To establish that they are does not tell us very much about the relationship between the audience and the media. The question that ought to be asked is to what extent is a member or group from the audience able to get their 'selections' and 'reactions' accepted. Stuart Hall, in his earlier work with the Birmingham Institute of Cultural Studies, recognised the problems that the findings of audience research pose for the 'mass society thesis'. Accordingly he argued that media texts could not be regarded as 'transparent'. He argued instead that the 'encoding' and 'decoding' of messages were both different moments of production. There is then a lack of equivalence between the two sides of the communicative exchange and this is how 'misunderstandings' or different readings arise. Nevertheless, in this asymmetry between the codes of the 'source' and the codes of the 'receiver', the former has the privilege of offering preferred meanings. But this still does not tell us anything about the ability of an individual or group to get their preferred meaning accepted. It simply suggests that there is the possibility for this to occur.[112]

It is Chomsky's view that what might be called 'the audience' includes the advertisers. The advertisers are the buyers of audiences and are the media's most valued customers. As we've seen, he argues that advertisers have the power to distribute 'flak and enforcement'. He also documents the many occasions when they exert this force, mainly through funding for various pressure groups, but also sometimes more directly.[113] This segment of the audience then has the opportunity to preclude certain messages from being encoded. As he states, 'it would hardly come as a surprise if the picture of the world they present were to reflect the perspectives and interests of the sellers, buyers and the product'.[114]

Then there are what he often refers to as the 'bewildered herd' or 'rabble'. He uses these terms with irony. In their non-ironical sense they express the view that elites have (sometimes explicitly) of the rest of the population.[115] It is this group of 'unimportant people', sometimes referred to by elites as 'special interests'' – meaning, women, black people, working people generally (in other words, non-corporate interests, posing as representatives of the 'national interest', but three-quarters of the population nevertheless) who must be kept in line. It is this group from whom consent must be engineered.[116] However, it is his view that this group is selective and reactive and can be shown to have views on issues that are different from those that the propaganda system seeks to spread. To this end Chomsky frequently makes reference to opinion polls and letters written to newspapers by the public. But it is the political system, which 'is essentially a one party system, what sometimes has been called the property party', that is successful in depoliticising people by removing channels for dissent.

> [This] is why you get these apparent paradoxes that polls, for example, reveal that the population is overwhelmingly pro-Reagan, while when people are asked: would the country be better-off or worse-off if Reagan's policies were enacted, about the same proportion say that the country would be worse-off. So you have a huge majority for Reagan and about an equivalent majority opposed to his policies. That is not unreasonable in a depoliticized society . . .[117]

However, the media can be found manipulating the results of opinion polls. Again with reference to the Reagan administration, Chomsky argues:

> The population overwhelmingly opposed the policies of his Administration, and even the Reagan voters in 1984, by about three to two, hoped that his legislative program would not be enacted. In the 1980 elections, 4 per cent of the electorate voted for Reagan because they regarded him as a 'real conservative'. In 1984, this dropped to 1 per cent. That is what is called 'a landslide victory for conservatism' in political rhetoric.[118]

It is his view that people are 'intelligent enough to understand that they are not voting the issues'.[119]

> State capitalist democracy has a certain tension with regard to the locus of power: in principle, the people rule, but effective power resides largely in private hands, with large-scale effects throughout the social order. One way to reduce the tension is to remove the public from the scene, except in form.[120]

The point is that this segment of the audience can be found to have views at variance with those of the corporate sector and the media but, unlike these sectors, they do not get the opportunity to have their views encoded.

This raises a question. If the propaganda system is not very effective, why does it have to be maintained? Chomsky seems to have two responses to this. First, he does think that there are occasions when the propaganda system has a short-term effect on the views of the public. Referring to Bush's so called drug war, he argues:

> The short-term impact was impressive. Shortly after the November 1988 elections, 34 per cent of the public had selected the budget deficit as 'George Bush's No. 1 priority once he takes office.' Three percent selected drugs as top priority, down from previous months. After the media blitz of September 1989, 'a remarkable 43% say that drugs are the nation's single most important issue,' the *Wall Street Journal* reports, with the budget deficit a distant second at 6 percent. ... The real world had hardly changed; its image had, as transmitted through the ideological institutions, reflecting the current needs of power.[121]

Also certain media campaigns are more effective than others:

> Part of the difficulty is that even the most efficient propaganda system is unable to maintain the proper attitudes among the population for long. The currently available devices have none of the lasting impact of appeal to the Soviet threat.[122]

The second explanation for the maintenance of the propaganda system is that it is actually 'educated elites who are the prime targets of propaganda'.[123] 'The dramatic difference between letters and professional commentary again illustrates the failure of the ideological offensive of the past years to reach beyond educated elites ...'[124] The reason for this, Chomsky argues, is

> [m]ost people are not liars. They can't tolerate too much cognitive dissonance. I don't want to deny that there are outright liars, just brazen propagandists. You can find them in journalism and in the academic professions as well. But I don't think that's the norm. The norm is obedience, adoption of uncritical attitudes, taking the easy path of self-deception.[125]

In other words: 'for the intellectual elite themselves, it's crucial that they believe it because, after all, they are the guardians of the faith. Except for a very rare person who's just an outright liar, it's hard to be a convincing exponent of the faith unless you've internalized it and come to believe it.'[126] It is Chomsky's view in fact that 'the intellectual elite is the most heavily indoctrinated sector'.[127]

In this sense intellectual elites are slightly different from those in the business community itself, whose interests are more directly served by the maintenance of the status quo. Chomsky argues that in fact: '[t]he

business community has demonstrated a high degree of class consciousness and an understanding of the importance of controlling what they
call "the public mind". The rise of the public relations industry is one
manifestation of this concern for "engineering of consent".'[128] Chomsky
also often quotes from corporate documents that are not designed for
public consumption, which again demonstrate this understanding. Nevertheless, even they will seek to justify their policies by reference to the
benefits of this course for others.

> The favored conception of development, for example, is commonly
> presented in terms of the alleged benefits to the indigenous popula-
> tion, not the interests of American investors and corporations or their
> local clients and associates. The belief that what you are doing is
> helpful to the peasants of north eastern Brazil doesn't harm your busi-
> ness operations, but just makes it psychologically easier to continue
> to act in your own interest.[129]

Like advertisers, if the correct line is not adhered to they can generate
'flak', and ensure that a more appropriate message is encoded.

In no sense then can Chomsky's views of the audience be described as
a view that sees the audience as an undifferentiated mass. His views are
much more nuanced. In general the media, by keeping the range of debate
narrow, encourage apathy and complacency. With a wider and more
searching debate of the real issues there could be, he believes, an 'improvement in the moral and intellectual climate'.[130] He argues '[t]here is reason
to believe that the substantial improvement in the general cultural and
moral levels set in motion in the 1960s continued to expand, imposing
conditions that any system of concentrated power must meet'.[131] Without
this wider debate however, the most powerful and damning effect that
the media can be said to have is that the fostered apathy allows governments to continue to get away with policies that are ruthless and
destructive.

> We regard it as wrong, indeed pathological, to steal food from a
> starving child. But we engage in such behavior on a massive scale
> without second thought when the act is disguised in terms of high
> policy: for example, when US power is employed to overthrow a
> moderate regime in Guatemala that is attempting to improve the lot
> of miserable peasants, replacing it by a successor devoted to export-
> oriented agriculture while tens of thousands starve and most of the
> work force labors under the conditions of semi-slavery (that is, those
> who survive the death squads run by the regimes placed and main-
> tained in power by the United States).[132]

The processes are complex:

... we have to try to understand our own societies. It is not a simple picture. In the United States we see, for example, the tiny Jesuit center Quest for Peace which, with no resources, was able to raise millions of dollars for hurricane relief in Nicaragua from people who have been able, somehow, to keep their independence of thought and their hold on simple moral values. On the other hand, we see the rigid fanaticism, wilful ignorance, and intellectual and moral corruption of the elite culture. We see a political system in which formal mechanisms function with little substance, while at the same time dissidence, activism, turbulence and informal politics have been on the rise and impose constraints on state violence that are by no means negligible.[133]

The media then do have an effect, but only on certain elite segments of the population. Lack of resistance to the status quo is less due to the media having a successful effect on the rest of the population, and more to do with the absence of channels for resistance.

Conclusion

It has been argued in this chapter that Chomsky's theory of the media is not merely instrumentalist. Like his analysis generally, he considers the crucial importance of the structural aspects in our society. However, these structures are not static or law-like. He clearly does want to emphasise agency and so to that extent his theory has an instrumentalist character that should not be obscured. It has become fashionable within the social sciences to 'bring the agent back in', and in particular society's 'victims'. This development is an attempt to move away from an analysis of society that sees the individual within society as a mere object, as a passive receiver of the messages of socialisation. Taken to its extreme, this shift can lead us up all sorts of relativistic blind alleys. More sophisticated attempts such as Paul Willis' *Learning to Labour* demonstrate that although, in the final analysis, the outcome of individual action may be functional to 'the system', the action itself, nevertheless, involved rational choice, given the institutional constraints.[134] Fiske's work which looks at the pleasures and attraction of quiz shows for many women would be another example.[135] This development is seen by many commentators to be progressive, especially if it avoids relativism.

It is accepted that it is important to avoid suggesting, in any analysis of society, that the 'oppressed' are mere unwitting victims. However, if one is going to do that it is only logical to also accept that one cannot treat the powerful as mere unwitting oppressors. Many social scientists seem resistant to this sort of conclusion. Chomsky's work has always focused upon the agents, but he has always located them within the structure of state capitalism. His prime line of attack is the elites, because in his view there is a fair degree of recognition amongst them that these structures facilitate their self-interest. However, running throughout his work, especially in the context of the media, he reminds us that the 'unimportant people' can and do make a difference. Nevertheless they are marginalised. Their marginalisation is not however an effect of the media, as has been argued by many media commentators. It is principally a lack of resources including a lack of institutional structures. Having said this it is his view that the media do encourage apathy and distraction.[136] But more importantly Chomsky wants to argue that the 'manufacture of consent' is important for reducing cognitive dissonance amongst the educated elite. Their repetitious debate within the safe confines of how best to manage state capitalism amounts to, he argues, censorship and a peddling of propaganda. This does not mean alternative views are not expressed in the media, as Chomsky shows they are, but the importance is the balance and emphasis. Chomsky seeks, among other things, to redress the balance for the historical record. He also hopes to encourage, support and give confidence to others who do, and others who may yet question the standard lines of debate, especially those good and honourable journalists that he recognises are already out there.[137] If more questions were asked, the moral support from the media that elites currently enjoy, may begin to crumble.

Notes

1 Inglis, F. (1990) *Media Theory: An Introduction*, Oxford: Basil Blackwell, p. 3.
2 A distinction can be made here between newspaper media, and the subsequent development of mass media. The latter is characterised by both a proliferation of media form, e.g. radio and latterly TV, as well as the conglomeration process typical of the Northcliff revolution which was facilitated by the introduction of advertising revenue and developments in technology. See Curran, J. and Seaton, J. (1981) *Power without Responsibility*, London: Fontana.
3 Inglis, F. (1990) *op. cit.*; Curran, J. and Seaton, J. (1981) *op. cit.*; McQuail, D. (1987) (2nd edn) *Mass Communication Theory: An Introduction*, London: Sage; Curran, J. and Gurevitch, M. (eds) (1991) *Mass Media and Society*, London: Edward Arnold.
4 Burnham, J. (1960) *The Managerial Revolution*, Bloomington, Indiana: Indiana University Press.
5 Schlesinger, P. (1980) *Putting Reality Together: The BBC and its News*, (revised edn), London: Sage. Seymour Ure, C. (1969) 'Editorial Policy Making in the Press' in *Government and Opposition* Autumn. Gans, H. J. (1979) *Deciding What's News*, New York: Pantheon. Blumler, J. G. and Katz, E. (eds) (1974) *The Uses of Mass Communications*, Beverly Hills, California and London: Sage. Curran, J. (1990) 'The New Revisionism in Mass Communication Research: A Reappraisal' in *European Journal of Communication*, vol. 5, pp. 135–64. Gurevitch, M. and Levy, M. 'Information and Meaning: Audience Explanation of Social Issues' in Robinson, J. P. and Levy, M. (eds) (1986) *The Main Source*, Beverly Hills, California: Sage. Katz, E. (1987) 'Communications Research since Lazarsfeld' in *Public Opinion Quarterly*, vol. 51: S25–S45.

6 Murdock, G. and Golding, P. 'Capitalism, Communication and Class Relations' in Curran, J., *et al.* (eds) (1977) *Mass Communication and Society*, London: Edward Arnold. Relatedly: Poulantzas, N. (1978) *State, Power, Socialism*, London: Verso; also the capital-logic school of analysis, see Jessop, B. (1990) *State Theory: Putting Capitalist States in their Place*, Cambridge: Polity Press.
7 Herman, E. S. and Chomsky, N. (1994) *Manufacturing Consent* (2nd edn), London: Vintage. Relatedly Miliband, R. (1969) *The State in Capitalist Society*, London: Weidenfeld and Nicolson.
8 Glasgow Media Group (1976) *Bad News*, London: Routledge and Kegan Paul; Glasgow Media Group (1980) *More Bad News*, London: Routledge and Kegan Paul; Glasgow Media Group (1985) *War and Peace News*, Milton Keynes: Open University Press.
9 Philo, G. (1987) 'Whose News?' *Media, Culture and Society*, 9 (4) pp. 397–406.
10 Hall, S. (ed.) (1984) *Culture, Media Language*, London: Hutchinson.
11 Golding, P. and Murdock, G. 'Culture, Communications, and Political Economy' in Curran, J. and Gurevitch, M. (1991) *op. cit.*, p. 18.
12 Murdock, G. 'Large Corportions and the Control of Communications Industries' in Gurevitch, M., *et al.* (eds) (1982) *Culture, Media and Society: An Open University Collection*, Oxford: Methuen.
13 Personal communication from Noam Chomsky, 21 February 1995. See also Chomsky, N. (1969) *American Power and the New Mandarins*, London: Penguin, p. 271.
14 Herman, E. S. and Chomsky, N. (1994) *op. cit.*, p. 2.
15 Herman, E. S. and Chomsky, N. (1994) *op. cit.*, p. 4.
16 Herman, E. S. and Chomsky, N. (1994) *op. cit.*, p. 5.
17 Herman, E. S. and Chomsky, N. (1994) *op. cit.*, p. 8.
18 Herman, E. S. and Chomsky, N. (1994) *op. cit.*, p. 11.
19 Herman, E. S. and Chomsky, N. (1994) *op. cit.*, p. 11.
20 Herman, E. S. and Chomsky, N. (1994) *op. cit.*, p.13.
21 Herman, E. S. and Chomsky, N. (1994) *op. cit.*, p. 14.
22 Raymond Williams 'The Press we Don't Deserve' in Curran, J. (ed.) (1978) *The British Press: A Manifesto*, London: Macmillan Press, p. 24.
23 Herman, E. S. and Chomsky, N. (1994) *op. cit.*, p. 16.
24 Herman, E. S. and Chomsky, N. (1994) *op. cit.*, p. 17.
25 Herman, E. S. and Chomsky, N. (1994) *op. cit.*, p. 18.
26 Herman, E. S. and Chomsky, N. (1994) *op. cit.*, p. 22.
27 Herman, E. S. and Chomsky, N. (1994) *op. cit.*, p. 26.
28 Herman, E. S. and Chomsky, N. (1994) *op. cit.*, p. 28.
29 Herman, E. S. and Chomsky, N. (1994) *op. cit.*, pp. 30–1.
30 Chomsky, N. (1992a) *Deterring Democracy*, London: Verso, p. 145.
31 Golding, P. and Murdock, G. 'Culture, Communications and Political Economy' in Curran, J. and Gurevitch, M. (eds) (1991) *Mass Media and Society*, London: Edward Arnold, p. 48.
32 Herman, E. S. and Chomsky, N. (1994) *op. cit.*, p. 2.
33 Chomsky does refer to and employ the propaganda model independently of Herman in Chomsky, N. (1989) *Necessary Illusions*, London: Pluto Press.
34 Milan, R. (1995) *Chomsky's Politics*, London: Verso, p. 174, n. 44.
35 Chomsky, N. in Otero, C. P. (ed.) (1988) *Noam Chomsky: Language and Politics*, Montreal: Black Rose Books, p. 303.
36 Chomsky, N. (1992a) *op. cit.*, p. 19.
37 Chomsky, N. (1992a) *op. cit.*, p. 20.

38 Chomsky, N. in Otero, C. P. (ed.) (1981) *Noam Chomsky: Radical Priorities*, Montreal: Black Rose Books, p. 103.
39 Chomsky, N. (1992a) *op. cit.*, p. 20.
40 Chomsky, N. (1992a) *op. cit.*, p. 21.
41 Chomsky, N. (1982) *Towards a New Cold War*, New York: Pantheon.
42 Chomsky, N. (1992a) *op. cit.*, p. 21.
43 Chomsky, N. (1982) *op. cit.*, p. 18.
44 Chomsky, N. (1989) *op. cit.*, p. 19.
45 Chomsky, N. (1992a) *op. cit.*, p. 50.
46 Chomsky, N. (1985) *Turning the Tide*, London: Pluto Press, p. 50.
47 'The United States did not then need Middle East oil for itself. Rather the goal was to dominate the world system, ensuring that others would not strike an independent course.' Chomsky, N. (1992a) *op. cit.*, p. 53.
48 Chomsky, N. (1989) *op. cit.*, p. 72.
49 Chomsky, N. (1992a) *op. cit.*, p. 27.
50 Chomsky, N. (1992) *What Uncle Sam Really Wants*, Berkeley, California: Odonian, p. 80.
51 Chomsky, N. (1985) *op. cit.*, p. 55. Chomsky notes that Fred Halliday 'interprets my observation that "the real rivals" of the United States are Japan and Europe, not the USSR (obvious at the time, and by now the merest truism) as implying that the conflict with the USSR was "but a pretext used by the USA for waging conflict" with the EEC and Japan – which of course it does not', see Chomsky, N. (1992a) *op. cit.*, p. 65, n. 17.
52 Chomsky, N. in Otero, C. P. (ed.) (1981) *op. cit.*, p. 134.
53 Golding, P. and Murdock, G. (1991) *op. cit.*, p. 19.
54 Chomsky, N. in Otero, C. P. (ed.) (1988) *op. cit.*, p. 303.
55 Chomsky, N. (1969) *op. cit.*, p. 256.
56 Chomsky, N. (1969) *op. cit.*, p. 257.
57 Chomsky, N. in Otero, C. P. (ed.) (1988) *op. cit.*, p. 369.
58 Chomsky, N. in Otero, C. P. (ed.) (1988) *op. cit.*, p. 369.
59 Chomsky, N. in Otero, C. P. (ed.) (1988) *op. cit.*, p. 371.
60 Chomsky, N. in Otero, C. P. (ed.) (1988) *op. cit.*, p. 371. He is not saying that people who work in this field do not do valuable work.
61 Herman, E. S. and Chomsky, N. (1994) *op. cit.*, p. xii.
62 Chomsky, N. (1969) *op. cit.*, p. 275.
63 Glasgow Media Group (1976, 1980 and 1985) *op. cit.*
64 Chomsky, N. (1989) p. 8.
65 Glasgow Media Group (1976, 1980, and 1985) *op. cit.*; and Harrison, M. (1985) *TV News: Whose Bias?*, London: Policy Journals.
66 Schudson, M. 'The Sociology of News Production Revisited' in Curran, J. and Gurevitch, M. (1991) *op. cit.*, p. 144.
67 See my paper (1995) on 'Chomsky and the State' in *Politics*, 15(3), pp. 153–9.
68 Chomsky, N. (1989) *op. cit.*, p. 23.
69 Schudson, M. (1991) *op. cit.*, p. 144. Schudson actually argues that: 'For an American that kind of conclusion was easier to come to before Watergate than after.'
70 Chomsky, N. (1989) *op. cit.*, p. 13.
71 Chomsky, N. in Barsamian, D. (1992) *Noam Chomsky: Chronicles of Dissent*, Stirling: A. K. Press, pp. 10–1, 64.
72 Chomsky, N. (1988) *The Culture of Terrorism*, London: Pluto Press, p. 69.
73 Chomsky, N. (1988) p. 69.
74 Chomsky, N. (1989) *op. cit.*, p. 13.
75 Chomsky, N. (1989) *op. cit.*, p. 45.

76 Chomsky, N. (1989) *op. cit.*, p. 8.
77 Galtung, J. and Ruge, M. H. 'The Structure of Foreign News' in Tunstall, J. (ed.) (1970) *Media Sociology*, London: Constable.
78 Herman, E. S. and Chomsky, N. (1994) *op. cit.*, p. 37.
79 Herman, E. S. and Chomsky, N. (1994) *op. cit.*, p. 31.
80 The picture is obviously more complex because 'friends' are also competitors.
81 Herman, E. S. and Chomsky, N. (1994) *op. cit.*, p. 39.
82 Herman, E. S. and Chomsky, N. (1994) *op. cit.*, p. 39.
83 Herman, E. S. and Chomsky, N. (1994) *op. cit.*, p. 45.
84 However, television coverage of sport is particularly good at establishing the historical record, despite the complexities. This suggests that as such this seeming inability to deal with social processes is more the result of intention than a constraint of the medium.
85 Chomsky, N. (1989) *op. cit.*, p. 40.
86 Chomsky, N. in Peck, J. (1988) *The Chomsky Reader*, London: Serpent's Tail, p. 33. See also Chomsky, N. in Otero, C. P. (ed.) (1988) *op. cit.*, p. 717.
87 Chomsky, N. in Otero, C. P. (ed.) (1988) *op. cit.*, p. 717.
88 Chomsky, N. (1989) *op. cit.*, p. 51.
89 Chomsky, N. (1989) *op. cit.*, p. 67.
90 Chomsky, N. (1989) *op. cit.*, p. 67.
91 Chomsky, N. in Barsamian, D. (1992) *op. cit.*, p. 1.
92 Chomsky, N. in Barsamian, D. (1992) *op. cit.*, p. 3.
93 Chomsky, N. (1989) *op. cit.*, p. 67.
94 Herman, E. S. and Chomsky, N. (1994) *op. cit.*, p. 43.
95 Chomsky, N. (1989) *op. cit.*, p. 45.
96 Chomsky, N. and Herman, E. S. (1979a) *After the Cataclysm*, Nottingham: Spokesman, p. vii.
97 Chomsky, N. and Herman, E. S. (1979a) *op. cit.*, p. 135.
98 Chomsky, N. and Herman, E. S. (1979a) *op. cit.*, p. 159.
99 Chomsky, N. and Herman, E. S. (1979a) *op. cit.*, p. 293.
100 Chomsky, N. and Herman, E. S. (1979a) *op. cit.*, p. 139.
101 Chomsky, N. and Herman, E. S. (1979a) *op. cit.*, p. 152.
102 Chomsky, N. and Herman, E. S. (1979a) *op. cit.*, p. 158.
103 Chomsky, N. and Herman, E. S. (1979a) *op. cit.*, p. 139.
104 Lukes, S. (1980) 'Chomsky's betrayal of truths' in *Times Higher Education Supplement*, 7 November.
105 Chomsky, N. and Herman, E. S. (1979a) *op. cit.*, p. 4.
106 Chomsky in an unpublished letter to Lukes invites him to 'repudiate' his claims 'publicly'. When after two months, Lukes fails to do so, Chomsky felt forced to write to *Times Higher Education Supplement* in February 1981, following the publication of further 'fabrications' by Michael Leifer.
107 Chomsky, N. in Barsamian, D. (1992) *op. cit.*, p. 19.
108 Chomsky, N. in Barsamian, D. (1992) *op. cit.*, p. 19.
109 Mills, C. W. (1956) *The Power Elite*, New York: Oxford University Press.
110 McQuail, D. (1987) *op. cit.*, p. 74.
111 See Blumler, J. G. and Katz, E. (eds) (1974) *op. cit.*; Gurevitch, M. and Levy, M. (1986) *op. cit.*; Katz, E. (1987) *op. cit.*
112 Hall, S. (ed.) (1984) *Culture, Media Language*, London: Hutchinson.
113 For an example see Chomsky, N. (1994) *op. cit.*, p. 17.
114 Chomsky, N. (1989) *op. cit.*, p. 8.
115 Chomsky, N. (1993) *Year 501: The Conquest Continues*, London: Verso, p. 18.

116 Chomsky, N., Lecture, *World Orders: Old and New*, 22 May 1994, Red Lion Square, London.
117 Chomsky, N. in Otero, C. P. (ed.) (1988) *op. cit.*, p. 601.
118 Chomsky, N. (1992a) *op. cit.*, p. 374.
119 Chomsky, N. in Otero, C. P. (ed.) (1988) *op. cit.*, p. 600.
120 Chomsky, N. (1992a) *op. cit.*, p. 375.
121 Chomsky, N. (1992a) *op. cit.*, p. 120.
122 Chomsky, N. (1992a) *op. cit.*, p. 134.
123 Chomsky, N. (1989) *op. cit.*, p. 38. See also p. 47.
124 Chomsky, N. (1992a) *op. cit.*, p. 187.
125 Chomsky, N. in Peck, J. (1988) *op. cit.*, p. 39.
126 Chomsky, N. in Peck, J. (1988) *op. cit.*, p. 35.
127 Chomsky, N. in Peck, J. (1988) *op. cit.*, p. 35.
128 Chomsky, N. in Peck, J. (1988) *op. cit.*, p. 45.
129 Chomsky, N. in Peck, J. (1988) *op. cit.*, p. 45.
130 Chomsky, N. in Peck, J. (1988) *op. cit.*, p. 53.
131 Chomsky, N. (1992a) *op. cit.*, p. 80.
132 Chomsky, N. in Otero, C. P. (ed.) (1988) *op. cit.*, p. 303.
133 Chomsky, N. (1992a) *op. cit.*, p. 73.
134 Willis, P. (1977) *Learning to Labour: How Working Class Kids Get Working Class Jobs*, London: Saxon House.
135 Fiske, J. (1989) *Reading the Popular*, London: Routledge.
136 Chomsky, N. in Achbar, M. (ed.) (1994) *Manufacturing Consent: Noam Chomsky and the Media*, Montreal: Black Rose Books, p. 91.
137 Chomsky, N. (1989) *op. cit.*, p. 11.

Conclusion
Chomsky – militant optimist

It has been the purpose of this book to argue that Noam Chomsky *does* have a political theory which explicitly rests upon a view of human nature. It has been argued further that this theory represents an important synthesis of a prevalent polarisation in social and political theory between an analysis of structure versus an analysis of agency.

The key to Chomsky's social and political thought it has been argued, lies with his essentialism. This means that in Chomsky's view human beings have certain essential biological characteristics which inform their social behaviour. Social behaviour here includes human capacities for productive work. Chomsky thus appears to be opting for the agency side of the structure/agency dichotomy. However, he does not accept that explanations are solely a product of an agent's will. Structures are influential on behaviour in complex ways, although some more predictably than others. The point is that Chomsky wants to emphasise agency, but without implying that structural features are not important for explaining why things are the way they are. The significance about Chomsky's analysis is that he does not claim to be able to explain how the connections between human intention and structural conditions work.[1] It is that he thinks there is strong evidence to suggest there are connections, and that any analysis should highlight this.

Essentialism is usually regarded pejoratively. This is because, given that human beings quite evidently display very different capabilities and capacities, it would perhaps follow from this that societies are stuck with the 'fact' that some people have useful or worthy capacities while others have less useful or even unworthy capacities. In other words because essentialism means that these capacities are biologically given, the implication is that there is no use in fighting for a more egalitarian society, because people are just born unequal. As such, essentialism is deemed reactionary. However, as Chomsky has been shown to argue, in his view this conclusion is only plausible if one accepts that different human capacities and capabilities ought to be differentially rewarded. In Chomsky's view there is no reason why this should be the case. In his view, if people were given the opportunity to organise themselves from the ground up, so to speak, different capabilities would be shown to complement one another, and the idea that they should be hierarchically evaluated, as is currently the case, would not apply. So in Chomsky's view human capacities have a biologically determined nature, and differences should be celebrated. Chomsky not only objects to the anti-essentialist position because it carries with it elitist assumptions, but he also feels that the logic of the anti-essentialist position implies that human beings are malleable. In other words it implies that differences between people are simply the result of an inegalitarian society and so can be ironed out by an enlightened engineer of the environment. Whilst Chomsky would accept that an inegalitarian environment is responsible for people not developing their abilities to their full potential, he objects to the idea that differences should be flattened out. What should be flattened out, in his view, is the differential evaluation of abilities, but not the differences between abilities.

So there is a very significant caveat to Chomsky's essentialism: although his work in linguistics offers very suggestive evidence for such a claim he has no scientific evidence as such to support a more specific explanation of such a proposition. His views are based upon a combination of both hope and hunches based upon his work in linguistics. Because of this caveat, as the first chapter makes clear, Chomsky does not believe he can claim his social and political writings constitute science. However, as he also points out the anti-essentialist argument has no scientific evidence either.

In Chapter 1 we see that, in Chomsky's view, pursuing scientific inquiry is a valuable and necessary human endeavour. He argues, '[e]liminate scientific and technological inquiry and, shortly, several billion people will die of starvation, rather more than will die in a nuclear war.'[2] 'It is far from clear that the recent population explosion could exist, even at bare subsistence level, without these factors.'[3] And he goes on to explain that scientific inquiry involves employing the 'scientific method' which means rational inquiry. 'The method of rational inquiry ... insists that conclusions should follow from premises and that theories should be subjected to empirical test.'[4] And on the subject of what constitutes an adequate theory Chomsky argues that it should 'give some sort of insight into some domain of phenomena, provide some explanation for puzzling things, or come up with principles that are less than obvious that have empirical support'.[5] Chomsky is aware that some findings made through scientific inquiry within the natural sciences have been and will continue to be superseded on the basis of new evidence or new tools designed for discerning evidence, however, the method for accepting new evidence remains the same; i.e. it remains rational. As far as Chomsky is concerned 'it has been a reasonably successful approach'.[6] However, this is only the case within the natural sciences. As he argues '[i]t's hard to do these things outside a very small core of natural sciences'.[7] 'The point is that as we move towards spheres of greater human concern (e.g., questions of choice and will, of creativity, of social structure) we find that science has nothing to say'.[8] In Chomsky's view then we can go some way to determining the laws of nature, but when it comes to introspecting about our own motivational forces we are a long way from having anything useful to say. Indeed in his view, as a species we may not even have the faculties to begin to answer such a question. As he argues: '[w]hen we get to the areas where we're talking about choice of action, or the fact that we're only incited and inclined but not compelled, I don't think there are any candidates for a theory or explanation. Whether we even have the right kind of intelligence to study those questions or whether they're just too difficult to study, or what, I don't know'.[9]

If social institutions are the result of human action, and because we cannot yet, if ever, scientifically explain human action, we should not claim scientific credentials for social and behavioural analysis. As is very evident, human behaviour has many different manifestations, in part as a result of the environment, so presumably social institutions in turn can and do have various manifestations. As Chomsky argues: '[t]hese are human institutions: we can affect them. They're not laws of nature that we're talking about.'[10] As such the label of science is inappropriate. To put this another way, when 'policy experts' or 'social scientists' comment upon their object of analysis, whatever their comment, they are either defending the status quo, or challenging it. Whichever position they take, ultimately they are taking it because they hold a certain view about what is good or necessary for human social existence.[11] Because, on this issue, we have no knowledge that comes close to being scientific, the analysis can be nothing more than speculative. And so those 'experts' that posture as 'scientists' are seriously misrepresenting their findings. But then as we have seen, in Chomsky's opinion, this indicates more about them.

As Chomsky points out, it is not just the case that social analysis which calls itself scientific is misrepresentation because rational enquiry is not open to us here. Given that we do not know enough about human nature, it is also the case that much of the work that goes under the banner of 'social science' does not even come close to rational enquiry. To offer a concrete example to support such a claim Chomsky would have us look at the disparity between political rhetoric and the consequences of actual policy. When looking at American foreign policy the rhetoric is always that America has some uniquely principled and moral mission to aid others in the pursuit of freedom and democracy. When one then turns to consider the consequences of policy, we find that its implementation has involved highly unprincipled acts, and has consequences that are far from democratic. (We might cite Nicaragua as an example here, although Chomsky considers many others.) However, 'policy experts' and 'social scientists' in making an analysis, will almost universally accept the rhetoric as the true intention and then, given the evidence of consequences, will resort to explaining the disparity between the two as mere 'blunder', good intentions gone awry or as principles that have been thwarted.

In Chomsky's view the regularity with which the 'blunders' occur rationally draws one to the conclusion that the rhetoric is just that – rhetoric – an attempt to mask hidden intentions. One can then try to draw conclusions about what those intentions might be, and looking at power distribution within American society is, in his view, a useful place to start. For Chomsky, looking at this disparity between input and output is the rational way to proceed. It cannot however be scientific because, when we proceed from a comparison between input and output to what this implies for human organisation, we are in the realm of making claims about human nature which cannot yet be substantiated scientifically. It is his belief, and it is only a belief, that freedom is good for human beings, and 'that *objective* scholarship free from the ideological restraints which are imposed by the general political consensus and distribution of force would lead to radical conclusions'.[12]

Chomsky's position on the natural sciences versus the social sciences is nicely summed up in the following story:

> Over the years, I've worked in areas ranging from mathematics and automata theory to philosophy to intellectual history to the domain of 'political science.' I've noticed something quite striking: when I'm invited to give a talk to a graduate math colloquium, or a physics or biology colloquium, at some major university, no one asks about my credentials, though it is obvious at once that I'm not a pro. Rather they ask whether what I'm saying is right, can it be improved, etc. Same in philosophy, where there is a tradition of intellectual honesty. In intellectual history, however, people go bananas and produce the most outrageous falsifications and absurdities to try to send what I am saying to 'oblivion.' And in 'political science,' the quite standard response is that I have no right to speak because I lack credentials. (There are, of course, exceptions.) The explanation is obvious: in the sciences, there is no need to worry about credentials since the fields have intellectual substance and integrity. In the humanities, where a substantial number of practitioners are people with tiny minds and limited understanding, it is necessary to keep outsiders from prying in (they might have ideas, which would be terrifying). In political science and other forms of ideology, it is obvious that protection is necessary. So this is all clear enough. In fact, such terms as 'Marxist' or 'Freudian' give the game away. In mathematics, one is not a 'Gaussian,' and in physics one is not an 'Einsteinian.' The interest is in the ideas, not cults and Gods.[13]

The first chapter concludes that even if we are to accept Chomsky's arguments that all social and political analysis ultimately relies upon some notion of human nature which cannot claim to be established scientifi-cally, this does not mean that observations are just a matter of interpretation. If, as Chomsky seems to accept, there are real connections and therefore consequences which can be derived from the relationship between social structures and human life chances, then presumably the consequences of social structure can be measured against very basic things like human survival. Information such as this must enable us to draw conclusions about human need and therefore human nature, giving us information about how we may best arrange things to meet these needs. In other words even if we can never scientifically explain the precise nature of human intention and the relationship between this and social organi-sation, this does not mean that given the experience of various forms of social organisation we cannot then make conjectures about our nature. Chomsky employs this methodology when he compares proclaimed policy intention with policy outcome. He makes rational conjectures based upon available evidence about what factors there might be, other than proclaimed intentions, which affect policy and thereby account for the outcomes. He finds such conjectures consistently work in explaining outcomes. These conjectures thereby become the framework or theory with which to understand new events.

The curious thing about Chomsky's position is that he claims not to have a theory. He certainly objects to describing his social and political analysis as scientific and yet he clearly thinks that it is possible to proceed rationally. He regularly claims that social scientists draw irrational conclusions which presupposes that it *is* possible to draw rational ones. Were it not for this we would be left with a rather Oakeshottian anti-rationalist perspective on things:

> In political activity, then, men sail a boundless and bottomless sea: there is neither harbour for shelter nor floor for anchorage, neither starting-place nor appointed destination. The enterprise is to keep afloat on an even keel, the sea is both friend and enemy, and the seamanship consists in using the resources of the traditional manner of behaviour in order to make a friend of every hostile occasion.[14]

Such a view is inimical to Chomsky's concrete analysis. Were this not the case, we would have to ask why Chomsky the political commentator and critic does what he does.

Having established that Chomsky's ideas are constitutive of theory, but one that is underpinned by a view of human nature, Chapter 2 looked at his ideas about human nature and how they inform his vision of the good society. It was found that Chomsky's essentialism holds that human beings are inherently creative. It is his belief in human creativity which leads Chomsky to the political position that human beings ought to enjoy conditions of freedom, in order to realise their creative potential. The point about Chomsky's essentialism is that he is not making claims about absolute characteristics, for example, that human beings are competitive and so by implication non-altruistic. He is arguing that human behaviour has many different manifestations and that the environment does act as a trigger. So while human beings are agents in the sense that their given inherent characteristics will, to an extent, determine their intentions, these intentions will also be subject to the constraints of the environment, in other words the social structure. It is this combination of essentialism with the recognition that the environment mediates essential characteristics, which is suggestive of the view that Chomsky is somehow bridging the agency/structure dichotomy.

If Chomsky is arguing that human beings have certain innate capacities, but that it is the environment which allows them to flourish or wither, is he not simply falling into the trap of concluding that human beings are malleable? In other words is his position not simply that it *is* the environment which is determining in the last instance, so that he ends up being a structuralist after all? As Haley and Lunsford argue, when discussing Chomsky's view on the 'televangelist who bilks an innocent widow of her life's savings':

> He [Chomsky] may see the evangelist, but believe that he has gotten caught up in the web of a human institution that has taken arbitrary authority. Having been trapped in this institution, the evangelist has begun to act in the customary way for humans to act in such institutions. This line of thought would make Chomsky sound much more like a behaviourist than he (or I) would like.[15]

Is there anything in Chomsky's argument which allow us to overcome this conclusion? As the second chapter shows, when Chomsky argues that humans are innately creative, and that conditions of freedom would allow this creativity to flourish, he is not saying: and therefore conditions of freedom *ought to be* imposed. In other words he is not taking a behaviourist line which implies that if 'we' (whoever 'we' is) impose certain conditions then a change of behaviour will follow, which implies plasticity. Rather in Chomsky's view human beings have an 'instinct for freedom'. As such if human beings could be given all the facts and control over the way they organise themselves, they would recognise the compatibility of libertarian socialist organisation with their natures. In other words human beings need free access to resources, or conditions of freedom and equality. Chomsky's alternative picture of life presents us with a picture in which we can be in control.

In Chapters 3, 4, 5 and 6, having established that Chomsky *does* employ a theory, and one which employs a theory of human nature, the implications of his theory for an understanding of various features of social and political life is considered. His critique of social and political life is looked at within the context of other theorists. To this end Chapter 3 attempts to locate Chomsky's ideas on the state and capitalism by comparing them with those of Marx. It was found that Chomsky's focus upon the international character of the state highlights the proactive role played by the state in the business community's interest for capital expansion. This suggests that the structural emphasis of capital's dynamic in Marx's analysis obscures the role of agency. If the role of agency through the state is acknowledged, especially in the light of what are often draconian foreign policy measures, then whether we define a state to be democratic or totalitarian, for example, comes into question.

Chapter 4 continues a concern with the state by comparing Chomsky's ideas on the state with contemporary state theories. In particular this chapter was concerned with the difficulties state theory has had with reconciling the question of structure and agency. It was found that although Chomsky emphasises agency in his analysis, this is not to the exclusion of structural characteristics, and particularly the paradox of competition, even a competition which is favourably engineered. National state competition requires there to be healthy competitors for there to be a competition at all, but the danger will be that despite state engineered head starts, the race could still have an unexpected outcome. At the international level, without an international state to prop up private accumulation generally, business interests will have to ally themselves to a nation state forcing themselves into competition with what may ultimately be a 'superior' nation state, in that it is able to achieve more for those interests in terms of public subsidy for private profit. Chomsky's theory is characteristically simple and yet allows for the complexity of contingency.

In Chapter 5 Chomsky's theory of the state is used to critically analyse theories of nationalism. While most of Chomsky's theory of the state is derived from his analysis of the American state, his ideas (as he often acknowledges) are generalisable to other states. What his analysis demonstrates is that a state's *raison d'être* is to promote the 'national interest' which according to Chomsky means elite interest. As such then, countries most successful in international competition must be acting nationalistically in the process. However, it was found that theories of nationalism fail to acknowledge this, and it is difficult to locate successful 'first world' nations within their typologies.

Chapter 6 considers Chomsky's theory of the media. His analysis of the media is crucial to his political theory because it explains the way in which elites seek to divert attention away from an acknowledgement of the power they wield. The other crucial reason to consider his analysis of the media is that the media is one of his principle tools for evidence in his analysis of society more generally. It is from the media that he finds evidence of the disparity between the political rhetoric and the political outcome. And he points out the media's failure to acknowledge this disparity. However, this failure illustrates the structural point that they are institutions operating in the business interest and so it becomes too dangerous to properly explore the disparities between rhetoric and action – too dangerous that is to elite interests. The chapter establishes that as with his theory generally he incorporates an analysis of both structure and agency. As such the notion that his ideas are merely instrumentalist is challenged. However, as before it is acknowledged that he does nevertheless seek to emphasise the agency aspect of social and political behaviour. Just as it is politically dubious to treat the 'workers' or the 'masses' as dupes, so too is dubious to suggest that elites are unconscious carriers of structural constraints.

Throughout, this book has sought not only to establish and locate Chomsky's social and political thought, it has also sought to do this within the context of other theories of society. Throughout, the research on comparative theories demonstates the ongoing problems of reconciling difficulties around structure and agency. All attempts to theorise about society seem dogged by this dichotomy. While this may not be the only reason, it is possible to make the conjecture that this failure to overcome the dichotomy of structure and agency has left social and political thought open to what is usually regarded as the fatal attack of the postmodern critique or cultural relativism. While theories concerned with structures may be more 'objective' and therefore more concrete and law-like, they nevertheless have difficulty remaining realistic without the incorporation of agency. Theories have been forced to incorporate agency, but with this they lose their decisive and predictive force. If we are not to be left with the politically apathetic (or worse, reactionary) conclusions of postmodern thought, Chomsky's theoretical humility, but *theory* nevertheless, must be the key to move us beyond such a hiatus.

Enlightenment ideals are too readily linked to the modernist project. With the modern period's failure to fully and successfully emancipate, the pursuit of Enlightenment ideals and progress comes under attack. But, as Ellen Meiksins Wood argues, the resort to postmodernism is to throw out the Enlightenment baby with the modernist bath water.[16] Chomsky's essentialist analysis which seeks to expose any constraint on human autonomy, be this economic or political, offers a conceivable analysis of how to theoretically nurture the Enlightenment baby.

Notes

1 Chomsky's equivocation here has been criticised for not offering us a view of 'what is to be done'. Arnove, A. (1997) 'In perspective: Noam Chomsky' in *International Socialism*, Spring, no. 74, pp. 117–40.
2 Chomsky, N. in Raskin, M. G. and Bernstein, H. J. (1987) *New Ways of Knowing: The Sciences, Society and Reconstructive Knowledge*, Rowmen and Littlefield, p. 108.
3 Chomsky, N. in Raskin, M. G. and Bernstein, H. J. (1987) *op. cit.*, p. 135.
4 Chomsky, N. in Raskin, M. G. and Bernstein, H. J. (1987) *op. cit.*, p. 147.

Elsewhere he argues that science involves having 'a theory that has a certain internal rigor and that provides explanations for empirical phenomena and insight into the principles that account for them, principles that are not obvious and that account for puzzling phenomena. But science is not the only way to come to an understanding of things.' In Otero, C. P. (ed.) (1988) *Noam Chomsky: Language and Politics*, Montreal: Black Rose Books, p. 465.

5　Chomsky, N. in Otero, C. P. (ed.) (1988) *op. cit.*, p. 464.
6　Chomsky, N. in Raskin, M. G. and Bernstein, H. J. (1987) *op. cit.*, p. 131.
7　Chomsky, N. in Otero, C. P. (ed.) (1988) *op. cit.*, p. 464.
8　Chomsky, N. in Raskin, M. G. and Bernstein, H. J. (1987) *op. cit.*, p. 109.
9　Chomsky, N. in Otero, C. P. (ed.) (1988) *op. cit.*, p. 464.
10　Chomsky, N. in Otero, C. P. (ed.) (1988) *op. cit.*, p. 280.
11　Chomsky, N. in Raskin, M. G. and Bernstein, H. J. (1987) *op. cit.*, p. 131.
12　Chomsky, N. in Otero, C. P. (ed.) (1981) *Noam Chomsky: Radical Priorities*, Montreal: Black Rose Books, p. 201.
13　Chomsky, N. in Raskin, M. G. and Bernstein, H. J. (1987) *op. cit.*, pp. 148–9.
14　Oakeshott, M. (1962) *Rationalism in Politics and Other Essays*, Indianapolis: Liberty Press, p. 127.
15　Haley, M. C. and Lunsford, R. F. (1994) *Noam Chomsky*, New York: Twayne, p. 193.
16　Wood, Ellen Meiksins (1995) *Democracy Against Capitalism: Renewing Historical Materialism*, Cambridge: Cambridge University Press.

Bibliography

Achbar, M. (ed.) (1994) *Manufacturing Consent: Noam Chomsky and the Media*, London: Black Rose Books.

Alter, P. (1989) *Nationalism*, London: Edward Arnold.

Anderson, B. (1991) (1983) *Imagined Communities: Reflections on the Origin and Spread of Nationalism*, 2nd edn, London: Verso.

Arblaster, A. (1994, 2nd edn) *Democracy*, Buckingham: Open University Press.

Arnove, A. (1997) 'In Perspective: Noam Chomsky' in *International Socialism*, Spring, no. 74, pp. 117–40.

Arthur, C. J. (1986) *Dialectics of Labour*, Oxford: Basil Blackwell.

Baker, J. (1987) *Arguing for Equality*, London: Verso.

Bakunin, M. (1973) *Bakunin on Anarchy* (Sam Dolgoff, ed. and trans.), London: George Allen and Unwin.

Ball, T. (1995) *Reappraising Political Theory*, Oxford: Clarendon Press.

Barrington Moore, Jr (1966) *Social Origins of Dictatorship and Democracy*, London: Penguin.

Barry, N. P. (1995) *A Introduction to Modern Political Theory*, London: Macmillan.

Barsamian, D. (1992) *Noam Chomsky: Chronicles of Dissent*, Stirling: A. K. Press.

Barsamian, D. (1994) *Noam Chomsky: Keeping the Rabble in Line*, Stirling: A. K. Press.

Barsamian, D. (1996) *Noam Chomsky: Class Warfare*, London: Pluto Press.

Barsky, R. F. (1997) *Noam Chomsky: A Life of Dissent*, Cambridge, Mass: MIT Press.

Berger, P. L. and Luckman, T. (1966) *The Social Construction of Reality*, London: Penguin.

Berlin, I. (1969) 'Two Concepts of Liberty' in *Four Essays on Liberty*, Oxford: Oxford University Press.

Bernstein, R. (1976) *The Restructuring of Social and Political Theory*, Oxford: Methuen.

Block, F. (1987) *Revising State Theory*, Philadelphia: Temple University Press.

Blumler, J. G. and Katz, E. (eds) (1974) *The Uses of Mass Communications*, Beverly Hills, California and London: Sage.

Bricianer, S. (1978) *Pannekoek and the Workers' Councils*, St Louis, Missouri: Telos.

Burnham, J. (1960) *The Managerial Revolution*, Bloomington, Indiana: Indiana University Press.

Carey, A. (1997) *Taking the Risk out of Democracy: Corporate Propaganda versus Freedom and Liberty*, Urbana: University of Illinois Press.

Carnoy, M. (1984) *The State and Political Theory*, Princeton, NJ: Princeton University Press.

Carter, A. (1971) *The Political Theory of Anarchism*, London: Routledge and Kegan Paul.

Chalmers, A. F. (1992) *What is This Thing Called Science?*, Milton Keynes: Open University Press.

Chomsky, N. (1966) *Cartesian Linguistics*, New York: Harper and Row.

Chomsky, N. (1969) *American Power and the New Mandarins*, Harmondsworth: Penguin.

Chomsky, N. (1970) *At War with Asia: Essays on Indo-China*, New York: Pantheon.

Chomsky, N. (1971) *Problems of Knowledge and Freedom: The Russell Lectures*, New York: Pantheon.

Chomsky, N. (1973) *For Reasons of State*, New York: Vintage.

Chomsky, N. (1974) *Peace in the Middle East? Reflections on Justice and Nationhood*, New York: Pantheon.

Chomsky, N. (1979) *Language and Responsibility*, New York: Pantheon.

Chomsky, N. (1982) *Towards a New Cold War*, New York: Pantheon.

Chomsky, N. (1985) *Turning the Tide*, London: Pluto Press.

Chomsky, N. (1987a) *On Power and Ideology*, Montreal: Black Rose Books.

Chomsky, N. (1987b) *Pirates and Emperors*, Montreal: Black Rose Books.

Chomsky, N. (1988) *The Culture of Terrorism*, London: Pluto Press.

Chomsky, N. (1989a) 'An Interview', *Radical Philosophy*, Autumn.

Chomsky, N. (1989b) *Necessary Illusions*, London: Pluto Press.

Chomsky, N. (1992a) *Deterring Democracy*, London: Vintage.

Chomsky, N. (1992b) *What Uncle Sam Really Wants*, Berkeley, California: Odonian Press.

Chomsky, N. (1993) *Year 501: The Conquest Continues*, London: Verso.

Chomsky, N. (1994) *World Orders: Old and New*, Lecture at Conway Hall, Red Lion Square, London, 22 May 1994.

Chomsky, N. (1996a) *Powers and Prospects: Reflections on Human Nature and the Social Order*, London: Pluto Press.

Chomsky, N. (1996b) 'A Painful Peace' in *Z Magazine*, January.

Chomsky, N. and Herman, E. S. (1979a) *After the Cataclysm: Post War IndoChina and the Reconstruction of Imperial Ideology*, Nottingham: Spokesman.

Chomsky, N. and Herman, E. S. (1979b) *The Political Economy of Human Rights*, Volumes 1 and 11, Nottingham: Spokesman.

Chomsky, N. and Herman, E. S. (1979c) *The Washington Connection and Third World Fascism*, Nottingham: Spokesman.

Chomsky, N. and Herman, E. S. (1979, 1988) *Manufacturing Consent: The Political Economy of the Mass Media*, New York: Pantheon Books.

Curran, J. (1970) *The British Press: A Manifesto*, London: Macmillan.

Curran, J. (1990) 'The New Revisionism in Mass Communiation Research: A Reappraisal' in *European Journal of Communication*, vol. 5, pp. 135–64.

Curran, J. and Gurevitch, M. (eds) (1991) *Mass Media and Society*, London: Edward Arnold.

Curran, J. and Seaton, J. (1981) *Power without Responsibility*, London: Fontana.

Dolgoff, S. (1973) *Bakunin on Anarchy*, New York: George Allen and Unwin.

Donald, J. and Hall, S. (1986) *Politics and Ideology*, Milton Keynes: Open University Press.

Dupre, L. (1966) *The Philosophical Foundations of Marxism*, New York: Harcourt, Brace.

Durkheim, E. (1952) *Suicide: A Study in Sociology*, (John A. Spalding and George Simpson, trans.) London: Routledge and Kegan Paul.

Edgley, A. (1995) 'Chomsky and the State' in *Politics*, 15(3), pp. 153–9.

Edgley, R. (1970) 'Innate Ideas' in Royal Institute of Philosophy Lectures III, *Knowledge and Necessity*, London: Macmillan.

Elders, F. (1974) *Reflexive Water*, London: Souvenir Press.

Evans, M. (1975) *Karl Marx*, Political Thinkers no. 3, Parry, G. (General Editor), London: George Allen and Unwin.

Feyerabend, P. (1975a) *Against Method*, London: New Left Books.

Feyerabend, P. (1975b) 'How to Defend Society Against Science' in *Radical Philosophy*, Summer.

Feyerabend, P. (1987) *Farewell to Reason*, London: Verso.

Fiske, J. (1989) *Reading the Popular*, London: Routledge.

Fleming, M. (1979) *The Anarchist Way to Socialism*, Totowa, New Jersey: Rowmen and Littlefield.

Foley, M. (1991) *American Political Ideas: Traditions and Usages*, Manchester: Manchester University Press.

Forbes, I. and Smith, S. (1983) *Politics and Human Nature*, London: Frances Pinter.

Foucault, M. (1977) *Discipline and Punish: Birth of the Prison*, London: Allen Lane.

Foucault, M. (1980) *Power/Knowledge*, Hemel Hempstead: Harvester Wheatsheaf.

Foucault, M. (1981) *The History of Sexuality, Volume 1: An Introduction* (Hurley, R. trans.), Harmondsworth: Penguin.

Fowler, R. B. and Orenstein, J. R. (1993) *An Introduction to Political Theory: Toward the Next Century*, London: HarperCollins.

Fukuyama, F. K. (1992) *The End of History and the Last Man*, London: Penguin.

Galtung, J. and Ruge, M. H. (1970) 'The Structure of Foreign News' in Tunstall, J. *Media Sociology*, London: Constable.

Gamble, A. (1981) *An Introduction to Modern Social and Political Thought*, London: Macmillan.

Gans, H. J. (1979) *Deciding What's News*, New York: Pantheon.

Gellner, E. (1970) 'Concepts and Society' in Wilson, B. R. (ed.) *Rationality*, Oxford: Basil Blackwell.

Gellner, E. (1983) *Nations and Nationalism*, Oxford: Basil Blackwell.

Giddens, A. (1977) *Studies in Social and Political Theory*, Hutchinson.

Glasgow Media Group (1976) *Bad News*, London: Routledge and Kegan Paul.

Glasgow Media Group (1980) *More Bad News*, London: Routledge and Kegan Paul.

Glasgow Media Group (1985) *War & Peace News*, Milton Keynes: Open University Press.

Golding, P. and Murdock, G. (1991) 'Culture, Communications, and Political Economy' in Curran, J. and Gurevitch, M. (eds) (1991) *Mass Media and Society*, London: Edward Arnold.

Goodwin, B. (1982) *Using Political Ideas*, Chichester: John Wiley and Sons.

Gramsci, A. (1971) *Selections from the Prison Notebooks* (Quintin Hoare and Geoffrey Nowell Smith, eds and trans), London: Lawrence and Wishart.

Guerin, D. (1970) *Anarchism*, New York, London: Monthly Review Press.

Gurevitch, M. and Levy, M. (1986) 'Information and Meaning: Audience explanation of Social Issues' in Robinson, J. P. and Levy, M. (eds) *The Main Source*, Beverly Hills, California: Sage.

Haley, M. C. and Lunsford, R. F. (1994) *Noam Chomsky*, New York: Twayne Publishers.

Hall, J. A. and Ikenberry, J. G. (1989) *The State*, Milton Keynes: Open University Press.

Hall, S. (ed.) (1984) *Culture, Media Language*, London: Hutchinson.

Harding, N. (ed.) (1984) *The State in Socialist Society*, London: Macmillan.

Harrison, M. (1985) *TV News: Whose Bias?*, London: Policy Journals.

Harvey, D. (1989) *The Condition of Post Modernity*, Oxford: Blackwell.

Hayek, F. A. (1944) (1986) *The Road to Serfdom*, London: Routledge and Kegan Paul.

Herman, E. S. (1996) 'The Propaganda Model Revisited' in *Monthly Review*, July/August.

Hobbes, T. (1973) *Leviathan*, London: Everyman's Library.

Hobsbawm, E. (1990) *Nations and Nationalism since 1780*, Cambridge: Cambridge University Press.

Hobsbawm, E. and Ranger, T. (eds) (1983) *The Invention of Tradition*, Cambridge: Cambridge University Press.

Hogan, M. J. (1992) *The End of the Cold War: Its Meanings and Implications*, Cambridge: Cambridge University Press.

Hollis, M. (1977) *Models of Man*, Cambridge: Cambridge University Press.

Hollis, M. and Lukes, S. (1982) *Rationality and Relativism*, Oxford: Basil Blackwell.

Holloway, J. and Picciotto, S. (1978) 'Towards a Materialist Theory of the State' in Holloway, J. and Picciotto, S. (eds) *State and Capital: A Marxist Debate*, London: Edward Arnold.

Horkheimer, M. and Adorno, T. W. (1944) *Dialectic of Enlightenment* John Lumming (trans.), New York: Seabury Press.

Hudson, W. D. (ed.) (1969) *The Is/Ought Question*, London: Macmillan.

Inglis, F. (1990) *Media Theory: An Introduction*, Oxford: Basil Blackwell.

Jaggar, A. (1983) *Feminist Politics and Human Nature*, Brighton: Harvester.

Jessop, B. (1990) *State Theory: Putting Capitalist States in their Place*, Cambridge: Polity Press.

Joll, J. (1969) *The Anarchists*, London: Methuen.

Kamenka, E. (eds) (1976) *The Nature and Evolution of an Idea*, London: Edward Arnold.

Katz, E. (1987) 'Communications Research since Lazarsfeld' in *Public Opinion Quarterly*, vol. 51: S25–S45.

Keane, J. (1991) in McLellan, D. and Sayers, S. (eds) *Socialism and Democracy*, London: Macmillan.

Kearney, R. (1995) *States of Mind: Dialogues with Contemporary Thinkers on the European Mind*, Manchester: Manchester University Press.

Keat, R. and Urry, J. (1975) *Social Theory as Science*, London: Routledge and Kegan Paul.

Kedourie, E. (1966) *Nationalism*, London: Hutchinson.

Keynes, J. M. (1936) *The General Theory of Employment, Interest and Money*, London: Macmillan.

Kidron, M. (1967) 'A Permanent Arms Economy' in *International Socialism*, Reprints: 2, 1: 28 (Spring); republished 1989, London: Socialist Workers Party.

Kuhn, T. S. (1962) *The Structure of Scientific Revolutions*, Chicago: University of Chicago Press.

Kymlicka, W. (1990) *Contemporary Political Philosophy*, Oxford: Oxford University Press.

Layder, D. (1981) *Structure, Interaction and Social Theory*, London: Routledge and Kegan Paul.

Lenin, V. (1975) *Imperialism, the Highest Stage of Capitalism*, Peking: Foreign Languages Press.

Locke, J. (1986) in Stewart, M. (ed.) *Readings in Social and Political Philosophy*, New York: Oxford University Press.

Long, P. (ed.) (1969) *The New Left*, Boston, Mass: Extending Horizons.

Lowy, M. (1976) 'Marxists and the National Question' in *New Left Review*, no. 96, April–May.

Lukes, S. (1974) *Power: A Radical View*, London: Macmillan.

Lukes, S. (1980) 'Chomsky's betrayal of truths' in *Times Higher Education Supplement*, 7 November.

Maguire, J. M. (1978) *Marx's Theory of Politics*, Cambridge: Cambridge University Press.

Mandel, E. (1978) *Late Capitalism*, London: Verso.

Marx, K. and Engles, F. (1848, 1935) *The Communist Manifesto*, Moscow, Lawrence and Wishart.

McCarney, J. (1996) Review of Killing Time: The Autobiography of Paul Feyerabend, unpublished.

McLellan, D. (1971a) *Marx's Grundrisse*, St Albans: Paladin.

McLellan, D. (1971b) *The Thought of Karl Marx*, London: Macmillan.

McLellan, D. (ed.) (1977) *Karl Marx: Selected Writings*, Milton Keynes: Open University Press.

McLellan, D. and Sayers, S. (eds) (1991) *Socialism and Democracy*, London: Macmillan.

McQuail, D. (1987) *Mass Communication Theory: An Introduction* (2nd edn), London: Sage.

Miliband, R. (1969) *The State in Capitalist Society*, London: Weidenfeld and Nicolson.

Miliband, R. (1973) 'Poulantzas and the Capitalist State' in *New Left Review*, no. 82, November–December.

Mills, C. W. (1956) *The Power Elite*, New York: Oxford University Press.

Morris, Stephen (1981) 'Chomsky on US Foreign Policy' in *Harvard International Review*, December–January, vol. 3, no. 4

Mosse, G. L. (1976) 'Mass Politics and the Political Liturgy of Nationalism' in Kamenka, E. (ed.) *The Nature and Evolution of an Idea*, London: Edward Arnold.

Mulhall, S. and Swift, A. (1996 reprint) *Liberals and Communitarians* (2nd edn), Oxford: Blackwell.

Mulkay, M. (1979) *Science and the Sociology of Knowledge*, London: George Allen and Unwin.

Murdock, G. (1982) 'Large Corporations and the Control of Communications Industries' in *Culture, Media and Society: An Open University Collection*, Oxford: Methuen.

Murdock, G. and Golding, P. (1977) 'Capitalism, Communication & Class Relations' in Curran, J. *et al.* (eds) *Mass Communication and Society*, London: Edward Arnold.

Nairn, T. (1977) *The Break up of Britain: Crisis and Neo-Nationalism*, London: New Left Books.

Neocleous, M. (1996) *Administering Civil Society: Towards A Theory of State Power*, London: Macmillan.

Nielsen, K. (1973) 'Social Science and Hard Data' in *Cultural Hermeneutics*, 1, pp. 115–43.

Nozick, R. (1986) *Anarchy, State and Utopia* (reprint), Oxford: Basil Blackwell.

Oakeshott, M. (1991) *Rationalism in Politics and Other Essays*, Indianapolis: Liberty Press.

Offe, C. (1975) 'The Theory of the Capitalist State and the Problems of Policy Formation' in Lindberg, L. N. *et al.* (eds) *Stress and Contradiction in Modern Capitalism*, Lexington, Mass.: D. C. Heath.

Offe, C. (1984) *Contradictions of the Welfare State*, London: Hutchinson.

Olin-Wright, E. (1978) *Class Crisis and the State*, London: New Left Books.

Osborne, P. (ed.) (1991) *Socialism and the Limits of Liberalism*, London: Verso.

Otero, C. P. (ed.) (1981) *Noam Chomsky: Radical Priorities*, Montreal: Black Rose Books.

Otero, C. P. (ed.) (1988) *Noam Chomsky: Language and Politics*, Montreal: Black Rose Books.

Otero, C. P. (ed.) (1994) *Critical Assessments* Volumes 1–4, London: Routledge and Kegan Paul.

Pannekoek, A. (1909, 1912) *Marxism and Darwinism*, Chicago: Charles H. Kerr.

Pannekoek, A. (1970) *Workers' Councils*, Summerville, Mass: Kont and Branch.

Peck, J. (1988) *The Chomsky Reader*, London: Serpent's Tail.

Philo, G. (1987) 'Whose news?' *Media, Culture and Society*, 9 (4), pp. 397–406.

Phillips, A. (1997) 'From Inequality to Difference: A Severe Case of Displacement?' in *New Left Review*, no. 224, July–August.

Plamenatz, J. (1976) 'Two Types of Nationalism' in Kamenka, E. (ed.) *The Nature and Evolution of an Idea*, London: Edward Arnold.

Plant, R. (1991) *Modern Political Thought*, London: Basil Blackwell.

Plato (1948) *The Republic* (Cornford, F. M., trans.), Oxford: Clarendon Press.

Poulantzas, N. (1973) *Political Power and Social Class* Timothy O'Hagan (trans. ed.), London: New Left Books.

Poulantzas, N. (1978) *State, Power, Socialism*, London: Verso.

Poulantzas, N. (1979) *Fascism and Dictatorship*, London: Verso.

Przeworski, A. (1979) *Economic Conditions of Class Compromise*, Chicago: University of Chicago, mimeo.

Rai, M. (1995) *Chomsky's Politics*, London: Verso.

Raskin, M. G. and Bernstein, H. J. (1987) *New Ways of Knowing: The Sciences, Society and Reconstructive Knowledge*, Rowmen and Littlefield.

Rawls, J. (1972) *A Theory of Justice*, Cambridge Mass: Harvard University Press.

Reimer, N. (1967) *American Political Theory: The Democratic Experience*, vol. 1, New York: D. Van Nostrand.

Robertson, D. (1986) *Dictionary of Politics*, Harmondsworth: Penguin.

Rocker, R. (1937) *Nationalism and Culture*, Los Angeles, California: Rocker Publications Committee.

Rocker, R. (1938, 1972) *Anarcho-Syndicalism*, New York: Gordon Press.

Rothblatt, B. (ed.) (1968) *Changing Perspectives on Man*, Chicago: University of Chicago Press.

Salkie, R. (1990) *The Chomsky Update: Linguistics and Politics*, Unwin Hyman.

Sandel, M. J. (1982) *Liberalism and The Limits of Justice*, Cambridge: Cambridge University Press.

Sarup, M. (1988) *An Introductory Guide to Post Structuralism and Post Modernism*, Hemel Hempstead: Harvester Wheatsheaf.

Schlesinger, P. (1980) *Putting Reality Together: The BBC and Its News* (revised edn.), London: Sage.

Schudson, M. (1991) 'The Sociology of News Production Revisited' in Curran, J. and Gurevitch, M. (eds) *Mass Media and Society*, London: Edward Arnold.

Schutz, A. (1980) *The Phenomenology of the Social World* (George Walsh and Frederick Lehnert, trans), London: Heinemann.

Schwarzmantel, J. (1991) *Socialism and the Idea of the Nation*, Hemel Hempstead: Harvester Wheatsheaf.

Seymour Ure, C. (1969) 'Editorial Policy Making in the Press' in *Government and Opposition*, Autumn.

Skillen, T. (1972) 'The Statist Conception of Politics' in *Radical Philosophy*, 2, Summer.

Skillen, T. (1977) *Ruling Illusions: Philosophy and the Social Order*, Brighton: Harvester.

Skocpol, T. (1979) *States and Social Revolutions*, Cambridge: Cambridge University Press.

Skocpol, T. (1985) 'Bringing the State Back In: Strategies of Analysis in Current Research', in Evans, P. R., Rueschemeyer, D. and Skocpol, T. (eds) *Bringing the State Back In*, Cambridge: Cambridge University Press.

Smith, A. D. (1971) *Theories of Nationalism*, London: Duckworth.

Smith, A. D. (1979) *Nationalism in the Twentieth Century*, Oxford: Robinson.

Smith, A. D. (1991) *National Identity*, London: Penguin.

Smith, A. D. (1998) *Nationalism and Modernism*, London: Routledge.

Taylor, C. (1967) 'Neutrality in Political Science' in Laslett, Peter and Runciman, W. G. (eds) *Philosophy, Politics and Society*, Oxford: Basil Blackwell.

Urmson, J. O. (ed.) (1975) *The Concise Encyclopedia of Western Philosophy and Philosophers*, London: Hutchinson.

Walzer, M. in Zelinsky, W. (ed.) (1988) *Nation into State: The Shifting Symbolic Foundations of American Nationalism*, Chapel Hill, North Carolina: The University of North Carolina Press.

Weber, M. (1930, 1974) *The Protestant Ethic and the Spirit of Capitalism*, London: Allen and Unwin.

Wilkin, P. (1995) *Noam Chomsky: On Knowledge, Human Nature and Freedom*, PhD thesis, University of Southampton.

Wilkin, P. (1997) *Noam Chomsky: On Knowledge, Human Nature and Freedom*, London: Macmillan.

Williams, R. (1978) 'The Press we Don't Deserve' in Curran, J. (ed.) *The British Press: A Manifesto*, London: Macmillan.

Willis, P. (1977) *Learning to Labour: How Working Class Kids Get Working Class Jobs*, London: Saxon House.

Wintonick, P. and Achbar, M. (eds) (1994) in *Manufacturing Consent: Noam Chomsky and the Media*, Montreal: Black Rose Books.

Wood, Ellen Meiksins (1995) *Democracy Against Capitalism: Renewing Historical Materialism*, Cambridge: Cambridge University Press.

Woodcock, G. (1986) *Anarchism* (2nd edn), Harmondsworth: Penguin.

Index